Female Genital Mutilation

A Guide to Laws and Policies Worldwide

Edited by Anika Rahman
and Nahid Toubia

ZED BOOKS
London & New York

in association with

CRLP
Center for Reproductive Law and Policy

and

RAINBO
Research, Action and Information Network
for the Bodily Integrity of Women

Female Genital Mutilation: A Guide to Laws and Policies Worldwide
was first published by Zed Books Ltd, 7 Cynthia Street, London N1 9JF, UK, and
Room 400, 175 Fifth Avenue, New York, NY 10010, USA in 2000

in association with

Center for Reproductive Law and Policy,
120 Wall Street, New York, NY 10005, USA

and

Research Action and Information Network for the Bodily Integrity of Women
(RAINB♀), 915 Broadway, Suite 1109, New York, NY 10010, USA

Distributed in the USA exclusively by Palgrave, a division of St Martin's Press, LLC,
175 Fifth Avenue, New York, NY 10010, USA.

Second impression, 2001

Designed and typeset by Illuminati, Grosmont.
Cover image: "Mother and child figure, Dogon, Mali,"
from *Secrecy: African Art that Conceals and Reveals,*
courtesy of the Museum for African Art, New York.
Cover designed by Andrew Corbett
Transferred to Digital Printing 2008
www.biddles.co.uk

A catalogue record for this book is available from the British Library

Library of Congress Cataloging-in-Publication Data applied for

ISBN 1 85649 772 0 (Hb)
ISBN 1 85649 773 9 (Pb)
ISBN 978-1-85649-773-2

"This book is a testament to the heroic victories being won by a number of countries against female genital mutilation. UNICEF welcomes this valuable exposition of the steps and processes involved in enacting legislation and policies to end this abuse of girls' and women's rights. It contributes towards a better understanding of what can and must be done – through education, mobilization, renewed and strengthened consensus, expanded partnerships and stronger legislative and policy foundations – to protect the rights of girls and women and end FGM."

Carol Bellamy, Executive Director, UNICEF

"For all those working on the elimination of female genital mutilation, this book – the culmination of extensive research and collaboration – provides a framework and recommendations for practical legal policy and action. It is very significant in that it shows the tremendous changes that are taking place around the world in safeguarding the rights of all people and in improving their well-being."

Nafis Sadik, Executive Director, United Nations Population Fund

"Female genital mutilation affects the physical integrity of women and children and as such should be condemned. In doing so, it is necessary to act with tact and patience, bringing communities to understand that their cultural values are not to be confused with cultural practices, and that those practices can be changed without adversely affecting values. This book will perform an educational function in setting out the international legal framework in detail."

Mary Robinson, United Nations High Commissioner for Human Rights

"Women's groups across the globe have mobilized around the important health, social and cultural dimensions of FGM and have gained its recognition as a critical human rights issue. But never before have we had such a comprehensive worldwide review of legislation addressing this harmful practice, which affects some 130 million women and girls. CRLP and RAINBQ have provided an indispensable resource for activists, scholars and advocates interested in women's bodily integrity and human rights."

Professor Rosalind Petchesky, Hunter College, City University of New York

ANIKA RAHMAN is Director of the International Program of the Center for Reproductive Law and Policy. The CRLP is a nonprofit legal and policy advocacy organization dedicated to promoting women's reproductive rights. The central mission of the CRLP's International Program is the achievement of enforceable reproductive health care for women around the world.

Rahman's work focuses on reproductive health and rights issues from both comparative legal and international human rights perspectives. In addition, she monitors and analyses US and international population policies that affect the reproductive health of women.

She was closely involved in the negotiations of the 1994 International Conference on Population and Development in Cairo and the 1995 Fourth World Conference on Women in Beijing. She has written and spoken on international reproductive rights and health, comparative law, and national and international population policies, and has consulted with women's groups worldwide on strategies to achieve women's reproductive rights. Her recent publications include *An International Human Right to Reproductive Health Care: Towards Definition and Accountability in Health and Human Rights*, Harvard School of Public Health, François-Xavier Bagnoud Center for Health and Human Rights.

Prior to joining the CRLP, she was a corporate associate working in the field of international law at the firm of Cleary, Gottlieb, Steen & Hamilton. In addition, she has worked on legal issues involving the rights of immigrants in the United States. A member of the New York bar, she received her Juris Doctor in 1990 from the Columbia University School of Law and her Bachelor of Arts, cum laude, from the Woodrow Wilson School of Public and International Affairs at Princeton University.

NAHID TOUBIA was born in Khartoum in 1951, and attended medical school in Egypt. In 1981 she became a fellow at the British Royal College of Surgeons and the first woman surgeon in Sudan. She served as the head of the Paediatric Surgery department at Khartoum teaching hospital for many years. Recently, she worked for four years as an Associate for Women's Reproductive Health at the Population Council in New York City. She is currently an Associate Professor at Columbia University School of Public Health and Director of RAINB♀. She is also a member of several scientific and technical advisory committees of the World Health Organization, UNICEF and UNDP, and Vice-chair of the advisory committee of the Women's Rights Watch Program of Human Rights Watch, where she serves on the Board of Directors. She publishes widely on issues of reproductive health, women's rights, and gender inequality, particularly in Africa and the Middle East.

Contents

Acronyms and Abbreviations

African Charter	African Charter on the Rights and Welfare of the Child
African Commission	African Commission of Human Rights
American Convention	American Convention on Human Rights
Banjul Charter	African Charter on Human and Peoples' Rights
Beijing Conference	1995 UN Fourth World Conference on Women
Beijing Declaration and Platform for Action	Fourth World Conference on Women Declaration and Platform for Action
CEDAW	Committee on the Elimination of Discrimination Against Women
Children's Rights Convention	Convention on the Rights of the Child
Civil and Political Rights Covenant	International Covenant on Civil and Political Rights
CRLP	Center for Reproductive Law and Policy
CSW	Commission on the Status of Women
Declaration on Religious Intolerance	Declaration on the Elimination of All Forms of Intolerance and of Discrimination Based on Religion or Belief
DHS	Demographic and Health Surveys
Economic, Social and Cultural Rights Covenant	International Covenant on Economic, Social and Cultural Rights
European Convention	European Convention for the Protection of Human Rights and Fundamental Freedoms

FC/FGM	Female circumcision/female genital mutilation
Human Rights Commission	United Nations Commission on Human Rights
IAC	Inter-African Committee on Traditional Practices Affecting the Health of Women and Children
ICJ	International Court of Justice
ICPD	1994 UN International Conference on Population and Development
ICPD Programme of Action	International Conference on Population and Development Programme of Action
IEC strategies	Information, Education and Communication strategies
Minority Rights Declaration	Rights of Persons Belonging to National or Ethnic, Religious and Linguistic Minorities
NGOs	Non-governmental organizations
OAU	Organization of African Unity
Political Rights Covenant	International Covenant on Civil and Political Rights
Race Convention	International Convention on the Elimination of All Forms of Racial Discrimination
RAINB♀	Research Action and Information Network for the Bodily Integrity of Women
Sub-Commission	Sub-Commission on the Promotion and Protection of Human Rights
Torture Convention	Convention Against Torture and Other Cruel, Inhuman or Degrading Treatment or Punishment
UNFPA	United Nations Population Fund
UNICEF	United Nations Children's Fund
Universal Declaration	Universal Declaration of Human Rights
WHO	World Health Organization
Women's Convention	Convention on the Elimination of All Forms of Discrimination Against Women

Note on Terminology

In approaching this topic, one of the most controversial issues is whether to use "female circumcision" (FC) or "female genital mutilation" (FGM) as the terminology to describe this procedure. Proponents of the term "female circumcision" are sensitive to the fact that the term "female genital mutilation" is often offensive to the circumcised women, who do not necessarily think of themselves as mutilated or of their families as mutilators. They also voice a concern that mutilation terminology is often used as a means to insult people and the cultures from which they come. Historically, the term "female circumcision" was used in the international literature until the early 1980s, when the term "female genital mutilation" was introduced and became more widely used.

The term FGM has been adopted by a wide range of women's health and human rights activists, both inside and outside Africa, because they believe it indicates the damage caused by the practice. This term has been a very effective policy and advocacy tool, and, since 1994, has been used in several United Nations conference documents. In the late 1990s, some writers and international institutions began using other terms such as "female genital surgeries" (FGS) and "female genital cutting" (FGC).

In consideration of all these concerns, the dual term "female circumcision/female genital mutilation" (FC/FGM) has been used in this publication in order to acknowledge the validity of both expressions: that the intent of the procedure is circumcision and the effect is mutilation. However, in the title of this book, we chose to use "FGM" because of the nature of the publication as a tool for legal policy and action.

Acknowledgements

The editors of this book wish to thank the following people for reviewing an earlier draft of this book and providing invaluable comments and suggestions:

- Ms Asma Abdel Halim, Michigan Fellow at the Health and Population Division of USAID;
- Prof. Abdullahi Ahmed An-Na'im, Professor of Law, Emory University School of Law;
- Prof. Rebecca Cook, Professor, Faculty of Law, University of Toronto;
- Prof. Lynn Freedman, Director, Law and Policy Unit, Columbia University School of Public Health.

The editors would also like to acknowledge the contributions of a large number of individuals at CRLP, RAINB♀ and organizations around the world who worked to bring this project to fruition. Major portions of this book were edited, researched and drafted by Laura Katzive, CRLP Staff Attorney. The following people in the CRLP's International Program also participated in the preparation of this book: Maryse Fontus, Staff Attorney, drafted an initial version of the chapter of this book pertaining to the human rights implications of FC/FGM; Cynthia Eyakuze, former International Program Associate, researched and drafted a number of the profiles of national-level efforts to address FC/FGM. From RAINB♀: Fatima Maiga, Program Officer, drafted Chapter 1; Susan Izett, Senior Consultant, and Zeinab Eyega, Program Officer, assisted in developing a questionnaire sent to national organizations and reviewed successive drafts.

The questionnaires, which provided the information on national-level laws and policies, were completed by the following individuals and organizations:

- Theresa U. Akumadu, Women's Centre for Peace and Development (Nigeria);
- Khamisa Baya, Women's Health in Women's Hands Community Health Centre (Canada);

- Codou Bop, Groupe de Recherche Femmes et Lois au Senegal (Senegal);
- La Cellule de Coordination sur les Pratiques Traditionelles Affectant la Santé des Femmes et des Enfants (CPTAFE) (Guinea);
- Martine Chaumont, Cabinet Ministre M. Smet (Belgium);
- Jenny Davidson, FORWARD (United Kingdom);
- Nikki Denholm, National FGM Education Programme (New Zealand);
- Pamela Greene, Program for Appropriate Technologies in Health – Kenya (Sierra Leone);
- Fana Habteab and Caroline Linuauder, Riksföreningen Stoppa Kvinnlig Könsstympning (RISK) (Sweden);
- Amal Abd-El Hadi, Cairo Institute for Human Rights Studies (Egypt);
- Suzanne Julin, Swedish National Board of Health and Welfare (Sweden);
- Josephine Kasolo, Safe Motherhood Initiative in Uganda (Uganda);
- Françoise Kaudjhis-Offoumou, Association Internationale pour la Democratie (Côte d'Ivoire);
- Kadiatou Korsaga, Direction de la Promotion de l'Education des Filles (Burkina Faso);
- Mariam Lamizana, Comité National de Lutte contre la Pratique de l'Excision (Burkina Faso);
- Ines Laufer, Terre des Femmes (Germany);
- Els Leye, International Centre for Reproductive Health (Belgium);
- Fatimata M'Baye, Association Mauritanienne des Droits de l'Homme (Mauritania);
- Asha Mohamud and Nancy Ali, Program for Appropriate Technology in Health (United States of America);
- Carole Morency, Department of Justice, Canada (Canada);
- Mpessa-Djessi Ndine, Association Camerounaise des Femmes Juristes (ACAFES) (Cameroon);
- Ananilea Nkya and Leila Sheikh Hashim, Tanzania Media Women's Association (Tanzania);
- Jacqueline Rizkallah, GAMS Belgique (Belgium);
- Ama R. Saran, Ama R. Saran and Associates (United States of America);
- Mary Small, the Gambia Committee on Traditional Practices Affecting the Health of Women and Children (GAMCOTRAP) (The Gambia);
- David B. Smith, United States Department of Health and Human Services (United States of America);
- Agnete Strøm, Women's Front of Norway (Norway);
- Hillina Taddesse Tamrat, Ethiopian Women Lawyers' Association (Ethiopia);
- Di Tibbits, Royal Australian College of Obstetricians and Gynaecologists (Australia);

- Linda Weil-Curiel, Commission Pour l'Abolition des Mutilations Sexuelles (CAMS) (France).

Assistance in researching and drafting sections of this book was provided by CRLP interns: Erica Auerbach, Tracey Kerr, Megan Knight, Sarah Netburn, Stacey Pinchuk, Jocelyn Pridgen and Eschrat Rahimi-Laridjani. Additional research was undertaken by Elizabeth Roff and Jennifer Tierney. RAINB♀'s intern Heidi Müller assisted in contacting organizations for questionnaire responses.

The editors would also like to thank Barbara Becker, the CRLP's Deputy Director of Communications, Kathy Hall Martinez, Deputy Director of the CRLP's International Program, and RAINB♀'s Junior Program Officers Jennifer Fredette, Fatima Shama and Jessica Stern for reviewing this book and providing helpful recommendations. Lisa Hibler, International Program Assistant at CRLP, provided research assistance and other valuable support during every phase of this project. Alison-Maria Bartolone, Danka Rapic and Katherine Tell, all International Program Assistants at CRLP, also contributed to the completion of this book. Carla Avni, Sophie Lescure and Lara Stemple, International Program Fellowship Attorneys at CRLP, are thanked for their assistance in finalizing this book. Carol Schlitt, a former Staff Attorney at CRLP, undertook research relevant to this project.

In addition, Charles Mwalimu, Senior Legal Specialist at the Library of Congress, is thanked for his assistance in locating materials. Jill Grinberg is also thanked for volunteering her assistance in consulting with CRLP. Special thanks are also due to Louise Murray, our editor at Zed Books, for her steady commitment to this project.

Finally, we thank the Gender Partnerships and Participation Section of the Programme Division of UNICEF for its support for this project. We further note that this book would not have been possible without the generous support of the Wallace Global Fund, guided by the far-reaching vision of the late Gordon Wallace.

While numerous individuals and organizations contributed to this book, the opinions contained herein reflect only the views of the editors and their collaborating organizations.

Preface

The customary practice of female circumcision or female genital mutilation (FC/FGM) has attracted much attention in the international and national policy arenas in the past two decades. One of the highly debated issues is the role – if any – of legislative action against a pervasive social practice that is strongly linked to cultural norms and beliefs. While history tells us that legislation alone cannot change social behavior, the fact that many African and Western countries have recently enacted laws prohibiting the practice creates a *de facto* role for legislation, the effect of which should be closely observed and documented in the coming years. Another commonly posed question is whether framing the issues in the language of human rights is meaningful or appropriate for the majority of women who believe in or suffer from this practice in the context of their specific families and communities. We believe that framing issues such as FC/FGM as violations of women's rights is not only appropriate, but is an important means by which to raise the political profile of these neglected rights and to generate dialogue on how best to stop them.

This book is the product of collaboration between the Center for Reproductive Law and Policy (CRLP) and the Research Action and Information Network for the Bodily Integrity of Women (RAINB♀). CRLP and RAINB♀ are independent, non-governmental organizations (NGOs) with a common goal of promoting women's reproductive and sexual health and rights. The work of CRLP's International Program is primarily devoted to advocating for laws and policies that secure women's equality in society and ensure that they have access to appropriate and freely chosen reproductive health care. RAINB♀ is an international, multicultural organization with a strong African leadership that works on issues within the intersection of health and human rights of women. RAINB♀ has broad experience working on the issue of FC/FGM in close collaboration with African national, non-governmental organizations and African immigrant community organizations in the United States.

The initial collaboration between the CRLP and RAINB♀ on FC/FGM began in 1996, prior to the enactment of a federal law criminalizing this practice in the United States. The two organizations were asked to review the draft legislation and offer their input. Out of this process grew an interest in developing a framework for promoting legislation that could help deter families from continuing to impose FC/FGM on their daughters while protecting immigrant and minority communities from cultural, religious and racial discrimination. The idea for this book arose as both the CRLP and RAINBQ noted the increasing global trend toward taking a legal approach to FC/FGM and saw the need to anchor future legal action within human rights principles and to enhance the technical aspects of legal development by providing a comprehensive and comparative review of laws developed so far.

The genesis of this book lies in the joint interest of our organizations in discussing the "rights" perspective of FC/FGM. We believe that this perspective sharpens the focus on the underlying issues raised by this and other "cultural" or "traditional" practices – women's low social, economic and legal status and the importance of providing women with tools to empower themselves and demand their rights. It is thus our conviction that linking international human rights to national-level legal enactments on FC/FGM will promote a more informed legal approach. Also, while the international community has established that FC/FGM is a violation of human rights, there is still much work to be done to bring this dialogue to the national and community levels. Such work has to be undertaken in a manner that is appropriate and meaningful so that it will produce the desired social change in favor of protecting women's rights.

Addressing cultural practices that discriminate against women and that are meant to control their sexuality is a complex and highly charged political process. Our two organizations support the fundamental human rights call for stopping FC/FGM. At the same time, through this book, we want to pose some of the complex questions that arise from using the broad standards of international human rights law in dealing with specific social belief systems. One of the clear difficulties is that the language of international human rights law is very broad, and, in some instances, was drafted with only political and civil violations in mind. Many of the earlier human rights treaties were drafted in an era in which women's issues were not high on the international agenda.

Finally, we have sought to make a contribution to the manner in which NGOs can undertake further rights-based work. Although both the CRLP and RAINBQ are international organizations, we are keenly aware that the social movements against FC/FGM must be indigenously based. The work of stopping FC/FGM can and must be done at the national level, relying on domestic instruments and mechanisms. However, since the international community continues to play a significant role in fostering recognition of FC/FGM as a rights violation, we have structured this book to emphasize the contribution of an international human rights framework to stopping FC/FGM in different countries around the world.

What is in this Book?

Chapter 1 provides background on the nature and prevalence of FC/FGM and gives a brief history of actions taken on the global level to bring attention to the practice. Chapter 2 looks in-depth at the internationally accepted human rights norms that support a woman's right to freedom from FC/FGM. Chapter 3 examines governments' duty to address FC/FGM under the provisions of human rights treaties, drawing from those provisions a framework for action. Chapter 4 translates that framework into concrete recommendations for governments engaged in the formulation of legal and policy responses to FC/FGM in their countries. Finally, Chapter 5 reviews past and current strategies used by various NGOs working to address FC/FGM with recommendations for specific legal actions that may be taken by NGOs at national, regional and international levels.

The country-by-country review section in the second part of the book is a summary of legal, regulatory and policy initiatives taken thus far in countries around the world. It consists of 41 country profiles covering the 28 African countries in which FC/FGM is prevalent as well as 13 countries with immigrant populations from countries where FC/FGM is practiced. The section is not comprehensive in its coverage of countries that have immigrant populations that may practice FC/FGM. It reviews only a sampling, drawn from those receiving countries that have either taken substantial steps to address the practice of FC/FGM or received a significant number of immigrants from countries in which FC/FGM is prevalent.

It should be noted that our review of national-level efforts to stop the practice of FC/FGM focuses on the actions of governments – not NGOs. Because this is a book primarily about the role of law in bringing about social change, we have emphasized legal initiatives and complementary governmental programs that target FC/FGM. We have not attempted to describe comprehensively the important work being done by NGOs worldwide to stop the practice of FC/FGM. By no means, however, do we wish to downplay the significance of this work. Indeed, in many countries, the efforts of NGOs to address FC/FGM have far outstripped those of governments. We hope that our emphasis on government action will be useful to policy-makers and NGOs alike in developing a multi-strategy approach to addressing FC/FGM.

We wish to draw attention to the research efforts of many different individuals and groups, particularly with respect to the country profile section of this book. This section is the product of extensive research conducted over the course of 18 months. Over 50 questionnaires were sent to NGOs and government ministries in the countries profiled in this report. The 30 responses received proved to be an invaluable source and the most original contribution to this book. They detailed legislative and policy developments in their countries and discussed education and outreach programs undertaken by both government and non-governmental bodies. These questionnaires were supplemented by research conducted by the CRLP and RAINB♀. The *Annual Review of Population Law* (published by the United Nations Population Fund and the Harvard Law School) and the *International Digest of Health Legislation* (published by the World Health Organization) provided the texts of a number of legal and policy measures undertaken worldwide. News sources were also reviewed. Several secondary sources were consulted, including *Cutting the Rose* by Efua Dorkenoo; *Female Genital Mutilation: A Call for Global Action* by Nahid Toubia; *Visions and Discussions on Genital Mutilation of Girls: An International Survey* by Jacqueline Smith; the newsletters of the Inter-African Committee on Traditional Practices Affecting the Health of Women and Children (IAC); *Awaken*, a periodical produced by Equality Now; and the reports of the United States Department of State on FC/FGM. Reports released by United Nations bodies, including the Committee on the Elimination of Discrimination Against Women (CEDAW) and the Human Rights Committee (HRC); *Female Genital Mutilation: An Overview* by the World Health Organization; and *The Progress of Nations* 1996 and 1997 by UNICEF provided additional information.

Finally, we must re-emphasize that while this book focuses on the international human rights aspects of FC/FGM and surveys and analyzes laws passed to address the practice in different countries, the authors are fully aware of the limited role laws play in changing human behavior. Laws can, and should, be viewed as instruments for social change. Such tools are ultimately only as strong or weak as those who use them and as the legal systems within which they operate. However, we do hold some hope that the political framework presented by the human rights perspective is one that will serve as a reference point for those wielding the instruments of law and policy. Moreover, while international or national laws will never substitute for the indigenous social movements necessary to stop FC/FGM, they can play a significant role in enhancing such movements. We hope that this book will help clarify the legal status of

FC/FGM, both internationally and in specific countries, and the way in which advocacy groups and individuals may use legal and policy tools effectively in their struggle to stop the practice.

Anika Rahman and Nahid Toubia

Part I

A Human Rights Approach

1

Background and History

What is FC/FGM?

Female circumcision/female genital mutilation (FC/FGM) is the collective name given to several different traditional practices that involve the cutting of female genitals.[1] The procedure is commonly performed on girls anywhere between the ages of four and twelve years of age as a rite of passage to womanhood.[2] However, in some cultures, it is practiced as early as a few days after birth and as late as just prior to marriage or after the first pregnancy.[3] Girls may be circumcised alone or with a group of peers from their community. FC/FGM is generally performed by a traditional practitioner – often an older woman – who comes from a family in which generations of women have been traditional practitioners. However, more recently, in some countries it is also performed by trained health personnel, including physicians, nurses and midwives.[4]

Initially, interest in the practice was focused primarily on the physical and psychological damage that FC/FGM can cause. However, the act itself – the cutting of healthy genital organs for non-medical reasons – is at its essence a basic violation of girls' and women's rights to physical integrity. This is true regardless of the degree of cutting or of the extent of the complications that may or may not ensue. In addition, it is important to note that this is a procedure that is performed primarily upon children, who have no say in the matter. While parents who have their daughters circumcised do not intend to hurt their children, the practice violates a number of recognized human rights, including those protected by the Convention on the Rights of the Child (Children's Rights Convention). The issue of FC/FGM is therefore increasingly being discussed and addressed in the overall context of girls' and women's rights, rather than strictly as a health or medical issue.

Indigenous populations use a variety of terms in local dialects to describe the practice. These are often synonymous with purification or cleansing, such as the terms *tahara* in Egypt, *tahur* in Sudan and *bolokoli* in Mali. Local terminology for types of FC/FGM also varies widely among countries. In literature from Sudan, for example, clitoridectomy is referred to as *sunna*, and infibulation is referred to as *pharaonic*. In literature associated with French-speaking Africa, FC/FGM is commonly referred to as *excision*; while in English-speaking Africa, the term "circumcision" is predominant.

Within the international community, the term "female circumcision" was used for many years to describe the practice. Other expressions, such as "female genital cutting," "female genital surgery," "ritual genital surgery" and "sexual mutilation," have also been used. However, in the past decade, the term "female genital mutilation" has been adopted by a wide range of women's health and human rights activists because it clearly indicates the harm caused by the practice. The World Health Organization (WHO) also adopted the term "female genital mutilation."[5] Similarly, in 1990, at a meeting in Addis Ababa, Ethiopia, the Inter-African Committee on Traditional Practices Affecting the Health of Women and Children (IAC) formally adopted this term. Subsequently, the international community has used this expression in several United Nations conference documents, including those relating to the 1994 International Conference on Population and Development in Cairo (Cairo Conference), the 1995 World Summit for Social Development in Copenhagen (Copenhagen Summit) and the 1995 Fourth World Conference on Women in Beijing (Beijing Conference).

Although the term "female genital mutilation" has been a very effective policy and advocacy tool, organizations working with communities that practice FGM have found that this term can be offensive or even shocking to women who have never considered the practice a mutilation. Out of respect and sensitivity, many organizations have opted to use local terminology or more neutral terms such as "female circumcision" or "female genital cutting" when working with these populations. In recognition of these two approaches, the dual term "FC/FGM" has been used for this book except when quoting materials from United Nations conference documents and national legislation.

The term "female circumcision" may seem to imply an analogy with male circumcision. However, while some may argue that both practices are a violation of a child's right to physical integrity, in important ways the two practices are distinct. Male circumcision is the cutting off of the foreskin from the tip of the penis without damaging the organ itself. The degree of cutting in female circumcision is anatomically much more extensive. The male equivalent of clitoridectomy, in which all or part of the clitoris is removed, would be the amputation of most of the penis. The male equivalent of infibulation – which involves not only clitoridectomy, but the removal or closing off of the sensitive tissue around the vagina – would be removal of all the penis, its roots of soft tissue and part of the scrotal skin.[6] Another important distinction is the social and sexual message associated with each practice. Male circumcision affirms manhood with its superior social status and associations to virility. Female circumcision is explicitly intended to show a woman her confined role in society and restrain her sexual desires. Further discussion of the gender role differences between male and female circumcision is to be found in Chapter 2 under "The Right to be Free from All Forms of Discrimination Against Women." For a full discussion of the similarities and differences between male and female circumcision, see Nahid Toubia's "Evolutionary Cultural Ethics and Circumcision of Children."[7]

The reasons for FC/FGM are complex, related to each other and woven into the beliefs and values communities uphold. Hence, it is extremely difficult to isolate explanations for the practice. FC/FGM represents not a singular value, but a single way to demonstrate physically otherwise socially constructed concepts like gender and sexuality. Thus, while we can explain FC/FGM, we must understand that it is dependent not on a single factor, but on an entire belief system and values that support it. The following are general descriptions of the four most common justifications for the practice.

Custom and tradition

In many communities, circumcision is performed as a rite of passage from childhood to adulthood, during which time the girl is equipped with skills for handling marriage, husband and children. The process of "becoming" a woman thus contributes to the maintenance of custom and tradition by linking the girl to the lifestyle and roles played by other women. FC/FGM represents an act of socialization into cultural values and a connection to family, community members and previous generations. Communities that practice FC/FGM affirm their relationship with the beliefs of the past by continuing the tradition; they maintain community customs and preserve cultural identity.[8]

Women's sexuality

A fundamental reason advanced for female circumcision is the need to control women's sexuality. Because sexuality is socially constructed, it has different meanings depending on its context. For many communities that practice FC/FGM, a family or clan's honor depends on a girl's virginity or sexual restraint. This is the case in Egypt, Sudan and Somalia, where FC/FGM is perceived as a way to curtail premarital sex and preserve virginity. In other contexts, such as in Kenya and Uganda, where sexual "purity" is not a concern, FC/FGM is performed to reduce the woman's sexual demands on her husband, thus allowing him to have several wives. Notwithstanding the different reasons to control women's sexuality, FC/FGM is intended to reduce women's sexual desire, thus promoting women's virginity and protecting marital fidelity, in the interest of male sexuality. FC/FGM also results in the reduction of women's sexual fulfillment, thus aiding in the construction of parameters around women's sexuality.

Religion

It is important to note that FC/FGM is a cultural, not a religious, practice. The practice predates the arrival of Christianity and Islam in Africa and is not a requirement of either religion. In fact, FC/FGM is practiced by Jews, Christians, Muslims and indigenous religious groups in Africa.

However, despite the fact that FC/FGM is not known in many Muslim countries, it is strongly identified with Islam in several African nations, and many members of the Muslim community advocate for the practice. While neither the Qu'ran, the primary source for Islamic law, nor the "hadith," collections of the sayings of the Prophet Mohammed, include a direct call for FC/FGM,[9] debate over interpretations of statements from one hadith continues. Most recently, during the International Conference on Population and Reproductive Health in the Muslim World at Egypt's Al Azhar University,[10] a traditional center of Islamic scholarship, it was agreed that certain harmful practices, including FC/FGM, were the result of misunderstandings of Islamic provisions.[11]

Social pressure

A common explanation for FC/FGM is social pressure. In a community where most women are circumcised, family, friends and neighbors create an environment in which the practice of circumcision becomes a component of social conformity. Circumcision goes from being a perceived need to a pervasive practice that is necessary for acceptance. In such a context, not circumcising may not be an option. Fear of community judgment, such as men's refusal to marry uncircumcised women, contributes to this pressure. The process becomes cyclical; by believing that circumcision is necessary for social homogeneity and ease, FC/FGM grows in importance.

How Widespread is FC/FGM?

Worldwide, an estimated 130 million girls and women have undergone FC/FGM. At least two million girls a year are at risk of undergoing some form of the procedure.[12] Historically, FC/FGM is thought to have originated in southern Egypt or northern Sudan and was practiced by many cultures, including the Phoenicians, Hittites and the ancient Egyptians.

Currently, FC/FGM is practiced in 28 African countries in the sub-Saharan and Northeastern regions. National estimates of prevalence have been generated for most of the 28 African countries. While many of these figures come from limited studies or anecdotal information, seven countries – the Central African Republic, Côte d'Ivoire, Egypt, Eritrea, Mali, Sudan and Tanzania – have reliable data based on specific questions related to FC/FGM in their Demographic and Health Surveys (DHS). Based on current estimates, 18 African countries have prevalence rates of 50 per cent or higher.[13] However, prevalence varies widely from country to country. It ranges from nearly 90 per cent or higher in Egypt, Eritrea, Mali and Sudan, to less than 50 per cent in the Central African Republic and Côte d'Ivoire, to 5 per cent in the Democratic Republic of Congo and Uganda. There are also great disparities in prevalence within countries. For example, in Mali, prevalence in the regions of Timbuctu and Gao is less than 10 per cent, while in Bamako and Koulikoro, the rates are 95 per cent and 99 per cent, respectively.[14] In Asia, the practice has been documented among the Daudi Bohra Muslims in India and a few Muslim ethnic groups in Sri Lanka. In the Middle East, there are reports of the practice in Yemen and Oman.

As recently as the 1950s, physicians in the United Kingdom and the United States also performed FC/FGM to "treat" hysteria, lesbianism, masturbation and other so-called "female deviations."[15] Women who have undergone FC/FGM are also found among African immigrant communities in Europe, Canada, Australia and the United States. However, there is little data about either the number of these immigrants or the prevalence of FC/FGM amongst them. The existing sporadic and incomplete data available are listed in the relevant country sections. Apart from judicial cases in France,[16] there is no systematic documented evidence of the practice occurring in immigrant settings.

What are the Health Consequences of FC/FGM?

Before discussing the health consequences of the practice, it is important to explain the different types of FC/FGM. While procedures differ greatly according to such factors as ethnic groups and geographic regions, they can be grouped broadly into four categories, as established by the WHO.[17]

- *Type I* (commonly referred to as "clitoridectomy"): Excision of the prepuce with or without excision of part or all of the clitoris.

- *Type II* (commonly referred to as "excision"): Excision of the prepuce and clitoris together with partial or total excision of the labia minora.
- *Type III* (commonly referred to as "infibulation"): Excision of part or all of the external genitalia and stitching/narrowing of the vaginal opening.
- *Type IV* (unclassified): All other procedures that involve partial or total removal of the female external genitalia and/or injury to the female genital organs for cultural or any other non-therapeutic reasons. Type IV refers to numerous other procedures that have been documented, such as pricking, piercing, stretching or burning of the clitoris and/or surrounding tissues.

FC/FGM has serious potential health consequences for girls and women. These include the risk of physical complications as well as psychological effects.[18]

Physical complications

Immediate complications

The possible immediate complications of all types of FC/FGM include severe pain and bleeding. If prolonged, the bleeding can lead to anemia, which may affect the growth of a girl and result in life-long weakness. Shock can also result from hemorrhage and the pain or trauma of the procedure. If bleeding is very severe and uncontrolled, it can result in death.

A very common and immediate complication associated with FC/FGM is infection caused by using unsterile cutting instruments. Such infection may also occur within a few days of the procedure, if the genital area becomes contaminated with urine or feces. Infection can lead to septicemia if the bacterium reaches the bloodstream. Acute urine retention can result from swelling and inflammation around the wound. Retention is usually irreversible and can lead to urinary tract infection.

Long-term complications

Long-term problems can arise from any FC/FGM procedure. However, Types II and III usually result in the severest complications. Common complications of infibulation include: repeated urinary tract infection; chronic pelvic infections (these may cause irreparable damage to the reproductive organs and result in infertility); stones in the urethra or bladder; excessive growth of scar tissue or cysts at the site of the cutting; and fistulae (holes or tunnels) between the bladder and the vagina or between the rectum and vagina. Another common long-term complication is pain during sexual intercourse. Women with FC/FGM may also suffer from problems during childbirth. A tightly infibulated woman must be cut open (defibulated) during delivery of her children. If this is not done, labor will be obstructed and this can cause life-threatening complications for both the mother and the child. Some reports suggest that infibulated women may also experience increased pain during menstruation,[19] although these findings have not been verified. Such pain may be attributable to infection, which causes increased pelvic congestion. Infibulation may also heighten a woman's anxiety about the condition of her genitals during menstruation, thus contributing to the pain she experiences at that time.[20]

Psychological effects

While there are few studies on the psychological effects of FC/FGM, available information indicates a strong potential impact on the lives of girls and women. Girls have reported disturbances in eating, sleep, mood and cognition shortly after experiencing the procedure. Many girls and women experience fear, submission or inhibition and suppressed feelings of anger, bitterness or betrayal. Studies from Somalia[21] and Sudan[22] indicate resulting negative effects on self-esteem and self-identity.

There are few studies on the effects of FC/FGM on the sexuality of adult women. Information from available studies[23] indicates that while all types of FC/FGM can interfere to some degree with women's sexual responses, the procedure does not necessarily eliminate the possibility of sexual pleasure and climax. When parts of the genitals are removed, other areas of the body, such as the breasts, can take over roles in sexual stimulation. However, the sexual experience of circumcised women is still not fully understood and further research is needed in this area.

Historical Account of Attempts to Bring Attention to or Stop FC/FGM

The first documented actions to bring attention to the practice of FC/FGM date back to the turn of the twentieth century. However, it is possible that undocumented efforts and initiatives by local populations aimed at stopping the practice were carried out prior to this time.

In the *early 1900s*, colonial administrations and missionaries in the countries of Burkina Faso, Kenya and Sudan attempted to stop the practice by enacting laws and church rules, but such actions only succeeded in provoking anger against foreign intervention. Later attempts by the governments of Sudan and Egypt to pass laws on FC/FGM in the *1940s and*

1950s were also ineffective, largely because of the lack of prior awareness campaigns against the practice.

In the *1960s and 1970s*, indigenous African activism against FC/FGM further developed. In many countries, women's groups led intermittent campaigns to educate the population about the harmful effects of the practice. In addition, doctors – mostly in Sudan, Somalia and Nigeria – who observed patients suffering from complications of FC/FGM began to document the procedure and write about its clinical complications in medical journals.

In *1979*, the WHO sponsored the first Seminar on Harmful Traditional Practices Affecting the Health of Women and Children, in Khartoum, Sudan. Fran Hosken, an American journalist who had traveled through Africa to collect information on FC/FGM, presented her findings. A strong presence of women from several African countries led a vote to end all forms of the practice, against a suggestion from the medical participants for a milder form of the practice to be performed under hygienic conditions. The recommendations included the establishment of national commissions for the coordination of activities against FC/FGM. Despite this historical triumph of women's advocates to stop all forms of FC/FGM, their efforts are still repeatedly undermined by the attempts of the medical community in Africa and the West to medicalize the practice.

In the *1980s*, African women continued to organize to address the practice of FC/FGM. In 1980 four African women activists attended the UN Mid-Decade Conference on Women and the NGO Forum in Copenhagen to present a panel discussion on female circumcision. In that conference, the conflict between the approaches of indigenous African women to stop the practice and those of outsiders was apparent. A few Western women who spoke out against the practice were perceived by African women to be condescending and confrontational.[24] Unfortunately that incident is still registered as the great schism between Western feminists and African cultural conservationists in a crude reading of the historical facts and a biased attempt to fuel the fire of cultural conflict. As a result of this conference, an informal African network was established to address the practice. In 1984, a group of African women organized a meeting of African NGOs in Dakar, Senegal,[25] which resulted in the formation of the Inter-African Committee on Traditional Practices Affecting the Health of Women and Children (IAC). Over the 15 years subsequent to the Dakar seminar, IAC affiliates were founded in over 26 African countries. This regional network has since worked to educate national governments as well as the general public about the harmful effects of FC/FGM.

Another development during the 1980s was critical to later efforts to frame FC/FGM as a human rights violation. This decade marked a period of growing scholarship and thinking by international feminist legal scholars and advocates. They began increasingly to question the lack of a gender lens on the law and on human rights. One critical step in this questioning was the feminist critique of the manner in which most traditional law and human rights analysis focused attention on the "public" sphere – that is, the world of politics, government and the state. Little attention was paid to the "private" domain of the family and society despite the fact that the most frequent violations of women's rights occurred in this context. As a result of this false dichotomy between "public" and "private" spheres, many of the injuries inflicted upon women by private individuals – in the form of domestic violence, dowry deaths and FC/FGM – were not generally viewed as human rights abuses for which governments could be held accountable. In 1981, recognition of governments' responsibility to address violations of women's rights by both government actors and private parties was made explicit in the Convention on the Elimination of All Forms of Discrimination Against Women (Women's Convention).[26] Also during the 1980s, Mrs Halima Embarek Warzazi, a member of the Sub-Commission on the Promotion and Protection of Human Rights (formerly the Sub-Commission on Prevention of Discrimination and Protection of Minorities), was appointed by that body to serve as Special Rapporteur on Traditional Practices Affecting the Health of Women and Children. She has produced several reports documenting national- and international-level action to address FC/FGM.[27]

In the *1990s*, strong African leadership on FC/FGM led to growing international awareness, which resulted in the recognition of FC/FGM as a fundamental violation of women's rights. In 1990, the Committee on the Elimination of Discrimination Against Women (CEDAW), the committee charged with monitoring states' compliance under the Women's Convention, released a general recommendation pertaining specifically to FC/FGM.[28] Moreover, the 1993 United Nations Declaration on the Elimination of Violence Against Women explicitly included FC/FGM within its definition of the phrase "violence against women."[29] The international community again addressed the human rights implications of harmful practices such as FC/FGM at a series of international conferences. These included: the World Conference on Human Rights, Vienna 1993; the International Conference on Population and Development, Cairo 1994; and the Fourth World Conference on Women, Beijing 1995. The Vienna and Cairo conferences were marked by the presence of a powerful women's lobby, which ensured that issues of women's rights remained critical on the world stage. It is thus not surprising that during these meetings and the subsequent women's conference in Beijing, the prevention of FC/FGM was given special attention and strategies for appropriate policies and actions were outlined in the final documents approved by the governments. One result of the increased pressure by the women's movement was the appointment, by the Commission on Human Rights, in 1994, of Rhadika Coomerswamy as Special Rapporteur on Violence against Women. Since her mandate includes FC/FGM, her reports have drawn attention to this subject.[30]

There is currently an extensive network of African organizations working to stop FC/FGM, including women's NGOs, and health, human rights and legal organizations. They have been aided, in part, by a number of national and international donor and technical agencies. For example, several United Nations agencies have been active in promoting FC/FGM prevention worldwide. The WHO, the United Nations Children's Fund (UNICEF) and the United Nations Population Fund (UNFPA) have provided technical, administrative and financial support to a wide range of organizations in many spheres of activity. These agencies have also adopted formal policies and program plans to address the issue.

More recently, as migration from Africa to other parts of the world has increased, there are a growing number of immigrant and refugee service organizations that are working to address the practice among their African immigrant communities. Additional issues that result from dislocation and adapting to a new environment have created the need for new strategies and approaches to address FC/FGM in a broader setting.

Just as discussions about FC/FGM have undergone a transition in the past ten years, so have program interventions. Initially, much of the focus was on basic Information, Education and Communication (IEC) strategies. These centered on informing the population about the harmful health effects of FC/FGM. While provision of information was useful, this in itself was not sufficient to change people's thinking about the practice. In recent years, there has been increased use of innovative methods to reach the population, such as through music, theater and films. There have also been efforts to engage members of the community – such as opinion leaders, religious authorities and village elders – in local campaigns. In addition, there has been the development of more integrated activities on FC/FGM, involving incorporation of information and materials into programs in the health sector, schools and youth groups.

Along with these advances, there is an increased focus on addressing the practice as a violation of women's rights. Legal and human rights organizations are including information on FC/FGM in training programs on women's rights for lawyers, judges and society in general. Moreover, laws criminalizing the practice have been enacted or introduced in many countries. Efforts to make the law responsive to FC/FGM, either by drafting a specific law on the practice, or by pressing for use of existing laws to prosecute cases involving FC/FGM, are also underway in several other countries. While use of legal measures needs to be carefully considered and used in conjunction with other education efforts, laws can be a useful tool for change, giving NGOs and individuals greater leverage in persuading communities to abandon the practice.

More and more, the various actors involved in the fight against FC/FGM acknowledge the strategic importance of framing the issue as a matter of international human rights and obtaining governments' firm commitment to taking appropriate steps to stop the practice. Placing a particular traditional practice within a global paradigm is important for validating a universal reality – discrimination against women. Moreover, the use of an international framework is important in creating and maintaining international pressure for change. Although devising effective international campaigns is a complex task, there is little doubt that international pressure has played a role in efforts to stop FC/FGM. This book thus examines governments' responsibilities under international human rights law, evaluates legal, regulatory and policy measures undertaken thus far, and provides recommendations for future efforts to stop FC/FGM. Speaking of FC/FGM as a human rights issue is a critical tool for long-term social justice.

Notes

1. N. Toubia, *Female Genital Mutilation: A Call for Global Action* (2nd edn), New York: RAINB♀, 1995, p. 9.
2. Ibid.
3. Ibid.
4. Ibid., p. 29.
5. N. Toubia and S. Izett, *Female Genital Mutilation: An Overview*, Geneva: World Health Organization, 1998.
6. Toubia, *Female Genital Mutilation*, p. 9.
7. Nahid Toubia, "Evolutionary Cultural Ethics and Circumcision of Children," in George C. Denniston, Fredrick Mansfield Hodges and Marilyn Fayre Milos, eds, *Male and Female Circumcision: Medical, Legal, and Ethical Considerations in Pediatric Practice*, New York: Kluwer Academic/Plenum Publishers, 1999.
8. Amnesty International, *Female Genital Mutilation: A Human Rights Information Pack*, London: Amnesty International, 1997.
9. Toubia, *Female Genital Mutilation*, p. 9.
10. Al Azhar University, which is one of the oldest Islamic academic institutions, acts as an authority in Qu'ranic interpretation and policy-making.
11. Final Report on the International Conference on Population and Reproductive Health in the Muslim World, Cairo, Egypt, February 21–24, 1998, p. 11.
12. United Nations Population Fund (UNFPA), *The State of the World Population 1999: 6 Billion, A Time for Choices*, New York: UNFPA, 1999, p. 2.

13. Toubia and Izett, *Female Genital Mutilation*, pp. 10–18.
14. Office of the Senior Coordinator for International Women's Issues, Bureau for Global Affairs and the Office of Asylum Affairs, Bureau of Democracy, Human Rights and Labor, US Department of State, *Female Genital Mutilation (FGM) or Female Genital Cutting (FC) in Mali*, 1999, p. 1.
15. Toubia, *Female Genital Mutilation*, p. 21.
16. For more details, please refer to the discussion of France in Part II of this book.
17. World Health Organization (WHO), *Female Genital Mutilation: Report of a WHO Technical Working Group*, Geneva: WHO, 1996, p. 6.
18. For a broader discussion of the health consequences of FC/FGM, see N. Toubia, *Caring for Women with Circumcision*, New York: RAINBQ, 1999; and Toubia and Izett, *Female Genital Mutilation.*
19. Toubia and Izett, *Female Genital Mutilation*, p. 29.
20. Ibid.
21. P. Gassivaro Gallo and E. Moro Moscolo, "Female Circumcision in the Graphic Reproduction of a Group of Somali Girls: Cultural Aspects and Psychological Experiences," *Psychopathologie Africaine*, 1985, pp. 185–6.
22. J. Boddy, *Wombs and Alien Spirits: Women, Men and the Zar Cult in Northern Sudan*, Madison: University of Wisconsin Press, 1989.
23. U. Megafu, "Female Ritual Circumcision of Africa: An Investigation of the Presumed Benefits among Ibos of Nigeria," *East African Medical Journal*, Vol. 60, No. 11, November 1983, p. 795; A.A. Shandall, "Circumcision and Infibulation of Females: A General Consideration of the Problem and a Clinical Study of the Complications in Sudanese Women," *Sudan Medical Journal*, Vol. 5, 1967; A. El Dareer, *Women, Why Do You Weep?*, London: Zed Books, 1982; O. Koso Thomas, *The Circumcision of Women: A Strategy for Eradication*, London: Zed Books, 1987.
24. S. Rich, *Historical Perspective of the FC/FGM Movement*, Presentation Given at the National Conference of the Ethiopian Community Development Council, Washington, DC, Sept. 12, 1997.
25. The Dakar International Seminar on Traditional Practices That Affect the Health of Mothers and Children, Dakar, Senegal, 1984.
26. Convention on the Elimination of All Forms of Discrimination Against Women, opened for signature Dec. 18, 1979, art. 2(e), 1249 UNTS 14 (entered into force Sept. 3, 1981).
27. United Nations General Assembly, "Traditional or Customary Practices Affecting the Health of Women," Report of the Secretary General, Fifty-third Session, Sept. 10, 1998, A/53/354.
28. Committee on the Elimination of Discrimination Against Women (CEDAW), General Recommendation No. 14 (Ninth Session, 1990): Female Circumcision, A/45/38 (General Comments).
29. United Nations General Assembly, Declaration on the Elimination of Violence Against Women, art. 2(a) (85th Plenary Meeting, 1993), A/RES/48/104.
30. United Nations General Assembly, "Traditional or Customary Practices Affecting the Health of Women."

2

International Human Rights Law: A Framework for Social Justice

While reference to "human rights" is common, the expression has not been authoritatively defined.[1] Human rights are generally thought to include those moral and political claims that every human being has upon her or his government or society as a matter of a right – not by virtue of kindness or charity.[2] To regard FC/FGM as a violation of the human rights of women and girls is to view this practice as an infringement by governments and societies upon the moral and political claims of women and children. However, to understand the implications of this powerful statement, it is necessary to have some basic information about the human rights framework and the strategies associated with it. Only then can activists and NGOs begin to view a human rights approach as part of a long-term process of political mobilization and advocacy for change.

This chapter seeks to examine FC/FGM in light of international human rights law. After providing some background about human rights, it discusses the international human rights affected by FC/FGM. The provisions of several key human rights treaties have been interpreted to support women's right to abandon the practice. However, to ensure comprehensive analysis, this chapter also considers the counter-arguments of those who believe that international law does not authorize governments to interfere with the practice of FC/FGM.

Background

Most contemporary human rights are based on international treaties signed by governments in the post-World War II era. Since the end of the war, human rights have been codified in legal instruments at both the international and the regional level. In general, these treaties sought to establish universal standards by recognizing fundamental rights of people and by requiring governments to take actions to ensure that such rights are respected. Most human rights treaties contain relatively short and simple statements regarding the rights of people; the texts of such treaties are usually comparable to national-level constitutions. Although the historical records regarding the negotiations relating to a treaty are often used to interpret these pithy statements, interpretation of the scope of these treaties is usually an ongoing process. The standards set by governments around the world are key to the development of human rights.[3] Since national-level laws and policies incorporate human rights principles and develop these norms, domestic laws are essential tools for interpreting international law standards. In addition, often a United Nations committee that monitors compliance with a particular human rights treaty issues recommendations that set forth the scope of some aspects of the treaty in question.[4] The international community may also gradually help interpret human rights principles, particularly when negotiating global action plans at high-profile international conferences.[5]

Critical to a discussion of FC/FGM as a human rights concern is some sense of the manner in which human rights have evolved. While cultures worldwide have historically recognized a concept of human rights, the origins of modern human rights law can be traced primarily to Europe in the eighteenth century.[6] The body of rights emerging from that period pertained to civil and political matters such as freedom of opinion, conscience and religion, freedom from arbitrary detention or arrest, the right to freedom of association and the right to own property. These rights have been referred to as the "first generation" of human rights.[7] Inspired by the socialist movements of the late nineteenth and early twentieth centuries, a "second generation" of rights focused on economic, social and cultural rights.[8] These rights included the right to decent working conditions, to social security, to education and to health. In the 1980s, scholars also identified a so-called "third generation" of rights.[9] Numerous concerns can be regarded as within this "third generation," and these include: environment, development, peace, communications, and humanitarian assistance. These "group rights" are predicated on solidarity and are regarded as being realizable only through the concerted efforts of numerous actors.[10] Some scholars and activists have criticized this so-called "third generation" as being too vague and representing a proliferation of rights.[11] Commentators have questioned the usefulness of the concept of generations of rights, particularly because it implies that each succeeding generation renders previous generations outdated.[12] However, the notion of generations is a helpful descriptive tool, for it reflects the historical developments within the human rights movement. These developments also form the backdrop against which discussions of the human rights of particular groups, such as women, have occurred.

Fueled by the successes of the human rights movement and by the need to develop new strategies by which to deal with global injustice, numerous political movements have used the human rights framework. Hence, the 1960s and 1970s witnessed the incorporation of racial and gender justice issues within the discourse of human rights. The International Convention on the Elimination of All Forms of Racial Discrimination (the Race Convention) entered into force in 1969, over a decade prior to the Women's Convention, which entered into force in 1981. One of the later developments in the field of human rights has been recognition of children's rights. The Children's Rights Convention entered into force only in 1991. These new areas of international human rights continue to be works-in-progress. While there is an established field of women's human rights law, the international community needs to elaborate upon this framework, particularly in terms of implementation. In newer areas such as children's rights, more needs to be done to strengthen the development and application of a human rights framework.

Notwithstanding the expansion of the human rights field to address social concerns, the means by which to enforce human rights remain limited. There is no global equivalent to national-level police forces. While atrocities committed during some armed conflicts have been addressed by international criminal courts – such as the International Criminal Tribunal for the Former Yugoslavia and the International Criminal Tribunal for Rwanda – these courts have limited jurisdiction.[13] The International Court of Justice (ICJ), which is devoted to deciding legal disputes between nations and to providing advisory opinions to certain international organs and agencies, has not focused primarily on matters of international human rights law.[14] However, the United Nations human rights system has set in place procedures for reporting on current human rights conditions. This system, at the core of which lies the Human Rights Commission, is focused on setting and monitoring human rights standards and using its political stature to make recommendations to governments to enhance human rights. In addition to international-level monitoring, some regional human rights mechanisms, particularly the European human rights system, have been active in enforcing human rights principles. Moreover, enforcement of many human rights principles can occur at the national level. Because the laws of many countries seek to respect and promote human rights, national-level courts are the first step toward the enforcement of human rights principles.

Enforcement of human rights has been aided by the increasing tendency to use the human rights framework as a tool for advocacy and raising public awareness. Highlighting violations of human rights – whether through the United Nations system, national legal and policy regimes or the media – can often be an effective means of enhancing government accountability. Reporting on the existence of human rights violations is also important to assist in the development of international norms. Many national-level movements have sought to build upon the advocacy potential of the human rights framework to promote their goals.

Sources of International Human Rights Law

To place FC/FGM within a human rights framework, it is critical to know more about contemporary human rights law. This body of law is based primarily upon human rights treaties at the international and regional levels, supplemented by United Nations declarations and other instruments.

Three of the earliest and most authoritative human rights instruments are the Universal Declaration of Human Rights (the Universal Declaration, 1948),[15] the International Covenant on Civil and Political Rights (the Civil and Political Rights Covenant, 1966),[16] and the International Covenant on Economic and Social Rights (the Economic, Social and Cultural Rights Covenant, 1966).[17] The Universal Declaration is one of the most influential legal and political instruments of the twentieth century.[18] The international covenants, which are legally binding upon nations that have ratified them, elaborate upon the rights contained in the Universal Declaration. Many nations have incorporated a number of these rights into their constitutions and laws. Strong legal support for action against FC/FGM is also found in more recent treaties. For example, the Women's Convention (1979)[19] and the Children's Rights Convention (1989)[20] focus on the rights of women and girls – the groups affected by FC/FGM.

These international treaties have been supplemented by regional treaties, which also contain provisions protecting the rights of women and girls. Such regional instruments are important because most of the countries in which FC/FGM is practiced are signatories to them. Regional instruments place legal obligations upon governments that may go beyond the obligations those states have agreed to under UN-sponsored treaties. In addition to their direct impact upon parties to those treaties, the regional conventions are evidence of emerging trends in international law, serving as persuasive authority in international settings and in other regions. The regional treaties include the African Charter on Human and People's Rights (the Banjul Charter, 1981),[21] the European Convention for the Protection of Human Rights and Fundamental Freedoms (the European Convention, 1950),[22] and the American Convention on Human Rights (the American Convention, 1969).[23] Nearly all of the African countries discussed in this book are parties to the Banjul Charter and all of the European countries with immigrant populations that practice FC/FGM are parties to the European Convention. However, neither Canada nor the United States –

the two countries in the Americas reviewed in this book – are parties to the American Convention. Nevertheless, the American Convention has been included in this discussion for its contribution to the development of globally accepted human rights norms.

The observations and recommendations of the various UN treaty-monitoring committees are of particular value in interpreting human rights treaties. Such committees have been established under the Women's Convention; the Civil and Political Rights Covenant; the Economic, Social and Cultural Rights Covenant; and the Children's Rights Convention, among others. These committees monitor national compliance with international human rights treaties. Nations that are parties to the human rights treaties are required to submit reports to these committees on a periodic basis to document their compliance with the norms of a particular treaty. Several of these committees have issued statements interpreting human rights instruments to prohibit FC/FGM.[24]

In addition to the above-mentioned sources of international human rights law, support for the elimination of FC/FGM is found in a number of declarations and resolutions adopted by inter-governmental international organizations. For example, the UN General Assembly has issued a Declaration on the Elimination of Violence Against Women, which characterizes FC/FGM as a form of violence.[25] Although not legally binding, these declarations or decisions may be considered evidence of international custom or general principles of law. In addition, they may be the basis for the formulation of a future treaty.[26]

Finally, calls for the elimination of FC/FGM are found in documents adopted at international and regional conferences, which also contribute to the development of human rights law. These include the Programme of Action of the Cairo Conference[27] and the Beijing Declaration and Platform for Action.[28] Again, while not legally binding, these conference documents contribute to the advancement of values recognized by the international community, and may assist in interpreting the scope of provisions contained within existing human rights instruments.[29] In the context of calls to improve women's status, reduce violence against women and improve women's health, both documents explicitly urge governments to take action to eliminate FC/FGM.[30]

The extent to which international human rights law explicitly deals with FC/FGM varies. The key earlier human rights treaties – such as the Civil and Political Rights Covenant and the Economic, Social and Cultural Rights Covenant – do not expressly mention traditional practices such as FC/FGM. Hence, the task of placing FC/FGM within these human rights treaties requires that this particular practice be interpreted within the scope of a broadly termed right, such as the rights to life, liberty and security

> It is important to recognize that most of the human rights protected in international and regional instruments are also enshrined in a number of national-level legal instruments such as national constitutions. Human rights advocates may be able to rely entirely on such instruments in framing legal and political arguments in support of women's rights. If domestic mechanisms are in place to ensure those rights, advocates may have little need to invoke international norms. International protections, however, may offer an avenue to uphold rights that governments have failed to ensure through national-level systems.

of the person. On the other hand, more recent treaties, such as the Women's Convention and the Children's Rights Convention, explicitly address harmful or discriminatory traditional practices. Nevertheless, because attempts to place FC/FGM within a human rights framework represent recent developments in international human rights, specific jurisprudence on this subject remains to be elaborated.

Major International Human Rights Violated by FC/FGM

Subjecting non-consenting girls and women to FC/FGM violates a number of recognized human rights protected in international and regional instruments and reaffirmed by international conference documents. This section discusses the key human rights that can be interpreted to support this view. While most human rights treaties do not refer specifically to traditional practices, this analysis examines the current understanding of the scope of a given human right in order to determine its application to FC/FGM. The following discussion sets forth the various treaties that recognize a particular right and then analyzes how this text is applicable to FC/FGM. This presentation identifies when the human rights community has expressly interpreted FC/FGM as infringing upon certain rights. However, given the general lack of jurisprudence on FC/FGM in human rights, some analysis is based on the authors' views of how certain human rights can be interpreted to support a call to stop FC/FGM.

The right to be free from all forms of discrimination against women

Article 1 of the Women's Convention takes a broad view of "discrimination against women," defining it as "any distinction, exclusion or restriction made on the basis of sex" that hinders a woman's ability to enjoy her human rights equally with men.[31] The prohibition of gender discrimination is supported in numerous international and regional instruments and conference documents. It is a fundamental principle of human rights law.

To view FC/FGM as an act of discrimination against women under human rights law, this practice must fall within the terms of Article 1 of the Women's Convention. This means that FC/FGM must meet two principal criteria: (1) it must be a distinction based on sex and (2) it must have the effect or purpose of impairing the equal enjoyment of rights by women. FC/FGM fits within this definition of gender discrimination. It is a practice reserved for women and girls that has the effect of nullifying their enjoyment of fundamental rights. FC/FGM, a practice aimed primarily at controlling women's sexuality, carries a strong message about the subordinate role of women and girls in society.[32] This procedure represents a societal impulse to repress the independent sexuality of women by altering their anatomy. By perpetuating the perception that women may play only the roles of mother and spouse, FC/FGM serves to reinforce women's subordination in political, economic, social and cultural realms. The view that FC/FGM is indeed a matter of gender discrimination is supported by the fact that CEDAW has issued a specific recommendation on this subject.[33]

Nevertheless, FC/FGM presents an unusual issue with respect to the Women's Convention's definition of discrimination against women. Since both men and women undergo types of circumcision, can FC/FGM be regarded as a "distinction" based on "sex"? The answer is "yes." It is indeed true that male circumcision and FC/FGM have certain features in common. Both involve the removal of healthy tissue and both are generally performed upon a child without capacity to consent. However, what distinguishes FC/FGM from male circumcision is both the severity of most forms of FC/FGM and the social message that is generally associated with the practice. In most situations, FC/FGM is a more severe procedure than male circumcision, and it results in a more extensive removal of a critical sexual organ.[34] In addition, justifications for FC/FGM often relate to societal control of women's sexuality.[35] The practice of FC/FGM thus serves to define the role of women and girls in society – a role that is, in most cases, subordinate to men.

The discussion here is focused on making a case for FC/FGM as a matter of gender discrimination. This analysis should not be interpreted to imply that male circumcision does not merit its own examination under human rights principles. The authors do not argue against the rights of activists opposing the practice of male circumcision to pursue their case.

- **Universal Declaration of Human Rights**, *Article 2*: "Everyone is entitled to all the rights and freedoms set forth in this Declaration, without distinction of any kind, such as race, colour, sex."
- **United Nations Charter**, *Articles 1 and 55*: One of the purposes of the UN is to promote "respect for human rights and for fundamental freedoms for all without distinction as to race, sex, language, or religion."
- **Women's Convention**, *Article 1*: "the term 'discrimination against women' shall mean any distinction, exclusion or restriction made on the basis of sex which has the effect or purpose of impairing or nullifying the recognition, enjoyment or exercise by women, irrespective of their marital status, on a basis of equality of men and women, of human rights and fundamental freedoms in the political, economic, social, cultural, civil or any other field."
- **Civil and Political Rights Covenant**, *Article 2(1)*: "Each State Party to the present Covenant undertakes to respect and to ensure to all individuals within its territory and subject to its jurisdiction the rights recognized in the present Covenant, without distinction of any kind, such as race, colour, sex, language, religion, political or other opinion."
- **Economic, Social and Cultural Rights Covenant**, *Article 2(2)*: "The States Parties to the present Covenant undertake to guarantee that the rights enunciated in the present Covenant will be exercised without discrimination of any kind as to race, colour, sex, language."
- **Banjul Charter**
  Article 18(3): "The State shall ensure the elimination of every discrimination against women and also ensure the protection of the rights of the woman and the child as stipulated in international declarations and conventions."
  Article 28: "Every individual shall have the duty to respect and consider his fellow beings without discrimination."
- **American Convention**, *Article 1*: "The States Parties to this Convention undertake to respect the rights and freedoms recognized herein and to ensure to all persons subject to their jurisdiction the free and full exercise of those rights and freedoms, without any discrimination for reasons of race, color, sex."
- **European Convention**, *Article 14*: "The enjoyment of the rights and freedoms set forth in this Convention shall be secured without discrimination on any ground such as sex, race."

The rights to life and physical integrity, including freedom from violence

The rights to life and physical integrity[36] are considered core human rights.[37] The Human Rights Committee has commented that the right to life should be broadly interpreted and that protection of this right requires states to adopt positive measures.[38] The right to physical integrity, while often associated with the right to freedom from torture,[39] encompasses a number of broader human rights principles, including the inherent dignity of the person, the right to liberty and security of the person,[40] and the right to privacy.[41] Acts of violence that result in death or severe harm obviously interfere with a person's rights to life and physical integrity. Also implicit in the principle of physical integrity is the right to make independent decisions in matters affecting one's own body. An unauthorized invasion or alteration of a person's body represents a disregard for that fundamental right. Recognition that pervasive violence against women is a violation of human rights is founded on these civil and political rights. It is a critical women's issue in the context of the right to physical integrity.

FC/FGM implicates the right to life in the rare cases in which death results from the procedure. Moreover, it violates numerous human rights associated with physical integrity. Since the practice is premised on the notion that women's bodies are inherently flawed and require correction, it does not respect women's inherent dignity. Respect for women's dignity implies acceptance of their physical qualities – the natural appearance of their genitals and their normal sexual function. A decision to alter those qualities should not be imposed upon a woman or a girl for the purpose of reinforcing socially defined roles. Similarly, because FC/FGM is an intervention into one of the most intimate aspects of a woman's life, her sexuality, her privacy rights are violated by the practice.

FC/FGM violates the liberty and security interests encompassed in the right to physical integrity, and is thus a form of violence against women. FC/FGM violates the right to liberty and security of the person. Girls are deprived of their rights to liberty and security when they are subjected to FC/FGM, either against their will or before they have reached an age at which they can give meaningful consent. Deprivations of liberty and security are most obvious when girls are forcibly restrained during the procedure. No less compromising of girls' liberty and security is the subjection of non-protesting girls and women to FC/FGM without their informed consent. Children who consent to FC/FGM are highly susceptible to coercion by adults, who may subject a child to various types of persuasion. Children are also unlikely to understand or have access to information about the consequences and potential complications of the FC/FGM procedure. It should also be recognized that even women over

- **Universal Declaration of Human Rights**
  Article 1: "All human beings are born free and equal in dignity and rights."
  Article 3: "Everyone has the right to life, liberty and security of person."
- **Civil and Political Rights Covenant**
  Preamble: Recognizes the "inherent dignity … of all members of the human family."
  Article 9(1): "Everyone has the right to liberty and security of person."
- **Economic, Social and Cultural Rights Covenant**, *Preamble*: recognizes that human rights "derive from the inherent dignity of the human person."
- **Children's Rights Convention**, *Article 19*: "States Parties shall take all appropriate legislative, administrative, social and educational measures to protect the child from all forms of physical or mental violence."
- **Banjul Charter**
  Article 4: "Human beings are inviolable. Every human being shall be entitled to respect for his life and the integrity of his person."
  Article 5: "Every individual shall have the right to the respect of the dignity inherent in a human being."
- **American Convention**, *Article 5(1)*: "Every person has the right to have his physical, mental, and moral integrity respected."
- **European Convention**, *Article 8(1)*: "Everyone has the right to respect for his private and family life."
- **Inter-American Convention on the Prevention, Punishment and Eradication of Violence Against Women** (Convention of Belem Do Para), *Article 1*: Defines violence against women as "any act or conduct, based on gender, which causes death or physical, sexual or psychological harm or suffering to women, whether in the public or the private sphere."
- **Declaration on the Elimination of Violence Against Women**
  Article 1: "[T]he term 'violence against women' means any act of gender-based violence that results in, or is likely to result in, physical, sexual or psychological harm or suffering to women … whether occurring in public or in private life."
  Article 2(a): "Violence against women shall be understood to encompass, but not be limited to … female genital mutilation and other traditional practices harmful to women."
- **Platform for Action of the Fourth World Conference on Women**
  Paragraph 107(d): "[E]nsure full respect for the integrity of the person, take action to ensure the conditions necessary for women to exercise their reproductive rights and eliminate coercive laws and practices."

Paragraph 118: "Violence against women throughout the life cycle derives essentially from cultural patterns, in particular the harmful effects of certain traditional or customary practices and all acts of extremism linked to race, sex, language or religion that perpetuate the lower status accorded to women in the family, the workplace, the community and society."
Paragraph 232(h): urges governments to "[p]rohibit female genital mutilation wherever it exists and give vigorous support to efforts among non-governmental and community organizations and religious institutions to eliminate such practices."

the age of 18 or mature minors may lack the conditions for consenting to the procedure. Refusing to undergo FC/FGM may jeopardize a woman's family relations, her social life or her ability to find a spouse.[42] The effects of refusing FC/FGM on both her emotional life and her financial security may make meaningful consent to the procedure impossible.

The international community, particularly the United Nations, has regarded FC/FGM as an act of violence against women. The numerous statements issued by the United Nations entities testify to this fact. These include: the General Assembly, in its Declaration on the Elimination of Violence Against Women;[43] CEDAW, in its General Recommendation Number 19 on Violence Against Women;[44] and the Special Rapporteur on Violence Against Women, in various reports.[45] Implicit in the international community's recognition that FC/FGM is a form of violence is its acknowledgement that the practice falls within the scope of Article 1 of the Declaration on the Elimination of Violence Against Women. FC/FGM is thus regarded as an "act of gender-based violence" that "results in … harm or suffering to women."

In viewing FC/FGM as an act of violence against women, it is important to note that the definition of such violence in the Declaration on the Elimination of Violence Against Women does not require intent to harm.[46] Parents who procure FC/FGM for their daughters and the practitioners who undertake the procedure are not motivated by a desire to harm. While those who practice FC/FGM are most likely aware of its harmful effects, they may feel that the benefits of FC/FGM outweigh the harm.

This issue of intent has also been central to not viewing FC/FGM as a form of torture. The Convention Against Torture and Other Cruel,

Inhuman or Degrading Treatment or Punishment (the Torture Convention)[47] defines "torture" as "any act by which severe pain or suffering, whether physical or mental, is *intentionally* inflicted on a person" (emphasis added) for such purposes as obtaining information, punishing, intimidating, coercing or discriminating.[48] This definition does not reflect the mental state of most FC/FGM practitioners and parents procuring FC/FGM for their daughters. Parents or family members, who may not recognize the discriminatory implications of FC/FGM, procure the procedure for girls and young women with hopes of securing their acceptance in society or meeting culturally defined obligations. Pain and suffering are not inflicted solely to cause harm or for the purposes contemplated in the Torture Convention's definition.[49]

There remains some uncertainty as to whether or not FC/FGM can be regarded as "cruel, inhuman or degrading treatment" within the terms of the Torture Convention. Since these terms remain largely undefined, it is difficult to make conclusive determinations. If, however, such treatment requires intent to harm, FC/FGM cannot fall within its parameters. On the other hand, if an act can be "cruel" or "inhumane" or "degrading" regardless of the mental state of the perpetrator, there is a possibility that such terms could cover FC/FGM.

The right to health

Under international human rights law, individuals are entitled to enjoy "the highest attainable standard of physical and mental health."[50] The World Health Organization has defined health as "a state of complete physical, mental and social well-being, not merely the absence of disease or infirmity."[51] According to the Cairo Programme of Action, reproductive health encompasses "sexual health, the purpose of which is the enhancement of life and personal relations."[52] While the right to health does not guarantee perfect health for all people, it has been interpreted to require governments to provide health care and to work toward creating conditions conducive to the enjoyment of good health.[53] CEDAW, in its recent General Recommendation on Women and Health, has recommended that governments devise health policies that take into account the needs of girls and adolescents who may be vulnerable to traditional practices such as FC/FGM.[54]

The complex question here is: how does FC/FGM infringe upon the right to health? Although this right is potentially vast in scope and much work remains to be done to determine its parameters, the right to health is not equivalent to a guarantee of perfect health for all. But does this right mean that people ought not to be subjected to procedures that can

- **Universal Declaration of Human Rights**, *Article 25*: "Everyone has the right to a standard of living adequate for the health and well-being of himself and of his family."
- **Economic, Social and Cultural Rights Covenant**, *Article 12*: "The States Parties to the present Covenant recognize the right of everyone to the enjoyment of the highest attainable standard of physical and mental health."
- **Banjul Charter**, *Article 16*: "Every individual shall have the right to enjoy the best attainable state of physical and mental health."
- **Additional Protocol to the American Convention on Human Rights in the Area of Economic, Social and Cultural Rights**, *Article 10(1)*: "Everyone shall have the right to health, understood to mean the enjoyment of the highest level of physical, mental and social well-being."
- **Programme of Action of the International Conference on Population and Development**, *Paragraph 7.2*: "Reproductive health is a state of complete physical, mental and social well-being and not merely the absence of disease or infirmity, in all matters relating to the reproductive system and to its functions and processes. Reproductive health therefore implies that people are able to have a satisfying and safe sex life.... It also includes sexual health, the purpose of which is the enhancement of life and personal relations."
- **Platform for Action of the Fourth World Conference on Women**, *Paragraph 89*: "Women have the right to the enjoyment of the highest attainable standard of physical and mental health.... Health is a state of complete physical, mental and social well-being and not merely the absence of disease or infirmity."

have a profoundly adverse effect on their health? In other words, can the right to health be interpreted at least to prevent actions that compromise health and prevent individual attainment of the highest possible standard of health? We believe so. Because the complications associated with FC/FGM can have devastating effects upon a woman's physical and emotional health, this procedure can be viewed as an infringement of the right to health. But even in the absence of such complications, FC/FGM compromises the right to health. Where FC/FGM results in the removal of bodily tissue necessary for the enjoyment of a satisfying and safe sex life, a woman's right to the "highest attainable standard of physical and mental health" has been compromised. In addition, any invasive procedure – no matter how "safely" performed – entails risks to the health of the person who undergoes it. Subjecting a person to health risks in the absence of medical necessity should be viewed as a violation of that person's right to health.

In talking about FC/FGM in terms of health, the issue of mental health is a complex one. The Economic, Social and Cultural Rights Covenant recognizes the right of everyone to the highest attainable standard of mental health and the World Health Organization's definition of health has a "social well-being" component. But while FC/FGM can result in negative emotional and psychological consequences, not undergoing FC/FGM can also cause anguish. Because FC/FGM is often a prerequisite for procuring a suitable marriage partner, a girl who has not been circumcised might suffer social, emotional and economic dislocation. However, as indicated by the numerous women who have advocated against FC/FGM in their own countries or sought political asylum in receiving countries in order to avoid the practice,[55] many women and girls view this procedure as emotionally and physically detrimental. Although it is unquestionable that women and girls will differ in the manner in which FC/FGM affects their mental health, there is little doubt about the physical, emotional and societal costs of the procedure. Even when a girl adjusts positively after being circumcised and does not clearly suffer grave psychological consequences, the risk she was put under is unjustifiable and the sacrifice of part of her body must not be the price of social acceptance and harmony.

The rights of the child

Because children generally cannot adequately protect themselves or make informed decisions about matters that may affect them for the rest of their lives, human rights law grants children special protections.[56] The right of the child to these protections has been affirmed in the Children's Rights Convention, one of the most widely ratified international human rights instruments. In the Children's Rights Convention, a "child" is defined as a person below the age of 18 unless majority is attained earlier under the law applicable to the child.[57] Under that Convention, states must respect the role of parents and family members in providing appropriate "direction and guidance" in children's exercise of their rights.[58] However, governments are ultimately responsible for ensuring that all children's rights recognized in the Convention are protected.[59] In so doing, they should be guided by the overarching principle that "the best interests of the child shall be a primary consideration."[60] While this principle may be broadly interpreted to accommodate varying cultural views on what constitutes a child's best interest,[61] such interpretations should be consistent with the Convention's other specific protections.

- **Children's Rights Convention**

  Article 2(1): "States Parties shall respect and ensure the rights set forth in the present Convention to each child within their jurisdiction without discrimination of any kind, irrespective of the child's or his or her parent's or legal guardian's race, colour, sex, language."
  Article 3(1): "In all actions concerning children, whether undertaken by public or private social welfare institutions, courts of law, administrative authorities or legislative bodies, the best interests of the child shall be a primary consideration."
  Article 6(1): "States Parties recognize that every child has the inherent right to life."
  Article 6(2): "States Parties shall ensure to the maximum extent possible the survival and development of the child."
  Article 16(1): "No child shall be subjected to arbitrary or unlawful interference with his or her privacy."
  Article 19(1): "States Parties shall take all appropriate legislative, administrative, social and education measures to protect the child from all forms of physical or mental violence."
  Article 24(1): "States Parties recognize the right of the child to the enjoyment of the highest attainable standard of health."
  Article 24(3): "States Parties [are to] take all effective and appropriate measures with a view to abolishing traditional practices prejudicial to the health of children."

- **African Charter on the Rights and Welfare of the Child** (African Charter):

  Article 4(1): "In all actions concerning the child undertaken by any person or authority the best interests of the child shall be the primary consideration."
  Article 5(2): "States Parties ... shall ensure, to the maximum extent possible, the survival, protection and development of the child."
  Article 10: "No child shall be subject to arbitrary or unlawful interference with his privacy."
  Article 14(1): "Every child shall have the right to enjoy the best attainable state of physical, mental and spiritual health."
  Article 21(1): "States Parties to the present Charter shall take all appropriate measures to eliminate harmful social and cultural practices affecting the welfare, dignity, normal growth and development of the child and in particular:
  (a) those customs and practices prejudicial to the health or life of the child; and
  (b) those customs and practices discriminatory to the child on the grounds of sex or other status."

The international community has generally regarded FC/FGM as a violation of children's rights. Because FC/FGM is commonly performed upon girls between the ages of 4 and 12,[62] those primarily affected by the practice meet the definition of "child" set out in the Children's Rights Convention.[63] Moreover, this treaty is explicit in its call to states to "abolish … traditional practices prejudicial to the health of children."[64] In fact, the concluding observations of the Committee on the Rights of the Child about particular countries often include a call for government action to stop FC/FGM.[65] The concern to stop traditional practices that are harmful to children is also evident in the African Charter, which was adopted by the Organization for African Unity in 1990, and entered into force in December 1999.[66]

Despite the Children's Rights Convention's clear stance against harmful practices, other language raises the the issue of children's ability to consent to a procedure such as FC/FGM. This instrument recognizes that children have an "evolving capacity" to make decisions affecting their lives. [67] It thus establishes the principle that a mature minor may be able to consent to procedures and events under certain conditions. In the context of FC/FGM, ensuring the conditions of consent to the procedure would require an assessment of a girl's capacity to consent and the provision of comprehensive information regarding the consequences of the procedure. Given the pressures faced by many young women in societies in which FC/FGM is practiced, governments should not take at face value even a mature minor's consent to undergo the procedure.

Finally, the Children's Rights Convention requires governments to promote the "best interests" of the child. The Convention can be interpreted as calling upon governments to promote the "best interests" of the child by intervening to prevent the practice of FC/FGM. As noted earlier, preventing girls from undergoing FC/FGM may not always appear at first glance to be in their best interests. Girls who have not experienced the procedure may suffer emotionally from certain social consequences, such as difficulty in finding a spouse or in gaining acceptance among peers.[68] However, the adverse social consequences faced by some girls and women must, of course, be viewed in light of the negative health effects of FC/FGM, as well as the implications of the procedure on women's subordinate status. Given the overall detrimental effect of FC/FGM for women and girls and their societal status, the "best interests" standard should be interpreted to support the call to stop FC/FGM. This view is supported by the fact that the Children's Rights Committee has called for the elimination of FC/FGM.[69]

There is thus ample support under international human rights law for holding governments accountable for the practice of FC/FGM in their countries. FC/FGM infringes upon a number of internationally recognized rights, including the right to be free from gender discrimination, the rights to life and physical integrity, the right to health and the right of the child to special protections. Yet, as is often the case with cultural practices that discriminate against women, a question arises about how to respond to those who argue for the immunity of cultural norms from scrutiny under human rights law. While numerous women's, human rights and other NGOs have called for stopping FC/FGM in various countries, there are also other interests that support the practice on grounds of culture, tradition, minority rights and even religious freedom. What guidance does the human rights framework present in dealing with these dual views? The next section will examine cultural, minority and religious rights and consider the extent to which government efforts to eliminate FC/FGM interfere with the enjoyment of these rights.

Other International Human Rights Raised by FC/FGM

The international human rights system recognizes and promotes a range of rights. Although these rights can sometimes be in conflict with each other, this system does not generally either adjudicate such differences or provide a clear solution. One recurring point of conflict is that between cultural and religious rights, on the one hand, and women's rights, on the other. A striking example of this reality is the almost universal manner in which religious and customary laws discriminate against women in matters relating to family law, particularly marriage, divorce and inheritance. Since international human rights law has begun to address the concerns of a worldwide women's movement and of a body of women's human rights law, this tension has generally been resolved, at least at the international level, in favor of women's status.[70]

In discussing the human rights implicated by FC/FGM, it is important to analyze those that its supporters can invoke. Events in different countries around the world indicate that those who oppose government actions to prevent FC/FGM may view such efforts as threatening to the right to enjoy one's culture or religion free of government interference. Although FC/FGM is not a requirement of any major monotheistic religion, some communities view it as a religious duty. Similarly, where FC/FGM is practiced primarily within a minority group, measures aimed at eliminating the practice have been perceived as an infringement upon the autonomy of the group. Cultural rights, the rights of minorities, and the right to religious freedom have all been recognized in human rights instruments. How are such rights to be viewed in light of the fact that numerous human rights support the call to end FC/FGM? This section seeks to present an answer to this query.

Right to culture

The right of people to participate in their culture is a human right. It was first recognized in the Universal Declaration of Human Rights and has been reiterated by the Economic, Social and Cultural Rights Covenant. In examining human rights associated with culture, it is critical to note that these important instruments are phrased to protect the right of people to take part in cultural life rather than to create a broad and indeterminate right to culture. However, it should be noted that the full scope of the right to participate in culture continues to be developed.[71] The Banjul Charter is particularly strong in its call to "preserve and strengthen positive African cultural values."[72]

Although international human rights instruments have recognized the right of peoples to enjoy and develop their cultures, this right is limited by governments' obligation to uphold other fundamental rights. The Universal Declaration of Human Rights and the Economic, Social and Cultural Rights Covenant contain general clauses stating that none of the rights they recognize should be interpreted to "destroy" any other right. This overall restriction thus applies to the right of people to participate in their culture. Limitations on rights associated with culture are also implicit in the Banjul Charter's call to preserve "*positive* African cultural values" (emphasis added), rather than all cultural practices. Furthermore, limitations on the right to culture are more explicit in later human rights documents such as the Declaration of the Principles of International Cultural Co-operation and the Declaration on Race and Racial Prejudice. For example, the former affirms that "[t]he principles of this Declaration shall be applied with due regard for human rights and fundamental freedoms."[73] While these declarations are not legally binding, they represent international consensus on key norms.

In the context of human rights associated with culture, the critical inquiry for FC/FGM is to assess whether this particular cultural practice infringes upon other human rights. Determining which cultural practices should be respected and preserved and which are unacceptable infringements upon human rights and fundamental freedoms is a complex task that must always be approached with caution. However, given that FC/FGM has been regarded by the international community as gender discrimination and an act of violence against women, this procedure should be regarded as an act that violates women's human rights. The human right to participate in cultural life does not protect this practice. This

- **Universal Declaration of Human Rights**
  Article 27(1): "Everyone has the right freely to participate in the cultural life of the community."
  Article 30: "Nothing in this Declaration may be interpreted as implying for any State, group or person any right to engage in any activity or to perform any act aimed at the destruction of any of the rights and freedoms set forth herein."
- **Economic, Social and Cultural Rights Covenant**
  Article 5(1): "Nothing in the present Covenant may be interpreted as implying for any State, group or person any right to engage in any activity or to perform any act aimed at the destruction of any of the rights or freedoms recognized herein."
  Article 15(1)(a): "The States Parties to the present Covenant recognize the right of everyone: To take part in cultural life."
- **Banjul Charter**, *Article 29(7)*: Gives the individual the duty "[t]o preserve and strengthen positive African cultural values in his relations with other members of the society."
- **Declaration of the Principles of International Cultural Co-operation**
  Article 1(1): "Each culture has a dignity and value which must be respected and preserved.... Every people has the right and the duty to develop its culture."
  Article XI(2): "The principles of this Declaration shall be applied with due regard for human rights and fundamental freedoms."
- **Declaration on Race and Racial Prejudice**, *Article 5*: "Culture, as a product of all human beings and a common heritage of mankind, and education in its broadest sense, offer men and women increasingly effective means of adaptation, enabling them not only to affirm that they are born equal in dignity and rights, but also to recognize that they should respect the right of all groups to their own cultural identity and the development of their distinctive cultural life within the national and international contexts."

conclusion is supported by Article 5 of the Women's Convention, which requires states parties to "take all appropriate measures ... to modify the social and cultural patterns of conduct of men and women, with a view to achieving the elimination of ... customary and all other practices which are based on the idea of the inferiority or the superiority of either of the sexes or on stereotyped roles for men and women."

Rights of minorities

International human rights law recognizes that members of minority groups – racial, ethnic, religious or linguistic – are entitled to special protection to enable them to maintain their own culture, free of interference and discrimination. Protections for the cultural identity of minorities are found in the Civil and Political Rights Covenant and in the Declaration on the Rights of Persons Belonging to National or Ethnic, Religious and Linguistic Minorities (the Minority Rights Declaration).[74] Both these instruments recognize the rights of minorities to enjoy their culture, practice their own religion and use their own language. They also provide, however, that the exercise of rights set forth therein should not imply the infringement of other rights recognized by each document.

The rights of minorities need to be discussed in any dialogue on FC/FGM because in many countries the communities who undertake this practice are members of a minority group. This is the case in non-African countries where FC/FGM is practiced primarily among immigrant groups ("receiving countries"). It is also true in some African countries in which the practice of FC/FGM is limited to a minority ethnic group. Under such circumstances, a decision made by the majority to eliminate FC/FGM is inevitably regarded as an infringement upon the autonomy of the minority group. Minorities are powerless to refute the judgment made upon their practices by the majority.

As with cultural rights, the key inquiry with respect to a minority community's practice of FC/FGM is to determine whether this practice infringes upon other human rights. Although a minority community has the right to practice its culture, the human rights of women in such communities need to be recognized. FC/FGM, with its severe physical effects on all women and girls, including those belonging to a minority community, and its discriminatory assumptions regarding women's sexuality, violates women's human rights and fundamental freedoms. Hence, because a cultural practice such as FC/FGM violates – and prejudices the enjoyment of – the human rights of women and children, governments are not required to respect this practice. Rather, states have a duty to intervene in the practice of FC/FGM. To do otherwise would be to negate the rights of certain women simply *because* they are members of a minority group.

Efforts to eliminate FC/FGM must be motivated by an interest in protecting the rights of women and girls. Such efforts must not be a pretext for the harassment or persecution of minorities. In stopping FC/FGM, governments should act without contempt for minority culture and endeavor to understand the many facets of the practice. In enacting laws

- **Civil and Political Rights Covenant**

  Article 3: States Parties "undertake to ensure the equal right of men and women to the enjoyment of all civil and political rights set forth in the present Covenant."

  Article 5(1): "Nothing in the present Covenant may be interpreted as implying for any State, group or person any right to engage in any activity or perform any act aimed at the destruction of any of the rights and freedoms recognized herein."

  Article 27: "In those States in which ethnic, religious or linguistic minorities exist, persons belonging to such minorities shall not be denied the right, in community with the other members of their group, to enjoy their own culture, to profess and practise their own religion, or to use their own language."

- **Declaration on the Rights of Persons Belonging to National or Ethnic, Religious and Linguistic Minorities**

  Article 2(1): "Persons belonging to national or ethnic, religious and linguistic minorities ... have the right to enjoy their own culture, to profess and practice their own religion, and to use their own language, in private and in public, freely and without interference or any form of discrimination."

  Article 8(2): The exercise of these rights "shall not prejudice the enjoyment by all persons of universally recognized human rights and fundamental freedoms."

and policies that relate to FC/FGM in contexts in which those who practice it belong to minority groups, governments must create safeguards against persecution of minorities. The debate over whether or not a receiving country has the right to pass a law prohibiting FC/FGM misses the crucial issue. The real issue is whether sufficient safeguards have been instituted to ensure that such a law does not become a means of persecuting cultural and racial minorities. The most important step to take when contemplating such a law is to involve progressive and sympathetic groups from the affected community. Extensive community consultations and outreach to community organizations are key to clarifying why such a law is necessary and getting advice on how best to make it effective. Moreover, in addition to legal measures, receiving countries should invest resources in community education and developing outreach programs. Leadership of these efforts should involve health and legal professionals from within the minority community. Finally, governments should: take measures to secure the legal status to refugee women and immigrant women, especially those experiencing domestic violence; invest in programs to empower refugee and immigrant women; and encourage such women to participate in the mainstream economy. Combining such steps with an approach that also criminalizes FC/FGM would increase the chances of stopping the practice and would avoid a top-down approach that could be viewed as patronizing.

Right to religious freedom

The right to religious freedom is an important human right. The Universal Declaration of Human Rights protects the "right to freedom of thought, conscience and religion." Although it was easy for the international community to agree on the general ideals of tolerance and non-discrimination on the basis of religion, the specific parameters of this right have proven more difficult to formulate.[75] In 1981, after nineteen years of negotiations at the United Nations, the Declaration on the Elimination of All Forms of Intolerance and of Discrimination Based on Religion or Belief (the Declaration on Religious Intolerance) was adopted in the General Assembly by consensus.[76] Although this declaration is not legally binding, it is regarded worldwide as articulating a right to freedom of religion and belief and is given significant weight.[77] The right to religious freedom, as defined in international instruments, is limited by governments' duty to protect public health and the fundamental rights of other members of society. For example, both the Civil and Political Rights Covenant and the Declaration on Religious Intolerance subject the manifestation of religion "to such limitations as are prescribed by law and are necessary to protect" "public safety," "health," "morals" or the "fundamental rights and freedoms of others."[78] Hence, restrictions on the manifestation of religion

- **Universal Declaration of Human Rights**
  Article 30: "Nothing in this Declaration may be interpreted as implying for any State, group or person any right to engage in any activity or to perform any act aimed at the destruction of any of the rights and freedoms set forth herein."
  Article 18: "Everyone has the right to freedom of thought, conscience and religion."
- **Civil and Political Rights Covenant**
  Article 5(1): "Nothing in this present Covenant may be interpreted as implying for any State, group or person any right to engage in any

activity or perform any act aimed at the destruction of any of the rights and freedoms recognized herein."

Article 18(1): "Everyone shall have the right to freedom of thought, conscience and religion."

Article 18(3): "Freedom to manifest one's religion or beliefs may be subject only to such limitations as are prescribed by law and are necessary to protect public safety, order, health, or morals or the fundamental rights and freedoms of others."

- **Banjul Charter**

  Article 8: "Freedom of conscience, the profession and free practice of religion shall be guaranteed. No one may, *subject to law and order*, be submitted to measures restricting the exercise of these freedoms" (emphasis added).

  Article 27(2): "The rights and freedoms of each individual shall be exercised with due regard to the rights of others, collective security, morality and common interest."

- **American Convention**

  Article 12(1): "Everyone has the right to freedom of conscience and religion."

  Article 12(3): "Freedom to manifest one's religion and beliefs may be subject only to the limitations prescribed by law that are necessary to protect public safety, order, health, or morals, or the rights or freedoms of others."

- **European Convention**

  Article 9(1): "Everyone has the right to freedom of thought, conscience and religion."

  Article 9(2): "Freedom to manifest one's religion or beliefs shall be subject only to such limitations as are prescribed by law and are necessary in a democratic society in the interests of public safety, for the protection of public order, health or morals, or for the protection of the rights and freedoms of others."

- **Declaration on Religious Intolerance**

  Article 1(1): "Everyone shall have the right to freedom of thought, conscience and religion."

  Article 1(2): "No one shall be subject to coercion which would impair his freedom to have a religion or belief of his choice."

  Article 1(3): "Freedom to manifest one's religion or belief may be subject only to such limitations as are prescribed by law and are necessary to protect public safety, order, health or morals or the fundamental rights and freedoms of others."

may come into effect under two simultaneous conditions – restrictions must be "prescribed by law" and "necessary" to protect specified goals. The former condition has been interpreted to refer to legislative acts.[79]

The issue of religious freedom arises because some communities practice FC/FGM as a matter of religious conscience. Although there is no clear support for the practice of FC/FGM in Islamic texts, a number of African communities in which Islam is practiced believe that FC/FGM is religiously mandated.[80] FC/FGM is also practiced in some African Christian and Jewish communities, again without support from textual sources of religious law.[81] Some may practice FC/FGM in adherence to other African religious faiths.

For communities that view FC/FGM as religiously mandated, state interference in the practice of FC/FGM can be perceived as an infringement upon religious rights. However, as noted above, under human rights law, religious rights are not absolute. They are limited by governments' mandate to protect, among other things, public health and the fundamental rights and freedoms of others. The detrimental effect of a cultural practice upon the health and human rights of women and girls can be a basis for restricting the human right to religious freedom so long as this restriction is embodied in a legislative act. In terms of FC/FGM, if a government enacts a law aimed at stopping FC/FGM in a country in which a community believes that the practice is mandated by its religion, the law would be regarded as a justifiable limitation on religious freedom.

Women and girls who wish not to undergo FC/FGM are themselves entitled to exercise their religious freedom. Where religious leaders are powerful, owing either to their political or to their social influence, they may compel participation in the practice of FC/FGM. Such compulsion is a denial of freedom of thought. Women whose religious convictions do not require them to undergo FC/FGM must be free to act consistently with their faith, abstaining from undergoing the procedure if they wish.[82]

Thus, assertions that the right to culture, the rights of minorities and the right to religious freedom preclude government action against FC/FGM lack support under international human rights law. These rights are not absolute and international law recognizes prescribed limitations. As indicated in human rights instruments, governments need to balance this set of rights against their duty to protect the fundamental rights of every member of society. However, in devising strategies by which to stop FC/FGM, governments need to be sensitive to the concerns related to religion, culture and the minority status of the affected community.

The international human rights framework provides a means for moving forward on FC/FGM. One of the fundamental contributions of this framework to the struggle to end the practice is to place this particular issue within a broader social justice agenda and to make it part of the long-term process of making governments accountable. A human rights approach clarifies that FC/FGM needs to be viewed through a prism that recognizes the complex relationship between discrimination against women, violence, health and the rights of the girl child. Because FC/FGM implicates several human rights, the means by which to redress the practice need to be multifaceted and reflect its complexity. Yet, while human rights principles can be invoked to support the right of women and girls to choose not to undergo FC/FGM, this framework's concern with a broad array of rights mandates that such support be provided in a manner that is sensitive to cultural, religious and minority concerns. Finally, because human rights instruments are focused on government actions, the rights framework spotlights the role of government in efforts to stop FC/FGM. What are the duties of governments in securing the rights of women and girls to be free of this practice? The answers to this question are complex and will be addressed next.

Notes

1. L. Henkin, R.C. Pugh, O. Schachter, and H. Smit, *International Law, Cases and Materials* (3rd edn), St. Paul: West Publishing Co., 1993, p. 597.
2. Ibid., pp. 597–8.
3. F. Newman and D. Weissbrodt, *International Human Rights: Law, Policy, and Process* (2nd edn), Cincinnati: Anderson Publishing Co., 1996, p. 23; Henkin et al., *International Law*, p. 617.
4. Newman and Weissbrodt, *International Human Rights*, p. 15.
5. Ibid., pp. 15–17.
6. S.P. Marks, "Emerging Human Rights: A New Generation for the 1980s," *Rutgers Law Review*, Vol. XXXIII, 1981, pp. 435, 437.
7. Ibid., p. 438.
8. Ibid.
9. Ibid., p. 440–41.
10. Ibid.
11. Ibid., p. 451.
12. Ibid.
13. K.D. Askin, "Sexual Violence in Decisions and Indictments of the Yugoslav and Rwandan Tribunals: Current Status," *American Journal of International Law*, Vol. 93, 1999, p. 97–8.
14. S.M. Schwebel, "Human Rights in the World Court," *Vanderbilt Journal of Transnational Law*, Vol. XXIV, 1991, pp. 945, 946.
15. Universal Declaration of Human Rights, adopted Dec. 10, 1948, GA Res. 217A (III), UN Doc. A/810 (1948).
16. International Covenant on Civil and Political Rights, opened for signature Dec. 16, 1966, 999 UNTS 171, 6 ILM 368 (entered into force Mar. 23, 1976).
17. International Covenant on Economic, Social and Cultural Rights, opened for

signature Dec. 16, 1966, 993 UNTS 3 (entered into force Jan. 3, 1976) (hereinafter Economic, Social and Cultural Rights Covenant).

18. Henkin et al., *International Law*, p. 608; L. Henkin, "The Universal Declaration at 50 and the Challenge of Global Markets," *Brooklyn Journal of International Law*, Vol. 25, 1999, pp. 17, 18.
19. Convention on the Elimination of all Forms of Discrimination Against Women, opened for signature Dec. 18, 1979, 1249 UNTS 13 (entered into force Sept. 3, 1981) (hereinafter Women's Convention).
20. Convention on the Rights of the Child, opened for signature Nov. 20, 1989, GA Res. 44/25, 44 UN GAOR Supp. (No. 49), UN Doc. A/RES/44/49, 30 ILM 1448 (1989) (entered into force Sept. 2, 1990) (hereinafter Children's Rights Convention).
21. African Charter on Human and Peoples' Rights, adopted June 26, 1981, OAU Doc. CAB/LEG/67/3/Rev. 5, 21 ILM 58 (1982) (entered into force Oct. 21, 1986) (hereinafter Banjul Charter).
22. European Convention for the Protection of Human Rights and Fundamental Freedoms, adopted Nov. 4, 1950, 213 UNTS 222 (entered into force Sept. 3, 1953).
23. American Convention on Human Rights, adopted Nov. 22, 1969, OAS Treaty Ser. No. 36, OEA/Ser.L./V/II.23.doc.21, Rev. 6 (1979), 9 ILM 673 (1970) (entered into force July 18, 1978).
24. See Committee on the Elimination of Discrimination against Women (CEDAW), General Recommendation No. 14 (Ninth Session, 1990): Female Circumcision, A/45/38 (General Comments); Committee on the Rights of the Child (CRC), Concluding Observations of the Committee on the Rights of the Child: Togo (Fifteenth Session, 1997), CRC/C/15/Add. 83; Human Rights Committee, Concluding Observations of the Human Rights Committee: Sudan (Sixty-first Session, 1997) CCPR/C/79/Add. 85.
25. United Nations General Assembly, Declaration on the Elimination of Violence Against Women, art. 2(a) (85th Plenary Meeting, 1993), A/RES/48/104.
26. Henkin et al., *International Law*, p. 129.
27. Programme of Action of the International Conference on Population and Development, Cairo, Egypt, 5–13 Sept. 1994, in Report of the International Conference on Population and Development, UN Doc. A/CONF.171/13/Rev.I, UN Sales No. 95.XIII.18 (1995) (hereinafter ICPD Programme of Action).
28. Beijing Declaration and Platform for Action, Fourth World Conference on Women, Beijing, China, 4–15 Sept. 1995, 1 UN Doc. DPI/1766/Wom. (1996) (hereinafter Beijing Declaration and Platform for Action).
29. R.J. Cook, "Human Rights and Reproductive Self-Determination," *American University Law Review*, Vol. XLIV, 1995, pp. 976, 977.
30. Beijing Declaration and Platform for Action, paras 107, 113, 124, 232, 277; ICPD Programme of Action, paras 4.22, 5.5, 7.6, 7.40.
31. Women's Convention, art. 1.
32. See Chapter 1 for discussion on the common justifications for FC/FGM.
33. CEDAW, General Recommendation No. 14 (Ninth Session, 1990): Female Circumcision, A/45/38 (General Comments).
34. N. Toubia, *Female Genital Mutilation: Call for Global Action* (2nd edn), New York: RAINBQ, 1995, p. 9.

35. See Chapter 1 for discussion of the common justifications for FC/FGM.
36. This right is often characterized as the right to "bodily integrity." In this text, the terms "physical" and "bodily" are assumed to be synonymous. For the sake of consistency, the term "physical" is employed throughout.
37. Y. Dinstein, "The Right to Life, Physical Integrity, and Liberty," in L. Henkin (ed.) *The International Bill of Rights*, New York: Columbia University Press, 1981, p. 114.
38. Human Rights Committee, General Comment 6: The Right to Life (art. 6): 30/07/82.
39. See ibid.
40. S.Y. Lai and R.E. Ralph, "Recent Development: Female Sexuality and Human Rights," *Harvard Human Rights Journal*, Vol. VIII, 1995, pp. 201, 207.
41. *X and Y* v. *The Netherlands*, European Court of Human Rights (1986), 8 EHRR 235, Mar. 26, 1985, para. 22.
42. See Chapter 1 for discussion of the common justifications for FC/FGM.
43. General Assembly Resolution adopting the Declaration on the Elimination of Violence against Women, A/RES/48/104 (Dec. 20, 1993), art. 2(a).
44. CEDAW, General Recommendation No. 19 (Eleventh Session, 1992): Violence Against Women, A/47/38 (General Comments).
45. See, e.g., Radhika Coomaraswamy, Preliminary Report Submitted by the Special Rapporteur on Violence Against Women, its Causes and Consequences, to the Commission on Human Rights (Fifty-first Session, 1995), E/CN.4/1995/42.
46. United Nations General Assembly, Declaration on the Elimination of Violence Against Women, art. 1 (85th Plenary Meeting, 1993), A/RES/48/104.
47. Convention Against Torture and Other Cruel, Inhuman or Degrading Treatment or Punishment, opened for signature Dec. 10, 1984, GA Res. 39/46, annex, 39 UN GAOR Supp. (No. 51) at 197, UN Doc. A/39/51 (1985) (entered into force June 26, 1987).
48. Ibid., art. 1.
49. See R. Copelon, "Intimate Terror: Understanding Domestic Violence as Torture," in R. Cook (ed.), *Human Rights of Women: National and International Perspectives*, Philadelphia: University of Pennsylvania Press, 1994, p. 128.
50. Economic, Social, and Cultural Rights Covenant, art. 12.
51. World Health Organization, Constitution of the World Health Organization, in Basic Documents, adopted on July 22, 1946 (14th edn, 1994).
52. ICPD Programme of Action, para. 7.2.
53. A. Rahman and R. Pine, "An International Human Right to Reproductive Health Care," *Health and Human Rights*, Vol. I, No. 4, 1995, pp. 405–6; B.C.A. Toebes, *The Right to Health as a Human Right in International Law*, Antwerp: Intersentia, 1999, pp. 245–58.
54. CEDAW, General Recommendation No. 24 (1999): Women and Health (General Comments), para.12(b).
55. See *in re* Fauziya Kasinga, Bd of Immig. Appeals, File A73 476 695, 1996 BIA LEXIS 15 (June 13, 1996).
56. Children's Rights Convention, preamble.
57. Ibid., art. 1.
58. Ibid., art. 5.
59. Ibid., art. 2.
60. Ibid., art. 3.

61. P. Alston, "The Best Interests Principle: Towards a Reconciliation of Culture and Human Rights," in P. Alston (ed.) *The Best Interests of the Child* , Oxford: Clarendon Press, 1994, p. 19.
62. Toubia, *Female Genital Mutilation*, p. 9.
63. In this Convention, a child is defined as "every human being below the age of 18 years unless, under the law applicable to the child, majority is attained earlier." Children's Rights Convention, art. 1.
64. Ibid., art. 24(3).
65. See, e.g., Convention on the Rights of the Child (CRC), Concluding Observations of the Convention on the Rights of the Child: Togo (Fifteenth Session, 1997), CRC/C/15/Add. 83.
66. Amnesty International, "Female Genital Mutilation and International Human Rights Standards," *Female Genital Mutilation: A Human Rights Information Pack*, London: Amnesty International, 1997.
67. Children's Rights Convention, arts 5, 14.
68. See Chapter 1 for discussion of societal pressures related to FC/FGM.
69. United Nations General Assembly, Traditional or Customary Practices Affecting the Health of Women, Report of the Secretary-General (Fifty-third Session, Sept. 10, 1998), A/53/354, paras 17–18.
70. See, e.g., *Lovelace* v. *Canada* (1981), United Nations Human Rights Committee, *Canadian Human Rights Yearbook*, Vol. 1, 1983, pp. 305–14. Some national courts in Africa have also given women's human rights preference over discriminatory customary practice. See, e.g., in Botswana *Attorney General* v. *Dow*, 1992 SACLR Lexis 7, in Tanzania *Ephrahim* v. *Pastory*, High Court of Tanzania (22 Feb. 1990).
71. For example, the cultural rights of indigenous people have been the subject of discussion in the Sub-Commission on the Promotion and Protection of Human Rights. See Human Rights of Indigenous Peoples, Report of the Working Group on Indigenous Populations on its Sixteenth Session (Geneva, July 27–31, 1998), E/CN.4/Sub.2/1998/16 (Aug. 19, 1998).
72. Banjul Charter, art. 29(7).
73. Declaration of the Principles of International Cultural Co-operation, proclaimed by the General Conference of the United Nations Educational, Scientific and Cultural Organization (UNESCO) (Fourteenth Session, Nov. 4, 1966), art. XI(2), in United Nations, *Human Rights: A Compilation of International Instruments*, Vol. 1 (2nd Part), New York: United Nations, 1993.
74. Declaration on the Rights of Persons Belonging to National or Ethnic, Religious and Linguistic Minorities, adopted by General Assembly resolution 47/135 of Dec. 18, 1992, in United Nations, *Human Rights.*
75. R. Clark, "The United Nations and Religious Freedom," *NYU Journal of International Law and Politics*, Vol. XI, 1978, pp. 196, 206.
76. Declaration on the Elimination of All Forms of Intolerance and of Discrimination Based on Religion or Belief, adopted Nov. 25, 1981, 21 ILM 205 (1982).
77. D. Sullivan, "Advancing the Freedom of Religion or Belief Through the U.N. Declaration on the Elimination of Religious Intolerance and Discrimination," *American Journal of International Law*, Vol. 82, 1988, pp. 487–8.
78. Declaration on Religious Intolerance, art. 1(3); Civil and Political Rights Covenant, art. 18(3).
79. A.C. Kiss, "Permissible Limitation on Rights," in Henkin (ed.), *The Inter-*

national Bill of Rights, p. 304.
80. Toubia, *Female Genital Mutilation*, p. 31.
81. Ibid., pp. 31–2.
82. Cook, "Human Rights and Reproductive Self-Determination," pp. 976, 1012.

3

Duties of Governments Under Human Rights Law

The right of girls and women to abandon FC/FGM has ample support in international law. What remains to be explored is the extent to which governments have a duty to ensure that girls and women in their jurisdictions are empowered to make such a choice. Achieving social justice for women requires recognition of a varied set of interconnected rights. These rights give rise to an equally diverse set of governmental duties. Once identified, these duties provide a useful framework for governmental action to address FC/FGM.

Duties of Governments

As a general rule, international human rights law governs the actions of states, not of private parties. This focus on government action may at first appear to be a barrier to holding governments accountable for FC/FGM. The practice is typically performed by private individuals – such as traditional practitioners and midwives – without the active participation of governments. However, this lack of direct government involvement does not relieve states of accountability before the international community for the practice of FC/FGM. Under international human rights law, governments are bound not only to refrain from violating rights but also to ensure that rights are universally enjoyed in their jurisdictions. Governments may thus be held responsible for failing to take steps to prevent or redress the practice of FC/FGM.

Governments' duty to take action against FC/FGM has its foundation in the provisions of international human rights treaties that require governments both to respect and to promote the enjoyment of individual rights in their jurisdictions. The Civil and Political Rights Covenant obligates states "to ensure" the rights guaranteed therein.[1] This language implies a duty to prevent violations of human rights, at the hands of either governments or private parties. Reflecting the international community's expanding view of state responsibility, more recently adopted

- **Women's Convention**
  Article 2: "States Parties ... agree to pursue by all appropriate means and without delay a policy of eliminating discrimination against women and, to this end, undertake: ...
  (e) To take all appropriate measures to eliminate discrimination against women by any person, organization or enterprise;
  (f) To take all appropriate measures, including legislation, to modify or abolish existing laws, regulations, customs and practices which constitute discrimination against women."
  Article 5(a): "States Parties shall take all appropriate measures to modify the social and cultural patterns of conduct of men and women, with a view to achieving the elimination of prejudices and customary and all other practices which are based on the idea of the inferiority or the superiority of either of the sexes."
- **Children's Rights Convention**
  Article 2(2): "States Parties shall take all appropriate measures to ensure that the child is protected against all forms of discrimination."
  Article 19(1): "States Parties shall take all appropriate legislative, administrative, social and educational measures to protect the child from all forms of physical or mental violence, injury or abuse."
  Article 24(3): "States Parties shall take all effective and appropriate measures with a view to abolishing traditional practices prejudicial to the health of children."
- **Civil and Political Rights Covenant**, *Article 2(1):* "Each State Party to the present Covenant undertakes to respect and to ensure to all individuals within its territory and subject to its jurisdiction the rights recognized in the present Covenant, without distinction of any kind, such as race, colour, sex, language, religion."
- **Economic, Social and Cultural Rights Covenant**, *Article 2(1):* "Each State Party to the present Covenant undertakes to take steps, individually and through international assistance and co-operation, especially economic and technical, to the maximum of its available resources, with a view to achieving progressively the full realization of the rights recognized in the present Covenant by all appropriate means, including particularly the adoption of legislative measures."

human rights treaties, including the Women's Convention and the Children's Rights Convention, place explicit obligations upon governments to prevent human rights violations by private parties. The Women's Convention requires states "to take all appropriate measures to eliminate discrimination against women by any person, organization or enterprise."[2]

Similar language is found in the Children's Rights Convention, which requires states to "take all appropriate legislative, administrative, social and educational measures" to protect children from violence and abuse, including that inflicted by private parties.[3]

Where the human rights at issue are guarantees of economic, social and cultural rights, international legal instruments do not place immediate obligations upon governments. Rather, most of these duties may be fulfilled incrementally, in keeping with governments' changing capacities. The Economic, Social and Cultural Rights Covenant requires states "to take steps ... to the maximum of [their] available resources" to realize the rights protected therein.[4] The Children's Rights Convention similarly specifies that "with regard to economic, social and cultural rights, States Parties shall undertake such measures to the maximum extent of their available resources."[5]

The incremental nature of governments' duties to uphold economic, social and cultural rights makes it difficult to ensure governmental compliance with treaty obligations in these areas. Commentators have developed a useful framework for rendering these duties more concrete. According to this framework, governments are obligated to respect, protect and fulfill economic, social and cultural rights.[6] The duty to "respect" rights requires governments to refrain from taking action that directly violates these rights. The duty to "protect" rights obliges states to prevent violations of rights by private parties or organizations. Finally, the duty to "fulfill" these rights requires governments to take measures and, in some cases, make expenditures that enable individuals to realize their rights.

In addition to the governmental duties that are inferable from general treaty provisions, international human rights instruments impose a number of specific duties upon governments. At least four such duties pertain directly to FC/FGM: the duties to (1) modify customs that discriminate against women; (2) abolish practices that are harmful to children; (3) ensure health care and access to health information; and (4) ensure a social order in which rights can be realized. The Women's Convention is unequivocal in its requirement that governments modify "social and cultural patterns of conduct" that discriminate against women. Similarly, the Children's Rights Convention obligates governments to abolish traditional practices harmful to the health of children. Moreover, the right to health care, particularly reproductive health care, implies that governments must ensure that women and men have access to services that improve their reproductive lives. This right can thus be interpreted to impose upon governments the obligation to provide information, education and appropriate services as they relate to FC/FGM. Finally, efforts to eliminate FC/FGM will not succeed until governments have made substantial progress in meeting their obligation to achieve a social order in which women may fully exercise their human rights. Taken together, these duties provide a framework for government action to eliminate FC/FGM.

The duty to modify customs that discriminate against women

The Women's Convention and subsequent United Nations conference documents establish governments' obligation to modify customs that discriminate against women. Governments should take affirmative measures to address discriminatory customs, even in the absence of demands to do so from female constituents. On the other hand, implicit in the obligation to modify discriminatory customs is women's right to participate in the process of social and cultural change. Governments should be responsive to women who call attention to discriminatory customs. Concerns for equality and overall development must be given priority over the interests of politically influential community leaders interested in preserving a status quo that discriminates against women.

- **Women's Convention**
  Article 2: "States Parties ... undertake: ... (f) To take all appropriate measures, including legislation, to modify or abolish existing laws, regulations, customs and practices which constitute discrimination against women."
  Article 5: "States Parties shall take all appropriate measures: (a) To modify the social and cultural patterns of conduct of men and women, with a view to achieving the elimination of prejudices and customary and all other practices which are based on the idea of the inferiority or the superiority of either of the sexes or on stereotyped roles for men and women."
- **Programme of Action, World Conference on Human Rights**, *Paragraph 38*: "[T]he World Conference on Human Rights stresses the importance of working towards the eradication of any conflicts which may arise between the rights of women and the harmful effects of certain traditional or customary practices, cultural prejudices and religious extremism."
- **Programme of Action of the International Conference on Population and Development**, *Paragraph 5.5*: Recommends that measures be "adopted and enforced to eliminate child marriages and female genital mutilation."
- **Platform for Action, Fourth World Conference on Women**, *Paragraph 224*: "Any harmful aspect of certain traditional, customary or modern practices that violates the rights of women should be prohibited and eliminated."

Governments attempting to eliminate FC/FGM face a challenge. FC/FGM is firmly rooted in custom, and in many cases its primary proponents are the women who practice it. As established in Chapter 2, however, claims of autonomy from public intervention in matters of culture and religion have little support in human rights law. Governments are bound to take action against FC/FGM to promote the interests of all women and protect their human rights.

The duty to abolish practices that are harmful to children

The Children's Rights Convention calls upon states to "take all effective and appropriate measures with a view to abolishing traditional practices prejudicial to the health of children."[7] This mandate is reinforced by the African Charter on the Rights and Welfare of the Child, which requires states to "abolish customs and practices harmful to the welfare, normal growth and development of the child and in particular: (a) those customs and practices prejudicial to the health or life of the child, and (b) those customs and practices discriminatory to the child on the grounds of sex or other status."[8]

- **Children's Rights Convention,** *Article 24(3)*: "States Parties [are to] take all effective and appropriate measures with a view to abolishing traditional practices prejudicial to the health of children."
- **African Charter,** *Article 21*: Requires member states of the Organization of African Unity (OAU) to abolish customs and practices harmful to the "welfare, dignity, normal growth and development of the child and in particular: (a) those customs and practices prejudicial to the health or life of the child; and (b) those customs and practices discriminatory to the child on the grounds of sex or other status."
- **Programme of Action of the International Conference on Population and Development,** *Paragraph 5.5*: "Measures should be adopted and enforced to eliminate child marriages and female genital mutilation."
- **Platform for Action of the Fourth World Conference on Women,** *Paragraph 39*: Girls are "often subjected to various forms of ... violence and harmful practices such as female infanticide and prenatal sex selection, incest, female genital mutilation and early marriage, including child marriage."
- **Programme of Action of the World Conference on Human Rights,** *Paragraph 49*: Urges "States to repeal existing laws and regulations and remove customs and practices which discriminate against and cause harm to the girl child."

The Children's Rights Convention, in its evaluation of state reports, has consistently characterized FC/FGM as a "harmful traditional practice" that governments must work to eliminate.[9] In addition, FC/FGM falls squarely within the African Charter's provision on harmful customs and practices, for it is unquestionably prejudicial to the health of the child, and may threaten a child's life. As discussed in the previous chapter, FC/FGM is also a form of discrimination against girls.

The duty to ensure health care and access to health information

The governmental duty to ensure health care has been articulated in a number of international and regional conventions. One critical component of this duty is the responsibility to ensure "access to specific educational information to help ensure the health and well-being of families."[10] Also encompassed in the duty to ensure health care is the government obligation to guarantee access to all necessary health services.

Health education is a crucial strategy for eliminating FC/FGM. Governments should undertake educational efforts at the community level to inform women of the health risks of FC/FGM – both to themselves and to future offspring. Educational programs should be designed to reach women and girls of every age, educational level and social and economic status. In addition, the right to health care has implications for women and children who have already been subjected to FC/FGM and who are suffering from the complications of the procedure. They should be given access to treatments for complications associated with FC/FGM. In countries with immigrant populations from cultures in which FC/FGM is prevalent, health care providers need to receive adequate training to enable them to provide appropriate care to women and girls suffering from the effects of the practice.[11]

CEDAW, in its general recommendation on women and health, characterized governments' obligation to provide health care as the duty to respect, protect and fulfill that right.[12] This framework elucidates governmental duties in the context of FC/FGM. The duty to *respect* the right to health care requires states to refrain from obstructing women's efforts to meet their health care needs.[13] When physicians perform FC/FGM in public hospitals upon a girl or upon a woman who has not given informed consent,[14] governments are implicated in a practice that interferes with women's and girls' right to health care. Public health care facilities should actively impart information to women and girls about the health consequences of FC/FGM. Governments, through their employees, should not perform the procedure upon girls and women who do not have a full understanding of its health effects or who are not in a position to consent

- **Economic, Social and Cultural Rights Covenant**, *Article 12(2)*: "The steps to be taken by States Parties to the present Covenant to achieve the full realization of [the right to health] shall include those necessary for: (a) The provision for the reduction of the still-birth rate and of infant mortality and for the healthy development of the child; ... (d) The creation of conditions which would assure to all medical service and medical attention in the event of sickness."

- **Women's Convention**, *Article 12*: Prohibits discrimination "in the field of health care," ensures equal "access to health care services, including those related to family planning," and requires States to "ensure to women appropriate services in connection with pregnancy, confinement and the post-natal period, granting free services where necessary, as well as adequate nutrition during pregnancy and lactation."

- **Children's Rights Convention**, *Article 24(1)*: "States Parties recognize the right of the child ... to facilities for the treatment of illness and rehabilitation of health. States Parties shall strive to ensure that no child is deprived of his or her right of access to such health care services."

- **Banjul Charter**, *Article 16(2)*: "States Parties to the present Charter shall take the necessary measures to protect the health of their people and to ensure that they receive medical attention when they are sick."

- **Additional Protocol to the American Convention on Human Rights in the Area of Economic, Social and Cultural Rights**, *Article 10(2)*: "In order to ensure the exercise of the right to health, the States Parties agree to recognize health as a public good and, particularly, to adopt the following measures to ensure that right: (a) Primary health care, that is, essential health care made available to all individuals and families in the community; (b) Extension of the benefits of health services to all individuals subject to the State's jurisdiction."

- **African Charter**, *Article 14(2)*: "States Parties ... shall take measures: ... (b) to ensure the provision of necessary medical assistance and health care to all children with emphasis on the development of primary health care; ... (f) to develop preventive health care and family life education and provision of services."

- **Platform for Action of the Fourth World Conference on Women**, *Paragraph 106(c)*: Recommends that governments "remove all barriers to women's health services and provide a broad range of health-care services."

to it freely. Governments' duty to *protect* the right to health care requires states to prevent violations of the right by private parties.[15] Knowing that FC/FGM is harmful to women's sexual health and that it may result in severe complications, governments should take action to prevent the practice of FC/FGM in all settings.[16] As discussed in Chapter 4, prevention efforts may take various forms, including educational programs and criminal legislation. In the context of health, this duty requires states to provide adequate health care and education. The duty to *fulfill* the right to health care obligates states to undertake measures that enable women to realize fully their right to health.[17] CEDAW, in its recent recommendation on Women and Health, stated that the duty to fulfill the right to health requires governments to address systemic barriers to health by taking "appropriate legislative, judicial, administrative, budgetary, economic and other measures to the maximum extent of their available resources to ensure that women realize their rights to health care."[18]

The duty to ensure a social order in which rights can be realized

It is the obligation of states to create an environment that is conducive to the full enjoyment of human rights. Article 28 of the Universal Declaration of Human Rights provides that "[e]veryone is entitled to a social and international order in which the rights and freedoms set forth in this Declaration can be fully realized."[19] This provision suggests that governments have a duty to identify and address the social and economic factors preventing some sectors of society from exercising their human rights.

- **Universal Declaration**, *Article 28*: "Everyone is entitled to a social and international order in which the rights and freedoms set forth in this Declaration can by fully realized."
- **Economic, Social and Cultural Rights Covenant**, *Preamble*: "[T]he ideal of free human beings enjoying freedom from fear and want can only be achieved if conditions are created whereby everyone may enjoy his economic, social and cultural rights, as well as his civil and political rights."
- **Civil and Political Rights Covenant**, *Preamble*: "[T]he ideal of free human beings enjoying civil and political freedom and freedom from fear and want can only be achieved if conditions are created whereby everyone may enjoy his civil and political rights, as well as his economic, social and cultural rights."

In a number of communities, women and girls who do not undergo FC/FGM may have difficulty entering into marriage. In societies in which there are legal and cultural barriers to women's economic independence, a woman's inability to marry deprives her of basic economic security.[20] Efforts to eliminate FC/FGM, therefore, must include action to improve the status of women in every sector of society. For example, governments must address women's status in the family, their access to education, and their economic position. Governments should revisit family laws that render women dependent upon their husbands or fathers. Property and labor laws that limit women's economic self-sufficiency should be reformed. Governments should also undertake efforts to remove barriers to women's education. Only when women have truly attained a status equal to that of men will they be empowered to make a genuine choice about whether or not to undergo FC/FGM.

Where human rights norms require governments to change their own policies or amend laws, measuring compliance is relatively straightforward. NGOs and members of the international community are well equipped to monitor a government's failure to make laws and policies conform to their duties under human rights law. However, in the context of FC/FGM, human rights law requires governments to do much more than change laws and policies. Governments must work to change social norms and individual behavior, fostering women's equality and autonomy in both public and private settings. Measuring governments' efforts to do so poses a significant challenge.

Measuring Compliance

While the duties of governments to address FC/FGM may be readily identifiable in human rights treaties, standards for measuring government fulfillment of those duties are less clear. Because private parties, and not governments, are the primary perpetrators of FC/FGM, it is not in governments' power to eliminate the practice outright. Governments must undertake long- and short-term strategies, and employ legal, regulatory and policy measures in an effort to shape social norms. Given the diverse legal, economic, social and political environments of the countries in which FC/FGM is practiced, there are no standard criteria by which to evaluate whether governments have met their various duties. Rather, under international law, the prevailing legal standard used to assess government action or inaction is the general one of "due diligence." Governments are required to exercise "due diligence" in preventing, investigating and punishing violations of human rights by both government actors and private persons.[21] Where governments fail to act with due diligence to ensure protected rights, they may themselves be held responsible for violations of those rights by private parties. In 1992, the treaty-monitoring body of the Women's Convention, CEDAW, endorsed the due diligence standard. CEDAW, in its General Recommendation on Violence Against Women, noted that "States may ... be responsible for private acts if they fail to act with due diligence to prevent violations of rights or to investigate and punish acts of violence, and for providing compensation."[22]

The "due diligence" standard has been applied and elaborated on in different international settings. In 1988, the Inter-American Court of Human Rights addressed the "due diligence" standard in the Velasquez Rodriguez case, which involved disappearances in Honduras.[23] The court determined that the government of Honduras could be held responsible for the kidnapping of Angel Manfredo Velasquez Rodriguez, even had there been no proof of direct government action. The court's opinion relied upon Article 1 of the American Convention, which requires states parties to "ensure" the free and full exercise of the rights and freedoms recognized therein.[24]

The Inter-American Court held that States must "take reasonable steps" to prevent and investigate human rights violations, identify and punish those responsible, and compensate the victims of those violations.[25] The Court emphasized that a failure to prevent or successfully investigate a single human rights violation did not necessarily give rise to state responsibility for that violation.[26] However, states must undertake efforts to address violations "in a serious manner and not as a mere formality preordained to be ineffective."[27] Governments that tolerate or condone a pattern of abuse may be deemed complicit in perpetuating that pattern.[28]

It is important to note that the due diligence standard must be adapted to the right in question, in some cases placing greater emphasis on the prevention of violations than on investigation and punishment. Preventing the practice of FC/FGM will require due diligence in, for example, carrying out efforts to empower women in various aspects of their lives. While some governments may find it appropriate to use law enforcement mechanisms to discourage the practice of FC/FGM, investigation and punishment in this context may not always be the most effective strategy for eliminating the practice. Nations should determine effective means of preventing FC/FGM and meet the standard of "due diligence" in pursuing those means.

Governments should acknowledge their responsibility to ensure that women and girls in their jurisdictions are free to reject the practice of FC/FGM. In designing a course of action, governments should be guided by their duties to change customs that discriminate against women, eliminate practices that are harmful to children, ensure access to health care, and ensure the existence of a social order in which women's rights can be realized. The next chapter translates these broad principles into concrete recommendations for government action.

Notes

1. International Covenant on Civil and Political Rights, opened for signature Dec. 16, 1966, art. 2(1), 999 UNTS 171, 6 ILM 368 (entered into force Mar. 23, 1976).
2. Convention on the Elimination of All Forms of Discrimination Against Women, opened for signature Dec. 18, 1979, art. 2(e), 1249 UNTS 13 (entered into force Sept. 3, 1981) (hereinafter Women's Convention).
3. Convention on the Rights of the Child, opened for signature Nov. 20, 1989, art. 19, GA Res 44/25, 44 UN GAOR Supp. (No. 49), UN Doc. A/RES/44/49, 30 ILM 1448 (1989) (entered into force Sept. 2, 1990) (hereinafter Children's Rights Convention).
4. International Covenant on Economic, Social and Cultural Rights, opened for signature Dec. 16, 1966, art. 2, 993 UNTS 3 (entered into force Jan. 3, 1976).
5. Children's Rights Convention, art. 4.
6. A. Eide, "The Right to an Adequate Standard of Living Including the Right to Food," in A. Eide, C. Krause and A. Rosas (eds), *Economic, Social and Cultural Rights: A Textbook*, Boston: Martinus Nijhoff, 1995, pp. 89–105.
7. Children's Rights Convention, art. 24(3).
8. African Charter on the Rights and Welfare of the Child, adopted 1991, art. 21, OAU Doc. CAB/LEG/24.9/49 (1990).
9. See, e.g., Committee on the Rights of the Child (CRC), Concluding Observations: Ethiopia, 24/01/97, para. 6; CRC, Concluding Observations: Sudan, 18/10/93, CRC/C/15/Add. 10, para. 13; CRC, Concluding Observations: Togo, 10/10/97, CRC/C/15/Add. 83, para. 24.
10. Women's Convention, art. 10(h).
11. For further information on appropriate clinical and counseling approaches, see N. Toubia, *Caring for Women with Circumcision: A Technical Manual for Health Care Providers*, New York: RAINBQ, 1999.
12. Committee on the Elimination of Discrimination Against Women (CEDAW), Women and Health: General Recommendation No. 24 (Twentieth Session, 1999) (General Comments), para. 13; see also D. Sullivan, "The Nature and Scope of Human Rights Obligations Concerning Women's Right to Health," *Health and Human Rights* Vol. 1, No. 4, 1995, pp. 369, 377.
13. CEDAW, Women and Health: General Recommendation No. 24 (Twentieth Session, 1999) (General Comments), para. 14.
14. According to the United Nations Resolution on Principles for the Protection of Persons with Mental Illness and for the Improvement of Mental Health Care, informed consent "is a consent obtained freely, without threats or improper inducements, after appropriate disclosure to the patient of adequate and understandable information in a form and language understood by the patient on: (a) diagnostic assessment; (b) the purpose, method, likely duration

and expected benefit of the proposed treatment; (c) alternative modes of treatment, including those less intrusive, and (d) possible pain or discomfort, risk and side-effects of the proposed treatment." Resolution 46/119 of Dec. 17, 1991. This definition has been endorsed by the Committee for the Study of Ethical Aspects of Human Reproduction, International Federation of Gynecology and Obstetrics (FIGO). Committee for the Study of Ethical Aspects of Human Reproduction, FIGO, *Recommendations on Ethical Issues in Obstetrics and Gynecology*, London, 1997.

15. CEDAW, Women and Health: General Recommendation No. 24 (Twentieth Session, 1999) (General Comments), para. 15(d).
16. Ibid., para. 15.
17. Ibid., para. 17.
18. Ibid.
19. Universal Declaration of Human Rights, adopted Dec. 10, 1948, art. 28, GA Res. 217A (III), UN Doc. A/810 (1948).
20. J. Fitzpatrick, "The Use of International Human Rights Norms to Combat Violence Against Women," in R. Cook (ed.) *Human Rights and Women – National and International Perspectives*, Philadelphia: University of Pennsylvania Press, 1994, pp. 532, 541.
21. Velasquez Rodriguez Case, judgment of July 29, 1988, Inter-Am.Ct.H.R. (Ser. C) No. 4 (1988).
22. CEDAW, Violence Against Women, General Recommendation No. 19 (Eleventh Session 1992), A/47/38 (General Comments), para. 9.
23. Velasquez Rodriguez Case.
24. Ibid., para. 166.
25. Ibid., para. 174.
26. Ibid., paras 175 and 177.
27. Ibid., para. 177.
28. Ibid., paras 173 and 176.

4

Recommendations for Governments

International human rights law gives rise to a governmental duty to ensure conditions that enable women to abandon the practice of FC/FGM. Once governments have acknowledged this duty, they should determine an effective course of action. Stopping FC/FGM involves a sea change in societal and individual thinking. Because FC/FGM plays a vital role in defining gender, women's status and self-identity for the majority of those communities that practice it, persuading them to view FC/FGM differently is not an easy challenge. Stopping the practice by providing women with the information and choices to abandon FC/FGM cannot be achieved by the simple act of drafting or interpreting a set of human rights principles or laws, even though such steps are necessary to enhance the process of change. To effect such profound social change, government action should take multiple forms and be part of a long-term process of obtaining social justice for all, particularly women.

Prior to commencing a discussion about the actions that governments can undertake to stop FC/FGM, it is useful to take note of a fundamental division of responsibilities within most governments, including those that are the concern of this book. There are generally three branches of government involved in the formation of law and policy. One is the legislature, which enacts legislation and whose members are usually elected officials. The second is the judiciary, which renders decisions on individual lawsuits and, in some nations, determines whether specific legislation or government action is in conformity with constitutional and international human rights norms. There is a hierarchy of courts in most countries and judges can be both appointed and elected. Finally, there is the executive branch, which oversees enforcement of the law and issues policies and recommendations to be implemented by government agencies. The distribution of power between these three principal branches of government varies. But this division of responsibilities is important in discussing the actions of governments since each branch should be involved in some manner to achieve an overall government objective.

While empowering women to make choices relating to FC/FGM requires government action in various forms, it is useful to review steps taken in a more limited sphere – law – to address this practice. As indicated in Part II of this book, none of the 41 countries reviewed has enacted a constitutional provision explicitly addressing FC/FGM. The constitutions of Ethiopia, Ghana and Uganda do, however, contain provisions that are applicable to FC/FGM. In addition, the constitutions of 29 other countries specifically guarantee the unconditional equality of women and men under law; 15 national constitutions explicitly protect the rights of children; and 20 constitutions declare the supremacy of constitutional protections and other formal law over customary or religious laws. Many countries have enacted criminal laws to address FC/FGM. To date, 16 countries – nine in Africa and seven industrialized countries elsewhere – have enacted laws criminalizing this practice (see Table 2, p. 101, for the names of these countries). In addition, one country, France, has consistently prosecuted cases of FC/FGM on the basis of general provisions of its Penal Code. (For more information on national-level action to address FC/FGM, see Part II.[1])

With the foregoing information on government legal actions serving as a backdrop, this chapter recommends actions for governments of African countries and governments of countries that receive immigrants from parts of Africa where FC/FGM is prevalent. The latter are referred to as "receiving countries." Suggested government action can be divided into roughly three categories: legal measures; regulatory measures; and broad policies. In the context of FC/FGM, legal measures should be viewed broadly to include reforms necessary to promote women's rights as well as laws specific to the practice. In terms of the latter, legal measures either create penalties for participation in the practice or provide protections for those who have undergone the procedure or are at risk of doing so. Regulatory measures can be aimed at specific groups, such as health professionals, who may be in a position either to discourage FC/FGM or to promote it. Policies addressing FC/FGM, which may encompass education and outreach programs, may be part of broader government initiatives aimed at promoting women's empowerment. Where possible, recommendations are accompanied by examples drawn from Part II of this volume on national-level government action. Because broad national policies aimed at women's empowerment fall beyond the scope of this book, examples of such policies have not been included.

It should be noted that measures addressing FC/FGM in African countries may differ from those adopted in receiving countries. In many African countries, where FC/FGM is deeply embedded in the culture of the majority, governments will have to devise strategies to contend with widespread resistance to change. In receiving countries, where FC/FGM occurs primarily among immigrants from parts of Africa where the practice is prevalent, governments should be sensitive to the situation of the minority and immigrant women and girls who are likely to be affected by the practice. Immigrant women may be wary of governmental efforts to prevent them from engaging in cultural practices that they take for granted. Receiving country governments should take care to ensure that their efforts to address FC/FGM do not result in alienating the community that they wish to assist.

Legal Measures

Ratify international and regional human rights instruments

As noted in previous chapters of this book, governments that ratify international and regional human rights treaties undertake a binding legal obligation to uphold the rights protected in those treaties. The effects of treaty ratification, however, are not solely legal. A clear government commitment to upholding human rights, as evidenced by ratification of international human rights treaties, can also have an impact on social justice movements. Social change can be achieved by advancing political movements that push behavioral norms from the accepted and emotionally familiar to the new, untested and potentially frightening. International human rights treaties and declarations, when ratified by governments and popularized by NGOs, can add legitimacy to such social movements. In doing so, human rights norms play the role of catalyst in a much larger process that must be initiated at the local or community level. In applying this strategy to FC/FGM, it is important to ensure that governments ratify appropriate international and regional human rights treaties. Those discussed in the previous chapter are particularly important.

As illustrated in Table 1 (p. 100), every country reviewed in this book is a party to some or all of the international and regional human rights conventions that are relevant to FC/FGM. These include: the Women's Convention; the Children's Rights Convention; the Civil and Political Rights Covenant; the Economic, Social and Cultural Rights Covenant; the Banjul Charter; the European Convention; and the American Convention. Of the 41 countries reviewed in this book 37 are parties to the Women's convention and four – Mauritania, Somalia, Sudan and the United States – are not. Thirty-nine countries have ratified the Children's convention and two, namely Somalia and the United States, have not. In fact, the United States is a party only to the Civil and Political Rights Covenant.

This is a noteworthy point, given the strong position government delegates from the United States have taken in support of women's human rights in international forums.

When governments ratify these treaties, it is important that they not undermine the force of these instruments by entering reservations. A handful of countries have made reservations to these treaties that potentially undercut state obligations to promote women's rights. For example, Egypt has made reservations to the Women's Convention asserting the precedence of Islamic Sharia law over articles of the treaty that prohibit discrimination against women and provide for equality in marriage and family relations. Similarly, Mauritania's reservations to the Children's Rights Convention declare the supremacy of the principles of Islam over all conflicting mandates of the Convention. As noted in Chapter 1, the legitimacy under international law of these broad reservations is questionable. Because reservations must be consistent with the "object and purpose" of the treaty, reservations that are so broad as to undermine the intended force of the treaty are regarded as invalid under international law.[2]

Government ratification of treaties is merely a first step toward social change. Much more needs to be done to transform the obligations of governments into concrete action that benefits people. Subsequent national-level action must be taken to ensure that all existing domestic legislation is compatible with the ratified treaty. In addition, once a treaty is ratified, future national-level legislation should be reviewed to determine its compatibility with the treaty. In some circumstances – as in the case of FC/FGM – governments may have to enact laws and create policies to address the widespread practices of private parties that violate the principles upheld in the treaty.

Ensure constitutional protections of the rights of women and girls

Most countries, as parties to international human rights treaties, have acknowledged a duty to protect women and girls from practices that threaten their physical integrity and health. These duties should be enshrined in national-level legal instruments, and have a force of law superior to that of other parliamentary and executive acts, as well as to that of customary and religious law. A nation's constitution is its law of highest authority. All legislation and government action should conform to the norms established in the constitution. Constitutional measures that uphold the rights of women and girls to be free from FC/FGM are thus critical and can shape governmental responses to the practice. In some countries, constitutional provisions provide legal remedies for women and girls who have been subjected to it.

Among the constitutions of countries where FC/FGM is practiced, none explicitly addresses FC/FGM. However, the constitutions of three countries contain provisions applicable to FC/FGM. The constitution of Ethiopia guarantees women protection from "harmful customs." Uganda's constitution declares that customs or traditions that are "against the dignity, welfare or interest of women or which undermine their status" are prohibited. The constitution of Ghana also provides that "traditional practices" injurious to people's health and well-being shall be abolished. While the constitutions of receiving countries tend to be less explicit than those of African countries in their protections of the rights of women and girls, such protections may be available in other sources of law, such as court decisions or legislation.

The constitutions of several African countries, including those of Kenya and the Gambia, explicitly declare that guarantees of non-discrimination are not applicable in matters governed by customary law. Because customary law in Africa frequently governs such matters as marriage and inheritance, a government's refusal to enforce women's equality when customary law is at issue may result in a perpetuation of conditions that lead to women's subordination. Women's weak social standing, in turn, reinforces their inability to reject FC/FGM. In matters affecting individual rights, constitutions of all countries should declare their supremacy over customary and religious law.

Where constitutions do not contain provisions that may be clearly interpreted to promote gender equality, including the elimination of cultural practices such as FC/FGM, governments should consider amending their constitutions. Constitutions should be unambiguous in securing the equality of women and men under the law in all matters, protecting the rights of children and guaranteeing women and children protection against harmful customs. The legal effects of such constitutional protections would vary according to each country's legal system. At the very least, a provision of constitutional status would guide members of the government in their drafting and implementation of law and policy. In addition, in many countries, a judicial body might have the power to strike down laws and policies that were inconsistent with such a protection. Moreover, the possibility for bringing lawsuits is enhanced. Women could sue governments for complicity in the perpetration of FC/FGM or, in some systems, bring claims against another private party, such as an FC/FGM practitioner, for violating the constitutional protection. Whatever the legal effects of a constitutional protection against FC/FGM, such a provision would represent a clear government commitment to protecting the rights of women and girls and could contribute to the legitimacy of a developing social movement.

Undertake other legal reform to promote women's equality

Because enabling women to make the choice to abandon FC/FGM requires profound social change and improvements in the status of women, governments should reform all existing laws that are barriers to women's equality. In particular, in African countries, it is critical for governments to reform customary and religious laws that discriminate against women. In many cases this means changing family laws, such as those that relate to marriage, divorce, custody and inheritance, as well as laws relating to property. Since many African countries have dual legal systems in which civil law operates alongside a customary/religious system governing personal and property law, women continue to face legal discrimination. In such situations, developing uniform civil laws relating to family law and the right of women to own property would represent an enormous step toward women's equality. In receiving countries, laws that prevent discrimination against immigrants and all racial and ethnic minorities would contribute to advancing the rights of women and girls who belong to communities in which FC/FGM is practiced. Moreover, reforms in immigration law that protect the rights of women would represent an advance. For example, women whose immigrant status is dependent upon that of their husband should be granted an independent status after a certain period of time or upon a showing of coercion or violence on the part of the spouse. In both African and receiving countries, additional legal reforms that would promote women's equality include laws that ensure that a percentage of legislative seats be held by women and affirmative action for women in education and employment.

Carefully consider application of criminal sanctions for FC/FGM

As does any legal measure condemning FC/FGM, criminal laws specifically prohibiting the practice help strengthen the position of those advocating for change. Where the laws are enforced, they may create incentives for change in individual behavior. Criminal sanctions have increasingly been employed to dissuade people from practicing FC/FGM. Nevertheless, criminal legislation addressing FC/FGM is a relatively recent phenomenon. In Africa, with the exception of the Central African Republic's Ordinance (1966) and Guinea's criminal code provision (1965), none of these laws was in place before 1994.

There are important reasons why, in most African countries, the instrument of the law should not be used too strongly or hastily to stop FC/FGM. First, law enforcement mechanisms are weak and lack resources, and the customary laws that govern private behavior are unlikely to support legislation that aims to abolish a customary practice such as FC/FGM. Second, in kinship-based societies, such as most of those in Africa, behavioral change at the individual level is difficult to achieve without the approval of the community to which the person belongs. Therefore, taking legal action against one's own relatives or tribe members may cause graver social and economic repercussions for the person filing a complaint than any penalty the court applies to the defendant. Third, when FC/FGM is common among one ethnic group and not another, enacting and applying a criminal law could fuel ethnic animosities.

However, a well-studied and strategically timed introduction of a criminal law prohibiting FC/FGM is a strong political and legal tool. If social change is well underway, with substantial popular backing and approval from the political establishment, the process of introducing, debating and successfully passing a law could itself serve to accelerate change. On the other hand, poorly timed or hastily introduced laws can backfire by truncating an emerging social dialogue, causing social rifts, and driving the practice underground.

> Under no circumstances should governments criminalize the practice of FC/FGM in the absence of a broader governmental strategy to change individual behavior and social norms.

If countries do elect to impose criminal sanctions for the practice of FC/FGM, they should take into account the following considerations.

Is new criminal legislation needed?

Criminal sanctions for the practice of FC/FGM may be imposed in one of two ways. Governments may enact a law specifically prohibiting the practice of FC/FGM, as was done, for example, in Senegal and Canada. Alternatively, governments may rely upon existing general criminal law provisions that assign penalties for a variety of actions that could include FC/FGM. France, for example, prosecutes cases of FC/FGM on the basis of general provisions of its Penal Code. The French Penal Code provides for penalties of imprisonment and a fine for violent acts that result in a "mutilation" or "permanent disability." The penalties are increased for those who commit these acts against a minor under the age of 15 years. While there is some variation among the types of general laws that may be applied to FC/FGM, they all address various forms of wounding or mutilation, often increasing penalties when this crime is committed against minors.

There are several difficulties that may be associated with arresting and prosecuting individuals for practicing FC/FGM in the absence of specific legislation prohibiting the practice. Most important is the problem of notice. In countries in which governments have traditionally tolerated the widespread practice of FC/FGM, the sudden enforcement of general criminal law provisions in cases of FC/FGM would take most people by surprise. Governments, through consistent non-application of such provisions in cases of FC/FGM, may have signaled that FC/FGM was not prohibited. Behavior considered legal one day would be the basis of a criminal arrest and prosecution the next. For this reason, enactment of a new criminal provision specifically prohibiting FC/FGM may be necessary to make clear that the practice constitutes a criminal offense. In the absence of new legislation, governments intending to prosecute cases of FC/FGM under general criminal law provisions should declare their intention to do so publicly, giving ample notice to those who might be unaware of the criminal law provisions to be applied. In addition, for reasons discussed in the next section, general criminal law provisions may be inadequate for defining with sufficient clarity the behavior that is subject to criminal sanctions.

Clear definition of crime

Governments that elect to enact legislation specifically criminalizing FC/FGM should ensure that the prohibited activity is clearly defined in the law. Because FC/FGM occurs in several different forms, penal laws should state clearly whether all procedures commonly referred to as FC/FGM are prohibited under the law. In addition to defining the condemned act, laws prohibiting FC/FGM should clearly state the categories of people who are potentially liable under the law. If parents who procure FC/FGM for their daughters – in addition to the practitioners themselves – are subject to prosecution, the law should make this clear.

Among the laws that have been enacted to address FC/FGM in African countries, specificity varies substantially. Those enacted prior to 1990, in Central African Republic and Guinea, merely state that the practice is prohibited and assign a penalty. Among the more recent laws, those of Djibouti and Tanzania similarly state only that FC/FGM is prohibited and subject to penalties. Other laws, including those of Burkina Faso and Ghana, are more complex. Both attempt to define precisely the behavior that is prohibited. Ghana's Criminal Code, for example, specifically prohibits the excision or infibulation of any part of the labia minora, labia majora and the clitoris, and the terms "excise" and "infibulate" are explicitly defined.[3] The laws of Burkina Faso, Côte d'Ivoire, Senegal and Togo provide for increased penalties when the procedure results in death. The laws of all of the receiving countries attempt to define the prohibited practice and distinguish it from procedures deemed medically justified.

Amongst African countries, only the laws of Burkina Faso, Senegal and Togo explicitly put parents or family members on notice of their potential liability under the law. Among receiving countries, the laws of Australia, Canada, New Zealand, Sweden and the United Kingdom have express provisions indicating that parents may be prosecuted. Burkina Faso and Togo explicitly make it a crime for a person with knowledge that FC/FGM has occurred to fail to report the act to the proper authorities. Senegal's law assigns criminal penalties to one who incites or instructs another to perform FC/FGM. Parents or family members of a girl subjected to FC/FGM would likely fall under either of these types of provision.

Canada, New Zealand and Sweden also prohibit arranging for the illegal practice of FC/FGM in a country in which the procedure is not prohibited. Burkina Faso and Senegal augment penalties for members of the medical profession who practice FC/FGM.

Punishment of parents

In keeping with the requirements of the Children's Rights Convention, "the best interests of the child" should be the guiding principle in formulating the law. Laws that provide criminal sanctions for parents who procure FC/FGM for their daughters may create undue hardship for the girls who have undergone the procedure. Long prison terms for parents of young children, involving separation of members of a family, can have severe effects on the emotional lives of the children involved. Such separations can be particularly difficult in countries in which those who practice FC/FGM are immigrants, with little support within the majority population. Governments should consider either assigning criminal sanctions only to the practitioners of FC/FGM themselves or assigning lighter penalties to parents than to practitioners. In addition, governments should seek to employ alternative legal mechanisms for influencing behavior, such as recognizing FC/FGM as an injury that gives rise to civil – as opposed to criminal – liability. This recommendation is further discussed below.

As currently written, all laws providing a basis for prosecution in cases of FC/FGM impose liability upon parents who procure FC/FGM for their daughters. As noted above, the laws of Burkina Faso, Senegal and Togo explicitly apply to parents and family members, as well as to practitioners of FC/FGM. Other laws render parents and family members guilty under general legal principles of accomplice liability, according to which anyone who procures the procedure or otherwise cooperates with the practitioner could be prosecuted.

Even where laws do potentially subject parents to prison sentences, judges may, in their discretion, elect not to impose such penalties on parents who have been convicted in cases of FC/FGM. In France, one of the few countries to have prosecuted parents for procuring FC/FGM for their daughters, the result of most prosecutions has been that convicted parents have not been assigned criminal penalties. In the most recent case of this type at the time of writing, for example, a practitioner of FC/FGM was sentenced to eight years in prison for performing the procedure on 48 girls. Most of the 25 parents who were tried as accomplices received suspended sentences from three to five years.[4] Those with suspended sentences are unlikely to spend any time in prison.

Conditions of consent

Governments should consider whether there are any circumstances under which FC/FGM should not be considered a crime. In particular, governments may wish to recognize an exception to a prohibition of FC/FGM when an adult who undergoes the procedure has given her informed consent. Informed consent, according to the United Nations General Assembly, is consent to a medical intervention that is "obtained freely, without threats or improper inducements."[5] Prior to giving consent, the patient must be provided with "adequate and understandable information in a form and language understood by the patient" on such matters as alternative treatments and "possible pain or discomfort, risks and side-effects of the proposed treatment."[6] Informed consent thus requires that a woman be free from coercion and that she have adequate information in order to make her decision. Where such conditions exist, laws should respect women's autonomy in making decisions about their bodies. Governments and women's advocates may not support or approve of a woman's choice to undergo FC/FGM. Still, provided that she has made her choice freely after being fully informed of the consequences of the practice, the choice of whether or not to undergo FC/FGM should be hers alone.

In many contexts, however, it may be difficult to ensure the conditions that will enable women to give their informed consent. For the reasons discussed in Chapter 2, children will generally not have the capacity to make a decision freely, with full understanding of the health consequences of their decision. Furthermore, enabling women and girls of any age to reject FC/FGM requires profound social change by which equal access to educational and economic opportunities are ensured. Because women may not be empowered to refuse FC/FGM, some women's groups have advocated that FC/FGM be a crime when committed even upon a consenting, adult woman. Governments should take these concerns into account when formulating criminal laws that address FC/FGM. At the same time, they should strive to create the conditions under which women will be free to reject FC/FGM in the absence of criminal sanctions.

Criminal laws addressing FC/FGM have generally not recognized circumstances in which a woman is deemed to have capacity to consent to undergoing the procedure. Only Canada, Tanzania and the United States have limited their prohibitions of FC/FGM to procedures performed upon a child under the age of 18. In the United States, this limitation was suggested by African immigrant women activists. They sought to avoid a situation in which adult immigrant women would be treated as legal minors in a country and legal system that allows adults to consent to body-altering operations – such as cosmetic surgeries – that are not necessary for their health. To these activists, stopping FC/FGM among adults should be a matter of persuasion, not legal coercion. The Tanzanian prohibition of FC/FGM is incorporated into a criminal provision pertaining to cruelty to children, which the law defines as persons under the age of 18.

Implicit in these laws is an assumption that by attaining the age of 18, a woman is in a position to consent to FC/FGM in the absence of coercion and with full understanding of the procedure's consequences. What remains in question is whether women will be given the information and true life choices necessary to abandon FC/FGM or whether the force of cultural norms and lack of economic and legal autonomy will prove stronger.

Effect on minorities

In countries in which FC/FGM is practiced primarily by a minority ethnic group, criminal laws prohibiting FC/FGM must not be used as a pretext for harassing or persecuting members of that group. Criminal legislation that is enacted in the absence of concerted governmental efforts to reach women and girls through education and empowerment programs should be considered suspect. Governments should show a consistent pattern of interest in eliminating FC/FGM as a means of improving the lives of women and girls. In countries in which minority rights are vulnerable, governments should take steps to show that their actions are not motivated by an interest in disrupting the lives of members of a minority ethnic group. Such steps may include increased consultations with minority organizations and enhanced appropriate educational programs, as well as the allocation of resources to community groups – particularly women's groups.

In countries in which FC/FGM is practiced primarily among immigrant groups, governments should avoid allowing xenophobic forces in the majority population to use FC/FGM as a pretext for discrimination or persecution. For this reason, governments should be sensitive to the effects of a criminal conviction upon the immigration status of a person who performs or procures FC/FGM. Governments should define the crime of FC/FGM in such a way as to avoid subjecting to deportation those convicted of the practice. Moreover, governments should engage in regular consultation with immigrant groups, appropriate training of law enforcement and immigration officials, and culturally appropriate educational programs developed by community-based organizations that are sensitive to the situation of refugee and immigrant groups. Such measures would reflect government sensitivity to immigrant and refugee concerns while not compromising the determination to prohibit FC/FGM.

Provide other legal protections against FC/FGM

In addition to criminal prosecution, there are a number of legal mechanisms that can be employed to discourage FC/FGM. For example, in countries with adequate mechanisms for adjudicating civil claims and enforcing judgments, FC/FGM can be recognized as an injury that gives rise to a civil lawsuit for damages or other remedies. Girls who have undergone FC/FGM can seek money damages from practitioners. Such lawsuits would have a long-term effect of deterring practitioners from performing FC/FGM. Other procedures may be available to prevent the procedure from occurring in the first place. In some countries, individual women and girls wishing to avoid undergoing the practice of FC/FGM have sought judicial intervention. For example, at least one girl in Uganda was able to avoid undergoing FC/FGM by obtaining the protection of a court.[7] However, while civil legal actions are a potentially effective means of influencing individual behavior and protecting girls and women from FC/FGM, such mechanisms have not consistently been utilized.

Most receiving countries have child protection laws that could potentially be applied to prevent girls from undergoing FC/FGM. Child protection laws provide for state intervention in cases of child abuse by a parent or guardian. Unlike criminal laws, child protection laws are concerned less with punishing parents or guardians than with ensuring that a child's interests are being served. These laws provide mechanisms for removing the child from his or her parent or guardian when the state has reason to believe that abuse has occurred or is likely to occur. A number of countries, such as the United Kingdom, have declared the applicability of child protection laws to FC/FGM. State authorities may thus remove a girl from her family if there is reason to believe that she will be subjected to FC/FGM. Authorities in the United Kingdom may also prevent a girl from being removed from the country if there is evidence that the girl will likely undergo FC/FGM in another country.

Regulatory Measures

Health professionals

Medical ethics standards should make it clear that the practice of FC/FGM upon non-consenting children or women violates professional standards. Medical practitioners who engage in the practice should be subject to disciplinary proceedings and should lose their licenses to work in the medical field. This regulatory development has occurred in several of the countries reviewed in this book. In Egypt, a Ministry of Health decree, upheld by the highest administrative court, has declared FC/FGM an unlawful practice of medicine, thereby making practitioners susceptible to criminal prosecution. In the Sudan, government health authorities have sanctioned traditional birth attendants and village midwives who participate in FC/FGM by confiscating their midwifery kits and placing them under close supervision.[8] The medical licensing and disciplinary bodies of Denmark, France and the United Kingdom have declared that physicians who practice FC/FGM may lose their licenses to practice medicine.

NGOs

NGOs should be permitted to organize and operate without government interference. NGOs play a crucial role in implementing activities aimed at stopping FC/FGM. They have also been instrumental in garnering community support for women's right not to undergo the practice. NGOs should be permitted to monitor government efforts to eliminate FC/FGM and to hold governments accountable for failure to fulfill their international obligations. In addition, governments should finance NGOs engaged in programs designed to stop FC/FGM and be willing to work with them.

Policy Measures

Education

Governments should devote resources to supplying information to FC/FGM-practicing communities about this practice and human rights in general. This information should: emphasize the potential psychological and physical impact of FC/FGM on women, girls and the community at large; examine the history and purpose of FC/FGM; promote human rights and demonstrate the manner in which human rights are affected by FC/FGM; and focus on the needs of women and girls while involving the entire community. Governments should rely on the assistance of NGOs, local leaders and health care professionals to collect and to provide this information in an effort to generate social dialogue. Moreover, governments' resources should support efforts to enable people to access health care services, skills development and training.

Governments of receiving countries should ensure that human rights education and FC/FGM-prevention programs are tailored to the needs of immigrant communities. Once again, such programs should address the entire community while centering on the needs of women and girls. Because of language barriers, cultural differences and immigration documentation issues, the ability of governments to reach out directly to immigrants may be limited. It is thus especially important to ensure that receiving governments work in cooperation with community-based immigrant NGOs in the creation and execution of programs. By working with such local groups and immigrants networks, governments will have the greatest chances of reaching girls and women affected by FC/FGM and disseminating culturally appropriate information.

Pursuant to legislation enacted in 1996, the United States Immigration and Naturalization Service is required to provide information concerning the harmful effects of FC/FGM and the legal consequences of its practice in the USA to immigrants and non-immigrants entering the USA from countries where FC/FGM is prevalent. This legislation requires that the information be compiled and presented in a sensitive and culturally appropriate manner. The United States Department of Health and Human Services worked closely with RAINB♀ and other community-based organizations on a series of community outreach consultations that have proved effective in garnering support for the legislation within the organized sector of the African immigrant community. Suggestions made in the course of these consultations were used to develop training and informational material for use in community settings.

Human rights principles and sensitivity to FC/FGM should also be infused throughout all governmental policies in both African and receiving countries. Through greater public awareness of human rights and the legal obligations of governments to enforce those rights, communities can begin to hold their governments accountable for failure to meet their obligations.

The media

Policies relating to the media, especially those that are owned by the government, should facilitate public dialogue on FC/FGM. In addition, in countries in which governments exert considerable control over the media, media outlets should be encouraged to discuss the right of women and girls to be free from FC/FGM. Moreover, groups or individuals advocating against FC/FGM should not be denied access to the media. Rather, policies should be established to facilitate the media's access to such advocates.

Empowering women

Women cannot abandon the practice of FC/FGM until they have the information, material conditions and skills to access different options. In countries in which FC/FGM is a prerequisite for marriage, women and girls whose economic security depends upon their ability to be married have little choice but to undergo FC/FGM. Governments should reform policies that prevent women from raising their economic, social and political status, including ensuring that both women and men have the right to work and the right to equal pay for equal work. They also have a responsibility and obligation to support women and encourage their participation in all aspects of community life. Barriers to women's ability to access credit and training should also be addressed. Governments should ensure girls' equal access to education by allocating sufficient resources and adopting gender-appropriate policies. Governments should also work to ensure women's participation in public office and decision-making.

As in African countries, women and girls who are members of immigrant communities may not feel they can exercise choice with regard to FC/FGM. Social compulsion may be compounded by xenophobia or racism from the host country, which makes immigrants reliant upon their families or their communities. Although not true for all people, these forces may make immigrants hesitant or unwilling to abandon practices from their home culture that distance them from the host culture. In the example of FC/FGM, women preserve traditions at the expense of their bodies while other elements of community life change. As in their home countries, immigrant women must have equal access to the systems of power so they can exert equal control over community values and cultural change.

There is much that governments of receiving countries can do to contribute to the empowerment of immigrant women. While respecting the importance of community life for new immigrants, they should ensure that immigrant women are able to make informed choices about their bodies and can access all the life options available within the host country. For this reason, governments should support programs that offer immigrant women instruction in the language of the majority, job training, and information regarding avenues for legal protection. Governments should also ensure adequate financial and social support network is available for immigrant women who sometimes must abandon their primary source of economic security – their families or their husbands – to exercise their right to make decisions about their bodies.

Ensure access to reproductive health services

Governments should not lose sight of the link between the practice of FC/FGM and the need for reproductive health services for all women. First, such services can be a critical avenue for supplying information to women about their own reproductive health. Women who understand the harmful health consequences of FC/FGM may be less likely to undergo the procedure or encourage their daughters to do so. Second, women who have already undergone FC/FGM have the greatest need for medical attention, particularly during pregnancy, childbirth and the post-partum period. These special health needs have explicit recognition in Togo's recent legislation prohibiting FC/FGM, which requires public and private health facilities to ensure that women and girls who have undergone the procedure receive the most appropriate medical care when arriving in these facilities. Finally, all efforts should be made to ensure that immigrant women have access to adequate reproductive health care.[9]

International legal standards establish not only that women and girls have the right not to undergo FC/FGM, but that governments must take action to ensure that women and girls are indeed enabled to make such a choice. In taking action against FC/FGM, the measures that governments employ should themselves conform to accepted human rights norms. The recommendations in this chapter are intended to guide governments toward compliance with those norms. Governments should therefore bear these recommendations in mind when formulating legal, regulatory and policy response to the practice of FC/FGM and when evaluating existing initiatives. By undertaking some or all of the recommendations presented, a country could take an important step toward promoting the well-being of its people.

Notes

1. Full citations to legal instruments and government policy documents appear in the endnotes following each national profile in Part II.
2. Vienna Convention on the Law of Treaties, opened for signature May 23, 1969, art. 2(d), UN Doc. A/CONF.39/27, 63 AJIL 875, 8ILM 679 (entered into force Jan. 27, 1980).
3. Criminal Code (Amendment) Act, 1994, reprinted in *International Digest of*

Health Legislation, Vol. 47, No. 1, 1996, pp. 30–31.
4. French Ministry of Employment and Solidarity, *Prevention des Mutilations Sexuelles en France* (n.d.), provided to CRLP on July 26, 1999 (on file with CRLP).
5. United Nations General Assembly, Principles for the Protection of Persons with Mental Illness and the Improvement of Mental Health Care, Resolution 46/119, Dec. 17, 1991, Principle 11, 2.
6. Ibid.
7. Dr Josephine Kasolo, Safe Motherhood Initiative in Uganda, Questionnaire (undated, Spring 1998).
8. Inter-African Committee on Traditional Practices Affecting the Health of Women and Children (IAC), "Sudan: Turning Point in the Sensitization Campaign," *Inter-African Committee Newsletter*, No. 19, June 1996, p. 8.
9. N. Toubia, *Caring for Women with Circumcision: A Technical Manual for Health Care Providers*, New York: RAINB♀, 1999.

5

Legal and Policy Strategies for NGOs with a Brief Review of Existing Approaches

While government action is necessary to create a political and legal environment that deters people from practicing FC/FGM, it is ultimately the women, their families and their communities who must be convinced to abandon the practice. Today it has become common wisdom that non-governmental, grassroots and community-based organizations are more likely to affect social behavior than government action alone. The profound social and political change required to recognize women's human rights and achieve gender equality requires the participation of broad sectors of society in an ongoing dialogue and consolidated efforts. Earlier chapters of this book have emphasized the human rights of women as individuals and as a social group and the corresponding duties of governments to protect and promote these rights. This chapter focuses on the role of non-governmental organizations (NGOs) in galvanizing governments as well as civil society to act. It also discusses the role of NGOs in holding governments accountable and monitoring their activities. Given the nature of this book and its focus on the legal and human rights aspects of social change, we concentrate on the practical aspects of legal and policy tools that NGOs can use. However, to complete the picture and place the role of legal and policy action within a broader context, we also include a brief review of programmatic approaches to stop FC/FGM that have been tried to date.

The NGO sector has tried a wide range of strategies to stop FC/FGM. Some seem to have failed and others have yielded varying degrees of success, whereas others still have not been adequately evaluated. Given the many differences amongst the countries and communities in which this practice occurs, it is impossible to identify one specific strategy for stopping the practice in all of them. Each organization or NGO movement must choose strategies that are relevant to its own political, economic and social realities. Moreover, the vision, political strategies, social values, expertise and resources of an organization will determine its plan of action. In most countries, there are a number of NGOs, each with its own expertise and political agenda. For example, some organizations work within communities to empower women to abandon the practice of FC/FGM. Others may work with governments, focusing primarily on legislation or policy initiatives. Still other NGOs engage in advocacy in international or regional forums. Cooperation among different types of NGOs to address FC/FGM is likely to increase the effectiveness of the overall movement.

A full review and evaluation of what amounts to twenty years of action by dozens of organizations in several countries is beyond the scope of this book and will not be attempted here. Some of the material from which this brief review is extracted can be found in the references. Readers who are interested in learning more about the evaluation of past and existing approaches to FC/FGM can contact RAINB♀ and the CRLP for the latest literature and work in this area – some of it is currently being drafted. As an organization specializing in studying and supporting various approaches to stop FC/FGM, RAINB♀ has a framework from which we approach the issue based on our understanding of its causes and the social context of its promotion. Our understanding of what constitutes more promising approaches is based on extensive exposure and critical study of the evidence which each approach presents to date. The framework from which we operate is based on the understanding that FC/FGM is only one action in a range of rules (customs) and practices that society devises to control women's sexuality and therefore ensure male dominance over women's reproductive power (children) as well as their economic production. FC/FGM is therefore not a disease or an isolated "harmful or bad practice" that occurs among ignorant people who simply need to be educated against it. It is one act that is a part of intricate and complex rules and a social construct to which all members of society subscribe to keep in place the existing social order that services the interest of male dominance. Because of this specific analysis and the understanding of the role FC/FGM plays in keeping the male-dominated status quo in the practicing societies, we believe that a human rights approach is necessary.

In our framework the first and most important principle is: as with all other issues of social justice, it is essential that those who lead the change are those who are aggrieved and therefore stand to benefit most from the correction of the injustice. Such were the principles behind the civil rights movement in the United States, the anti-apartheid movement in South Africa and the indigenous rights movement in many South American countries. It is therefore important that the movement to stop FC/FGM and all other gender-based violations in Africa be led by African women and all other supporters must become allies and not attempt to take the leadership. Even within each African country, or even within each community in one country, leadership should always be for women from the country and the community. This basic principle does not only contribute to a justifiable "rights" approach but has proven more effective when applied. For women to feel strong enough to stand up and demand their rights, they must be given the tools and choices for self-empowerment. These are usually a combination of all or some of the following: information (which would include health facts, human rights principles, religious interpretations favorable to women, etc.), material resources, analytical tools, organizational skills, legal protection, exposure to alternatives and, for most, literacy.

Another important principle is that women cannot stand alone in their demand for justice and must involve the widest possible sectors of their society. In reality, women are not just individuals or even a stand-alone group. Their lives are intricately woven and interdependent with their families, their children and their community. Issues of identity, social well-being and emotional and economic support systems cannot be ignored or dismissed if a realistic approach to social change, including stopping FC/FGM, is to be achieved. Therefore, any attempts to mobilize women to stand up against FC/FGM must bring along the whole community in a dialogue of common interests. In that dialogue, evidence can be invoked from the health facts (that FC/FGM is harmful to women), from human rights principles to which governments subscribe, from religious and cultural values that stand by the right to well-being for all members of society, and so forth. A successful movement away from existing social norms will not be achieved by women alone since they hold the least power and in very restricted domains. Women need allies among politicians, religious leaders, health and legal professionals and all other influential individuals or social groups in society.

A third principle that we advocate is that efforts to stop FC/FGM cannot be separated from calls to establish women's reproductive and sexual rights as fundamental to building a democratic society in the twenty-first century. So to work to stop genital cutting while leaving all other aspects of physical, sexual or emotional violence against women intact is a gross negligence and represents a tunnel vision that is difficult to justify. Despite the grave economic and health conditions that most women in Africa experience, it is important to respect the totality of their humanity, including their right to their physical integrity and to the full enjoyment of their sexuality and their reproduction without the threat of death, disease, social sanctions or abuse in war and political conflict.

The following is a brief, almost cursory, review of the many programs attempted in a number of countries, which cannot be adequately synthesized or evaluated in this publication. It is meant as a simplified summary to provoke thoughtfulness and to put in context the role of legal and policy efforts. Unlike the rest of the efforts in this book, we do not wish to recommend any specific approach or condemn another since we are unable to give them the full exposure and assessment they deserve. Such an effort will be attempted in a future body of work.

Review of Programmatic Approaches

The health risk or harmful traditional practice approach

This is the most widely used and oldest approach attempted to date. Historically, advocates for the elimination of FC/FGM, wishing to avoid both cultural conflict and being labeled culturally insensitive, have invoked the health risks of the practice, particularly the physical complications related to pregnancy and childbirth, as their main, and sometimes only, argument against it. Under this approach, authority figures from the health field have delivered messages about physical complications such as bleeding or infection, and risk to the fetus or to the mother. They have often been backed with supportive statements by religious authorities. The idea is that people need to be educated against their own ignorance, and if they receive enough messages about how detrimental FC/FGM is to health, the practice will be eliminated. Little community participation or dialogue is invoked and ongoing dialogue or continuity of presence is rare. Women or their social status are not given any special attention and the dynamic of social power or interests are not addressed. Although this has been the most applied and emulated approach, there is little evidence that it has resulted in any change in the twenty years it has been unquestionably replicated. In fact, a scientific evaluation of this approach in Egypt shows that it may have been counter-productive.[1] The Egyptian Demographic and Health Survey conducted in 1995 showed that the prevalence of the practice is still 97 per cent. One of the most interesting findings is that while most mothers were circumcised by traditional midwives, most daughters were circumcised by doctors.[2] This is widely interpreted as a direct result of the health risk/harmful traditional practice approach since families switched to doctors in order to avoid physical complications but saw no reason to stop the practice altogether.

Comprehensive economic and social development prioritizing women's empowerment

Some NGOs have designed programs aimed broadly at economic and social development coupled with a specific effort to empower women and to persuade the community to abandon FC/FGM. The wider social development activities include income generation, the provision of health services and literacy training. Programs that build income-generation and decision-making skills are particularly aimed at women in social contexts where men are emigrating to earn money abroad and women are becoming the heads of households as a result. Religious leaders are also involved in the project. This long-term effort is concluded with the signing of a declaration by all groups in the community (including the traditional midwives and barbers who act as the circumcisers) stating that they will abandon FC/FGM. Although this outreach strategy is a long-term one, it has provided uncontroversial proof of success in some settings, such as most of the Egyptian village of Dir El Barsha and among communities and families in other parts of the country.[3]

Participatory educational programs for women's empowerment

Another approach is based on participatory education, which includes literacy training, analytical skills and problem solving, health information and human rights principles provided to women over a period of time. This approach seeks to empower women and provide them with the information and self-confidence that enables them to abandon FC/FGM. The women then decide to make a public declaration to abandon FC/FGM. The success of this strategy was evident in Senegal where this approach was tried over a period of two years in a village in which women decided to abandon FC/FGM in 1997, without direct instructions on the practice. These Senegalese women negotiated support from their husbands and religious leaders and made a public declaration never to practice FC/FGM again. In Senegal, the movement spread to different villages and sparked a national debate that ultimately led to the 1999 enactment of a national law prohibiting FC/FGM. This approach has two elements in common with the previous one in Egypt: the emphasis on women's empowerment and the involvement of the community, which culminated in a public declaration to which all are signed or sworn.[4]

Ceremonies for alternative rites of passage for girls

A widely popularized approach to stopping FC/FGM is the development of alternative rites of passage for girls. In determining alternative rites, community-based NGOs usually consult with the community, particularly tribal and religious leaders. Different organizations have developed different components for the rituals, which substitute the cutting ritual with a non-cutting festivity and gift giving with or without extensive training.

The ceremonies are seen by some as a declaration of abandoning the practice in public. In some parts of Kenya, the alternative ritual for girls is combined with a separate training for the parents of the girls to be initiated. The girls' training covers such topics as health, sexual behavior, decision-making, marriage and behavior towards the elderly. A non-cutting ceremony is organized in which the community celebrates with gifts and food. While it is too early to assess fully the effectiveness of this approach, Kenyan groups have claimed success based on the increasing numbers of families enrolling in the rituals and the number of organizations emulating the approach. Currently there are efforts to evaluate these approaches by third-party evaluators.[5]

The positive deviant approach

Some organizations are currently promoting a new method of outreach based on identifying individuals who oppose FC/FGM in communities and then promoting them as role models. Potential role models include families, teachers, religious figures and others who have abandoned the practice, advised others against it, or made public statements in opposition to it. The effectiveness of this strategy is enhanced by documenting the stories of how these individuals reached their decisions and how they dealt with confusion, opposition and taking a stand against the majority. The organization then creates community forums at which these individuals testify to their experiences. At the time of writing, the positive deviant approach has been implemented in Egypt for less than one year and is too recent an experiment for any viable evaluation.[6]

Intensive social marketing to community leaders

This approach is based on reaching out with a social marketing message to the power holders or chiefs of a community or tribe, showing them through a cost–benefit analysis that FC/FGM is not good for the community, and persuading them to denounce the practice publicly. The approach also includes annual cultural days and an awards ceremony for the leaders who stand by their decisions to send an unambiguous order to the girls to stop circumcision. This outreach plan was initiated by an NGO in Uganda among the small minority Sabini community in which girls are circumcised at the age of 16, just before marriage. The Ugandan experience has reportedly resulted in stopping the practice amongst the majority of girls in the first circumcision seasons. Recent reports give strong evidence that during the following season most girls were circumcised and the leaders' opposition to the practice was not sustained. Many girls expressed a desire to be circumcised since they were not involved in the decision to stop and did not understand why such a privilege had been taken away from them.[7]

Educating circumcisers and providing them with alternative income

Programs focused on educating circumcisers and training them for alternative sources of income target the supply side of FC/FGM and have been seen as possibly faster and more effective than efforts to reach women and girls likely to undergo or procure the practice. This approach has been applied in many countries for over ten years but all anecdotal and scientific evaluation suggests that it has failed to affect the demand side and that families can successfully find alternative suppliers. Also, most circumcisers who abandoned FC/FGM because of the initial financial incentives have eventually returned to the practice to boost their income.[8]

It is clear from the above that many approaches have been attempted and many more will be developed until effective means of stopping FC/FGM are reached. Despite the specificity and diversity of NGO strategies that need to be developed according to the circumstances and needs of each community, it may be useful to identify action as occurring at four levels – community, national, regional and international. This chapter reviews and suggests strategies for NGOs to stop FC/FGM and advance women's rights at the four levels.

Strategies

Community level

Community-level NGOs are most effective in undertaking awareness and outreach programs designed to provide women with the information and choices to abandon FC/FGM. In fact, NGOs in several countries have developed outreach programs that have proven successful in reducing the practice of FC/FGM. Governments should be aware of the special strengths of community-level NGOs and make every effort to support them and learn from their experience. If appropriate, governments can allocate resources and facilitate access to media and training curriculums for approaches that have been proven to be effective.

The role of community-level NGOs or community-based organizations (CBOs) is of particular importance in receiving countries and in African countries where only a minority community practices FC/FGM. The ties of such organizations to their communities are crucial in implementing effective information dissemination and outreach programs. Such NGOs are capable of creating an atmosphere that is welcoming and non-threatening to immigrant and minority women. They may also have greater insights than government agencies and other broadly representative organizations into the needs and priorities of women from their own communities.

National level

Although it is extremely difficult to discuss national-level strategies in a manner that is applicable to all the countries in which FC/FGM is practiced, a few general recommendations are possible. All of these recommendations are focused on ensuring legal and policy change and undertaking long-term advocacy efforts.

Lobby for effective legislation and policy on FC/FGM

NGOs can and should play a crucial role in the development of legislation, an effective tool for stopping FC/FGM. Legislative acts that reflect the experiences and expertise of NGOs working on behalf of the human rights of women and children can be powerfully responsive to the problem of FC/FGM. In countries in which the groups that practice FC/FGM are in the minority, NGOs can represent the interests of minority women and advocate on their behalf before the majority population. However, undertaking national lobbying efforts to influence the legislative process is a long-term and intensive goal. Such work requires numerous resources, including the necessary finance, knowledge of the legislature and connections to government officials. Moreover, successful legislative lobbying is most often combined with advocacy efforts that seek to change public opinion. The enormous task of influencing public opinion against FC/FGM requires strategic thinking and effective use of limited resources. Ideally, such campaigns would involve all the strategies recommended in this section.

Senegal provides a successful example of NGO involvement in the legislative process to stop FC/FGM. The law enacted in Senegal was hailed as a product of a movement initiated by women at the grassroots level.[9] Women testified at legislative hearings before Parliament to support the prohibition of FC/FGM.[10]

Build broad coalitions to support an end to FC/FGM

When attempting to change societal attitudes and government positions toward a deeply ingrained cultural practice such as FC/FGM, an effective

NGO strategy would be to build broad national coalitions of individuals and groups interested in taking a stand against it. Such coalitions could consist of representatives of diverse fields, including human rights groups, community-level organizations, health professionals and providers and religious communities. Because members of these diverse sectors can bring expertise from different fields, their joint participation could influence policy makers concerned with the interests of their various constituencies. In the context of FC/FGM, it is particularly important to identify providers of the practice and religious leaders and convince them to speak out against FC/FGM. In a country where governments or other organizations are attempting to recognize the appropriateness of FC/FGM performed in hospital settings, it would also be critical for NGOs to lobby medical associations to take an ethical position against the procedure. This has happened in the Netherlands, Egypt and in a hospital in Seattle, Washington, in the USA, where there were attempts to legitimize the provision of FC/FGM within a hospital setting.[11] In all three countries activists' groups opposed the recommendation and lobbied strongly until such propositions were defeated.

Monitor government action

To achieve a long-term goal such as enabling women to have the information and choices necessary to ensure their abandonment of FC/FGM, NGOs should monitor the actions that governments are taking to deal with the practice. Monitoring government actions is often a role for which many such organizations are well suited. For FC/FGM, it is particularly important for NGOs to be aware of the activities being undertaken by the government, to express their views regarding such actions, and to dialogue with government representatives about future plans. To undertake such activities, NGOs may have to identify the government agencies and departments involved in FC/FGM and determine the manner in which such branches are working together. Such organizations should maintain a dialogue with the government on FC/FGM. When government actions are inappropriate or not forthcoming, NGOs should consider whether additional dialogue or public criticism is more useful. Where the government is undertaking desirable actions, NGOs would face a similar choice.

Disseminate and collect information regarding FC/FGM

NGOs should ensure that the information they have regarding FC/FGM in their country is as complete as possible. Effective advocates for any issue, including FC/FGM, should be regarded by others as experts in that field. NGOs promoting an end to the practice of FC/FGM should collect data on a regular basis regarding prevalence rates; who is affected by the practice; the activities of different levels of governments and other sectors; and the legal framework and policies relating to providers. Groups may then determine strategies by which to present and disseminate this information, which may be made available through publications, short briefing papers and, where appropriate, the Internet.

Engage in litigation

Because legal systems differ around the world, no formula for litigation can be recommended in this publication. However, NGOs should consider ways to use the judicial branch in efforts to stop FC/FGM. Litigation may be pursued for a number of different purposes. Lawyers may use the courts to attract publicity to the continued practice of FC/FGM, to obtain a remedy for an individual who has undergone the practice, to enforce a law intended to prevent FC/FGM, or to challenge an existing law that is detrimental to the struggle against it.

In countries in which constitutional protections exist for women's equality and bodily integrity, for example, NGOs may challenge governmental endorsements of the practice of FC/FGM. In some countries, civil suits may be brought against practitioners of FC/FGM by women or girls who were subjected to the practice. It should be noted that for lawyers in many countries, particularly in Africa, litigation may not be an effective strategy for upholding women's rights. Where legal protections are weak, judges are subject to political pressures, or lawyers' resources are limited, NGOs may achieve greater success through other forms of advocacy.[12] In addition, in some cases, non-adversarial methods of solving disputes may be more appropriate than litigation. NGOs should explore the availability of alternative dispute mechanisms that may advance NGO efforts to stop FC/FGM.

One example of NGO participation in litigation is found in Egypt, where NGOs challenged a 1994 decree issued by the Minister of Health permitting the practice of FC/FGM in hospitals.[13] The NGOs argued that the Minister's decree contradicted the recommendations of a committee that he had formed to assess the harmfulness of FC/FGM.[14] The case was postponed in the courts for nearly two years and became moot in 1996 when a new Minister of Health issued a decree prohibiting the practice of FC/FGM in all public hospitals.[15] Some NGOs again took the opportunity to participate in litigation when the 1996 ban of FC/FGM came under legal attack from conservative medical and religious forces.[16] While NGO attempts to intervene in the lawsuit were unsuccessful in the highest administrative court, their legal action was a concrete show of support for the Minister of Health's decree, which was ultimately upheld by that court.[17]

In France, litigation of a different nature has been a primary strategy for addressing FC/FGM. The Commission for the Abolition of Sexual Mutilations, a French NGO, has participated in the criminal prosecutions of practitioners of FC/FGM and of parents of girls who have undergone the procedure.[18] In 1998, a case was brought forward on the initiative of a Parisian law student whose family is from Mali. She underwent FC/FGM as a child, as did her sister several years later.[19] While criminal prosecution may not always be the most effective means of influencing people's behavior, NGOs should be aware of all of the avenues for legal action available to them.

Undertake public information and media campaigns

NGOs should undertake public information and media campaigns on an ongoing basis. Such work is key to ensuring that FC/FGM remains on the public agenda and can serve as a catalyst for action. Public education activities can include producing educational materials in different languages, making or using videos as a tool for education, and conducting training workshops. An organization needs to tailor its media strategies to the specifics of a given context. Actions to consider would be identifying individuals respected by the community and persuading them to speak out, and using newspapers, radio and television to publicize messages.

Regional level

At the regional level, the strategies pursued by NGOs to ensure government action to eliminate FC/FGM are different from those at the community and national levels, but more similar to work that can be undertaken at the international level. The recommended two-prong NGO regional strategy focuses on human rights monitoring bodies and regional institutions that work in health and population.

Work through regional human rights monitoring bodies

In three regions around the world, nations have established regional human rights organizations and have adopted regional human rights treaties containing human rights provisions similar to those in international human rights conventions. The Banjul Charter, which has been signed by members of the Organization of African Unity, creates the African Commission of Human Rights (African Commission). The Banjul Charter requires states to submit reports to the African Commission every two years to document compliance with human rights norms. The African Commission also may receive and review communications from other sources. Victims of violations, or anyone acting on behalf of victims, may submit complaints to the Commission.[20] Unlike the African human rights system, the European and Inter-American systems do not rely upon a reporting mechanism as their principal means of enforcement. Rather, both systems employ a centralized body that deliberates upon individual claims of human rights violations. These mechanisms are available to individuals making claims against their governments, provided that they have exhausted all remedies that are available in their own countries.

For FC/FGM, the work of NGOs with respect to these regional institutions should focus on advocacy and the promotion of women's ability to abandon the practice. In terms of advocacy, objectives can include the issuance of a regional declaration on FC/FGM. NGOs may have to lobby government representatives and explain the significance of such a statement. If such a declaration has already been made – as is the case with the OAU statement of 1997[21] – NGO actions could emphasize follow-up to this statement by organizing symposia for legislators and government officials from the region. NGO advocacy at the regional level should also include enhancing the knowledge of regional bodies regarding FC/FGM. NGOs could supplement information contained in states' reports and influence the commissions in their questioning of government representatives. Moreover, groups can attempt to dialogue with members of different commissions and attend the working sessions of regional bodies.

Create greater awareness amongst other regional institutions

Several UN commissions work at the regional level to assist governments to address population issues, train population specialists, disseminate population information and conduct demographic research. These organizations include the Economic Commissions for Africa, Asia, Europe and Latin America and the Caribbean. In addition, the WHO has six regional sub-offices, including those for Africa, Latin America and the Caribbean (referred to as "Pan-American World Health Organization") and one for Europe.

The United Nations' regional attempts at stopping FC/FGM have been underway for at least twenty years. In 1979, the WHO organized the first regional conference on female circumcision in Sudan. The conference issued the first declaration condemning all forms of the practice. After the conference, a few physicians and political leaders in some countries started publicly opposing the practice. In 1984, a meeting of women's organizations supported by UN agencies was held in Senegal. At the end of that meeting, the Inter-African Committee on Traditional Practices Affecting the Health of Women and Children (IAC) was born.[22] Within the next decade, affiliates to the IAC were established in almost all African countries where FC/FGM is practiced.

NGO activities focused on these commissions and organizations, particularly those in Africa and Europe, should be encouraged to integrate the international community's recommendations on FC/FGM into their policies and procedures. They should also be urged to promote and assist in monitoring the implementation of these recommendations, in particular by developing a plan of action for implementation, and coordinating activities with other UN agencies and regional organizations, UN human rights treaty monitoring bodies and NGOs. NGOs should continue to lobby regional organizations to commit resources to FC/FGM and to encourage other donors to do the same.

International level

At the international level, there are two arenas in which NGOs can act to promote actions aimed at facilitating women's abandonment of FC/FGM. Both focus on the United Nations and on raising implementation issues within the operations of its various agencies and bodies. The first strategy involves working within the procedures established for monitoring human rights around the world. The second seeks to enhance the activities the United Nations undertakes to deal with FC/FGM.

Work through the UN human rights system

NGOs have access to a number of UN human rights mechanisms that they can use in efforts to stop FC/FGM. Those mechanisms fall into two general categories: bodies created pursuant to international human rights instruments and bodies that exist independent of such conventions.

National compliance with international human rights treaties is monitored by UN committees. Nations that are parties to the human rights treaties are required to submit reports to these committees on a periodic basis to document their compliance with the norms enumerated in a particular treaty. Some committees also have the authority to issue Recommendations and General Comments about how treaty provisions are to be interpreted. The treaties under which such committees have been established include the Women's Convention, the Civil and Political Rights Covenant, the Economic, Social and Cultural Rights Covenant, and the Children's Rights Convention. In addition, some human rights treaty-monitoring committees have also been empowered to examine individual complaints of specific types of human rights violations within a country. A major limitation in the use of these committees is that even a country that is a party to a treaty with an individual complaints procedure must have given specific consent for individual complaints to be brought with respect to its activities.

The other set of human rights bodies at the UN consists of the various commissions that have been created outside of the treaty framework to review state compliance with UN human rights norms. In contrast to the treaty-monitoring bodies, these forums do not either examine country reports submitted by countries or, in general, deal with individual claims. Instead, they examine information provided to them from various sources on serious countrywide human rights violations. Although such bodies are more subject to political pressure than treaty bodies, they have a significant advantage – all countries are subject to their jurisdiction and there is no requirement that a nation must have ratified a particular instrument.

The most important of these non-treaty-based human rights bodies is the United Nations Commission on Human Rights (Human Rights Commission), which consists of 53 members who act as representatives for their countries, and the Sub-Commission on the Prevention of Discrimination and Protection of Minorities (Sub-Commission). Among other things, these bodies receive information sent to them from individuals and NGOs and, if warranted, adopt public resolutions on abuses. The Human Rights Commission is also authorized to establish a mechanism or body to study country conditions in greater depth and then ultimately issue a report.

Another commission established outside the treaty system is the Commission on the Status of Women (CSW). It consists of 45 members who are appointed by governments and elected by the Economic and Social Council for four-year terms. Among other things, the CSW is charged with overseeing the implementation of the recommendations adopted at the Fourth World Conference on Women in Beijing.

In addition to these commissions, other non-treaty mechanisms, known as the "thematic mechanisms," have been established by the Human Rights Commission to deal with specific kinds of human rights violations. Among these are the Special Rapporteur on Violence Against Women and the Special Rapporteur on Harmful Traditional Practices. The mandate of these individuals is to undertake studies of the issue for which they have been appointed rapporteur. Activities can include: receiving and seeking information from governments and NGOs; informing governments of alleged violations; visiting countries upon invitation; and filing annual reports with the Human Rights Commission containing recommendations for national and international actions. Moreover, in carrying out these activities, these rapporteurs are empowered to examine individual complaints in the context of countrywide abuses.

These numerous forums and procedures at the UN relating to human rights can be utilized to advance efforts to eliminate FC/FGM. In particular, NGOs can enhance these efforts by working within these UN forums and procedures by undertaking three types of actions: (i) providing the relevant treaty and non-treaty bodies with independent factual information regarding government action at the national level to combat FC/FGM; (ii) lobbying for policy Recommendations and General Comments on the subject of FC/FGM to be issued by the treaty monitoring bodies; and (iii) supporting individual complaints regarding FC/FGM that are brought before both types of bodies.

Provide independent factual information

NGOs can be of great service by providing treaty-monitoring bodies with independent factual information with which to assess national reports regarding the actions governments have undertaken to stop FC/FGM. Commonly referred to as "shadow reports," these materials enable members of these bodies to formulate questions on the statements presented in reports, take issue with country representatives and make observations on compliance, including suggestions for improvement. Summaries of these comments and recommendations will appear in the official reports prepared by the treaty-monitoring bodies and can serve as an important moral prod for change at the national level. Shadow reports can be submitted to CEDAW, the Human Rights Committee, the Economic and Social Rights Committee and the Committee on the Rights of the Child. These reports could be used as a means of monitoring government progress in addressing FC/FGM by discussing the areas in which governments could be doing more. The use of shadow reports as a tool for national-level advocacy is enhanced if NGOs use the opportunity of government reporting at the international level to dialogue with the government representatives and other organizations about the activities that should be undertaken for stopping FC/FGM. Shadow reports may also be a means of informing the broader international community about the situation with respect to FC/FGM in a given country. Finally, the comments of the committee, incorporating information from NGOs, can be widely distributed at the national level and used by NGOs to advocate for further changes in the government's approach.

Lobby for recommendations and general comments condemning FC/FGM

NGOs can be instrumental in lobbying human rights treaty-monitoring bodies to adopt Recommendations and General Comments that clarify further government responsibility to work toward providing women with information and choices to abandon FC/FGM. While NGO involvement in the process of establishing such Recommendations and General Comments varies with each human rights body, NGOs can play an important role by lobbying for the adoption of measures specifically on FC/FGM. For example, CEDAW has already made Recommendations relating to FC/FGM (Recommendation 14). Additional Recommendations and General Comments on FC/FGM from the other human rights treaty bodies, which to date have not issued such statements, would represent an advance in the advocacy of such rights. NGOs should call upon other treaty-monitoring committees, such as the Human Rights Committee and the Economic and Social Rights Committee, to issue general recommendations on FC/FGM based on the provisions in those treaties that are relevant to the practice of FC/FGM.

Support individual complaints

Another useful NGO strategy at the international level is supporting the individual complaints of women subjected to FC/FGM that are brought before either treaty-monitoring committees or the thematic rapporteurs. The Human Rights Committee, which monitors implementation of the Civil and Political Rights Covenant, has jurisdiction to hear such complaints. While NGOs are themselves prohibited from bringing complaints on behalf of others, they can provide valuable technical, documentary, financial and moral support for individual victims filing such complaints. NGOs should also lobby for increasing the powers of the treaty bodies to examine individual complaints.

The UN General Assembly recently adopted the Draft Optional Protocol to the Women's Convention.[23] This protocol allows CEDAW to review complaints brought by individuals or groups alleging government violation of rights or failure to carry out its treaty obligations, adopt views on the merits of complaints, and make recommendations for government action. It would also authorize CEDAW to initiate its own inquiries concerning serious or systematic violations of the Convention. For example, it could appoint a special rapporteur on violence against women or harmful traditional practices. NGOs should encourage their governments to become parties to this optional protocol.

Increase activities in other UN contexts

Other bodies within the UN system can assist NGO efforts to enable women to have the information and choice to abandon FC/FGM. The mandates of various divisions within the UN Secretariat require action to protect the rights of women and girls. The Human Rights Commission and the Commission on the Status of Women should be lobbied to play a prominent role in efforts to eliminate FC/FGM. Several important steps have already been taken in this respect. As noted above, the General Assembly approved the Declaration on the Elimination of Violence

Against Women, which specifically cites FC/FGM as a form of violence against women that should be eliminated.[24] Similar efforts focused on FC/FGM should be promoted within the UN system.

The UN specialized agencies can also be further engaged in efforts to eliminate FC/FGM in Africa. In 1997, the World Health Organization (WHO), the United Nations Children's Fund (UNICEF) and the United Nations Population Fund (UNFPA) issued a joint statement committing their support to policies and programs aimed at eliminating FC/FGM.[25] In their statement, all three agencies declare their intention to work with NGOs in their efforts to eliminate the practice.[26] NGOs should encourage these agencies to engage in further dialogue with governments. NGOs can also provide these agencies with valuable ideas for effective programs to eliminate FC/FGM.

UN-sponsored international conferences present another opportunity for NGOs to bring international attention to the continued practice of FC/FGM and to government progress in efforts to eliminate it. At the World Conference on Human Rights in Vienna in 1993, African activists named FC/FGM as a cultural practice that violates women's human rights. This and the explicit inclusion of FGM as a reproductive and sexual health and rights issue for women in the ICPD and Beijing documents have led women's health and rights groups, international technical support agencies and donors to include FC/FGM as a priority issue on their agenda.

Conclusion

Efforts to address FC/FGM are part of a long-term process that seeks to make governments accountable for women's rights. A crucial means by which to develop a social justice approach to FC/FGM is to regard this practice as a matter of human rights. Characterizing FC/FGM as a violation of the human rights of women and girls has significant consequences for NGOs and governments. By invoking human rights standards, advocates can hold governments accountable for their inaction in response to FC/FGM. They can thus spur governments to address the practice of FC/FGM in their countries, through legal initiatives and other policies aimed at discouraging the practice with education and outreach. At the same time, NGOs that address FC/FGM as a human rights violation are given access to a wide range of international and regional mechanisms to combat the practice – mechanisms that can support their national-level efforts. From the perspective of governments, human rights raise questions regarding government action and inaction, and the need to ensure that national standards are consistent with global norms.

The experiences of nations around the world in addressing FC/FGM reveal that no single approach can eliminate FC/FGM. Criminal laws by themselves will not change people's behavior. Likewise, educational efforts, while often successful, cannot entirely eliminate adherence to the practice. Governments must be willing to devote attention and resources to a multi-strategy approach to eliminating FC/FGM. They should be receptive to the efforts of NGOs and international organizations that are also engaged in the struggle. All of these activities must be guided by a respect for the human rights of women and girls and an awareness of the lessons learned thus far in the global effort to eliminate FC/FGM.

The challenges associated with stopping FC/FGM should awaken us to the reality of the profound social and political changes that must occur to eliminate discrimination against women. Women's inequality is a global phenomenon that must be combated by a host of strategies and means that are responsive to the specifics of any given context. As NGOs and governments seek to deal with FC/FGM, it is critical to view such efforts as part of a worldwide attempt to move into a new millennium marked by equality and justice for all.

Notes

1. "Experiences of Non-governmental Organizations Working towards the Elimination of Female Genital Mutilation in Egypt," a study prepared by Samiha el Katsha, Sherine Ibrahim and Noha Sedky (November 1997), study paper available in English through CEDPA's Partnership Projects for Girls and Young Women Project. Also published in book form in Arabic by the Egyptian Task Force Against Female Genital Mutilation, 1997.
2. *1995 Egyptian Demographic and Health Survey*, Cairo: National Population Council, p. 171.
3. Amal Abd-El-Hadi, *We are Decided: The Struggle of an Egyptian Village to Eradicate Female Circumcision*, Cairo: Cairo Institute for Human Rights Studies, 1999.
4. Tostan, *Breakthrough in Senegal: A Report on the Process to End Female Genital Cutting in 31 Villages*, New York: Population Council, 1998.
5. Program for Appropriate Technology in Health (PATH), "Improving Women's Sexual and Reproductive Health: Review of Female Genital Mutilation Eradication Programs in Africa," 1998, submitted to the WHO, p. 35.
6. See *Positive Deviance: An Introduction to FGM Eradication*, Cairo: Center for Development and Population Activities, 2000.
7. Elaine Eliah, "Reaching for a Healthier Future," *Populi*, Vol. 23, No. 1, March 1996; Tom Masland, "The Ritual of Pain," *Newsweek*, July 5, 1999.
8. Population Council, *Evaluation de la Stratégie de Reconversion des Exciseuses pour l'Eradication des Mutilations Génitales Féminines au Mali*, New York: Population Council, Dec. 1998.
9. "UNICEF Welcomes Senegal Ban on Female Circumcision," AP Worldstream, Jan. 14, 1999.

10. Ibid.
11. For the Netherlands and Egypt, see country profiles in Part II. For the USA, see C.M. Ostrom, "Harborview Debates Issue of Circumcision of Muslim Girls," *Seattle Times*, Sept. 13, 1996, p. A1.
12. C.E. Welch, Jr, *Protecting Human Rights in Africa: Strategies and Roles of Non-Governmental Organizations*, Philadelphia: University of Pennsylvania Press, 1995, p. 59.
13. Amal Abd-El-Hadi, Personal Communication, July 10, 1998 (on file with CRLP).
14. Ibid.
15. Ibid.
16. Legal Research and Resource Center for Human Rights, Verdict Regarding the Prohibition of FGM in Egypt (visited Nov. 17, 1998), <http://www.geocities.com/CapitolHill/Lobby/9012/FGM/Circum/.htm>.
17. Ibid.
18. Linda Weil-Curiel, Commission Pour L'Abolition des Mutilations Sexuelles (CAM), Questionnaire, June 1998.
19. M. Simons, "8-Year Sentence in France for Genital Cutting," *New York Times*, Feb. 18, 1999.
20. Welch, *Protecting Human Rights in Africa*, p. 59.
21. OAU in Addis Ababa, Ethiopia, on September 12, 1997.
22. Welch, *Protecting Human Rights in Africa*, p. 93.
23. Optional Protocol to the Convention on the Elimination of All Forms of Discrimination Against Women, Adopted by General Assembly resolution A/54/4 on October 6, 1999, opened for signature on December 10, 1999.
24. United Nations General Assembly, Declaration on the Elimination of Violence Against Women, art. 2(a) (85th Plenary Meeting, 1993), A/RES/48/104.
25. World Health Organization, *Female Genital Mutilation: A Joint WHO/UNICEF/UNFPA Statement*, 1997.
26. Ibid., pp. 17–19.

Part II

Reference

National-level Legal Measures

This reference section consists of 41 country profiles covering the 28 African countries in which FC/FGM is prevalent as well as 13 receiving countries with immigrant populations from countries where FC/FGM is practiced. This section is not comprehensive in its coverage of countries that have immigrant populations that may practice FC/FGM. It reviews only a sampling, drawn primarily from those receiving countries either that have taken substantial steps to address the practice of FC/FGM or that have received a significant number of immigrants from countries in which FC/FGM is prevalent.

Information Contained in National Profiles

Statistical information

Each country profile provides basic statistical information. These data are intended to provide a contextual backdrop for discussion of national responses to FC/FGM. In the profiles of each African country, information is included on the prevalence rate of this practice. This information is not available for the receiving countries profiled in this report. While every effort was made to provide the most accurate statistics on the prevalence rate of FC/FGM in each African country, it should be noted that such information is difficult to determine with precision. In addition, where available, information on the religious and ethnic groups that practice FC/FGM is included in the African country profiles. This information, however, is not uniformly available, and it is absent from several of the country profiles.

The information appearing in the statistics boxes is drawn from the following sources (unless otherwise specified in the notes):

- N. Toubia, *Caring for Women with Circumcision: A Technical Manual for Health Care Providers*, New York: RAINBQ, 1999, p. 25.
- OECD, *Trends in International Migration: Annual Report 1996*, Paris: OECD, 1997,

pp. 224, 232, 256–8, 263.
- J. Smith, *Visions and Discussions on Genital Mutilation of Girls: An International Survey*, Amsterdam: Defence for Children International, 1995, p. 143.
- N. Toubia and S. Izett, *Female Genital Mutilation: An Overivew*, Geneva: World Health Organization, 1998, pp. 10, 12–18, 25.
- UNFPA, *The State of World Population 1998*, New York: UNFPA, 1998, p. 70.
- United Nations, *The World's Women 1995: Trends and Statistics*, New York: United Nations, 1995, pp. 24–5.
- World Bank, *World Development Indicators 1999*, Washington, DC: World Bank, 1999, pp. 12–14, 248.

Information regarding human rights treaty ratification and reservations was drawn primarily from the following Internet resources: United Nations Treaty Collection; United Nations High Commissioner for Human Rights Treaty Bodies database; University of Minnesota, African Human Rights Resource Center; and Council of Europe, European Treaties site. Website addresses for these resources appear below Table 1. Information on reservations to human rights instruments is included only where such reservations are relevant to a discussion of FC/FGM.

Sources of law and other measures to address FC/FGM

Legal and policy measures pertaining to FC/FGM are found in a variety of sources, including international and regional treaties, constitutions, criminal laws, decrees and regulations, child protection laws and medical ethics codes.

The types of sources relied upon in each country profile are described below. The set of measures discussed in the profiles of the African countries varies from that discussed in the receiving countries. In both groups, international and regional treaties, constitutions, penal codes and other governmental and non-governmental measures aimed at eliminating FC/FGM have been examined. In the profiles of receiving countries, additional information has been provided on child protection laws, the standards of health professionals, and donor policies for stopping FC/FGM in African countries. The differences in the profiles of African countries versus those of receiving countries reflect, in part, the differences in the legal strategies being employed in the two sets of countries. It should be noted, however, that information was not consistently available on child protection laws and the regulation of health professionals in African countries. Where such information was available, it was included under the heading "Other Measures."

The laws of a number of countries have been translated into English from the language in which they appear in official publications. Unless otherwise indicated, translations are by the authors of this publication.

Measures reviewed in all countries

International and regional human rights treaties

As discussed in Chapter 1, international and regional human rights treaties give rise to a number of governmental obligations. Governments that have signed and ratified these treaties are bound by international law to uphold them. Treaties can be enforced in three different ways. In some countries, the protections outlined in international treaties have been given the status of domestic law, allowing individuals to enforce those protections in private lawsuits against their governments in domestic courts. Some treaties create a central enforcement body, such as a commission or a court, which hears individual challenges of national-level government action. Currently, the most common means of enforcing a human rights treaty is through a reporting mechanism. States that are parties to certain treaties are obligated to report regularly to committees on their progress in implementing the terms of the treaties.

Each country profile includes a list of the international and regional treaties to which countries are parties. The date on which the government officially became bound to each treaty appears in parentheses next to the name of each treaty. In most cases, this date refers to the date of ratification, which is the date upon which governments that have signed treaties become bound through a process of ratification at the national level. In some cases, the date refers to the date upon which a government "accedes" to a treaty. Accession occurs when a government that is not a signatory to a treaty nevertheless becomes a party. Other governments may have "succeeded" to a treaty, which occurs when a new national government agrees to be bound by the international obligations accepted by the previous government. For the sake of clarity and simplicity, the term "ratified" is used throughout this section to refer to all three of the means of becoming bound to a treaty: ratification, accession and succession.

Constitution

A nation's constitution is its law of highest authority. All legislation and government action should conform to the norms established in the constitution. Most constitutions contain provisions ensuring individual rights, often protecting such rights from infringement by both government actors and private parties.

Criminal law

Criminal laws describe acts deemed unlawful by the state, carrying penalties such as imprisonment and fines. Criminal law provisions are generally enacted by a country's legislative body, in accordance with the formal procedures mandated by the constitution of that country. Violators of a country's criminal law could face arrest and prosecution by law enforcement officials. Criminal laws that specifically address FC/FGM are reproduced in their entirety. Other potentially relevant laws are paraphrased in part. When laws provide for monetary fines, the amount specified in the text is followed by a converted figure in US dollars in parentheses.

Other measures: laws, regulations and policies

This category covers decrees and regulations pertaining to FC/FGM and government policy statements. Decrees and regulations emanate from the executive branch of government – the sector usually charged with implementing and enforcing the law. Unlike criminal law provisions, decrees and regulations may be issued without the approval of the legislature. For this reason, they are more often subject to revision and rescission. Decrees and regulations pertaining to FC/FGM have typically been issued by ministries of health and of women's affairs. A decree or regulation cannot in itself be the basis of a criminal prosecution. However, it can declare FC/FGM an unlawful medical practice, subjecting perpetrators to prosecution under national criminal law. More commonly, decrees announce a governmental policy to address FC/FGM, often creating a plan of action and a body charged with overseeing the government's activities in this area.

Additional measures reviewed in receiving country profiles

Three additional categories of measures were included in the profiles of receiving countries, reflecting the dimensions of the legal and policy responses to FC/FGM in those countries. Each receiving country profile examines the manner in which child protection laws, professional standards of health professionals, and overseas assistance programs are employed in national efforts to eliminate FC/FGM. For the reasons noted above, these categories do not appear in the profiles of African countries. Where information related to these subjects is available, it appears under the heading "Other Measures."

Child protection laws

Child protection laws provide for state intervention in cases of child abuse by a parent or guardian. Unlike criminal laws, child protection laws are concerned less with punishing parents or guardians than with ensuring that a child's interests are being served. These laws provide mechanisms for removing the child from his or her parent or guardian when the state has reason to believe that abuse has occurred or is likely to occur.

Standards of health professionals

Physicians in most countries are subject to the authority of the licensing and disciplinary bodies of the medical profession. The extent to which governments play a role in determining the ethical standards to which medical professionals are held varies from country to country.

Policies for eliminating FC/FGM in Africa

A number of donor governments have issued policy statements pertaining to FC/FGM. In some cases, efforts to address FC/FGM have been integrated into ongoing foreign assistance activities.

Table 1 Treaty Ratification by Country

	Women's conv.	*Children's rights conv.*	*Civil & pol. rights cov.*	*Economic, social & cult. rights cov.*	*Banjul charter*	*European conv.*	*African charter*
Australia	•	•	•	•			
Belgium	•	•	•	•		•	
Benin	•	•	•	•	•		•
Burkina Faso	•	•	•	•	•		•
Cameroon	•	•	•	•	•		•
Canada	•	•	•	•			
C. African R.	•	•	•	•	•		
Chad	•	•	•	•	•		
Côte d'Ivoire	•	•	•	•	•		
D.R. of Congo	•	•	•	•	•		
Denmark	•	•	•	•		•	
Djibouti	•	•			•		
Egypt	•	•	•	•	•		
Eritrea	•	•					
Ethiopia	•	•	•	•			
France	•	•	•	•		•	
Gambia	•	•	•	•	•		
Germany	•	•	•	•		•	
Ghana	•	•			•		
Guinea	•	•	•	•	•		
Guinea-Bissau	•	•		•	•		
Italy	•	•	•	•		•	
Kenya	•	•	•	•	•		
Liberia	•	•			•		
Mali	•	•	•	•	•		•
Mauritania		•			•		
Netherlands	•	•	•	•		•	
New Zealand	•	•	•	•			
Niger	•	•	•	•	•		•
Nigeria	•	•	•	•	•		
Norway	•	•	•	•		•	
Senegal	•	•	•	•	•		•
Sierre Leone	•	•	•	•	•		
Somalia			•	•	•		
Sudan		•	•	•	•		
Sweden	•	•	•	•		•	
Tanzania	•	•	•	•	•		
Togo	•	•	•	•	•		•
Uganda	•	•	•	•	•		•
UK	•	•	•	•		•	
USA			•				

Sources: United Nations High Commissioner for Human Rights, Status of Ratification of the Principal International Human Rights Treaties <http://www.unhchr.ch/pdf/report.pdf>; University of Minnesota African Human Rights Resource Center <http://www1.umn.edu/humanrts/instree/ratz1afchar.htm>; Council of Europe Treaty Office <http://conventions. coe.int/treaty/EN/cadreprincipal.htm>.

Table 2 Prevalence Rates of FC/FGM and Official Action Against FC/FGM

Country (% prevalence)	*Specific FC/FGM laws/regulations*	*Existing laws recognized as applicable to FC/FGM*
Australia	♦[1]	♥
Belgium		
Benin (50)		
Burkina Faso (70)	♦	
Cameroon (20)		
Canada	♦	♥
Central African Republic (43)	♦	
Chad (60)		
Côte d'Ivoire (43)	♦	
Dem. Republic of Congo (5)		
Denmark		♦
Djibouti (98)	♦	
Egypt (97)	o	♦
Eritrea (95)		
Ethiopia (90)	•	
France		♦ ♥
The Gambia (80)		
Germany		♦
Ghana (30)	♦ •	
Guinea (50)	♦	
Guinea-Bissau (50)		
Italy		
Kenya (50)	o	♦
Liberia (60)	¤	
Mali (94)		♦
Mauritania (25)		♦
Netherlands		♦
New Zealand	♦	♥
Niger (20)		
Nigeria (60)		
Norway	♦	
Senegal (20)	♦	
Sierra Leone (90)		
Somalia (98)		
Sudan (89)		
Sweden	♦	
Tanzania (18)	♦	
Togo (50)	♦	
Uganda (5)	•	¤
United Kingdom	♦	♥
United States	♦	♥

♦ Criminal law ♥ Child protection law • Constitutional law ¤ Civil law o Ministerial decree

[1] Six of eight states have enacted legislation. Two have indicated that existing penal code provisions are applicable.

Source: (for prevalence rates) N. Toubia, *Caring for Women with Circumcision: A Technical Manual for Health Care Providers*, New York: RAINBQ, 1999.

Australia

Size (1,000 km^2): 7,741

Income (per capita GNP in US$): 20,650

Population (millions): 19

Immigrant population: In 1991, there were 75,968 women in Australia from countries in which some form of female circumcision is practiced. In 1991, there were 33,200 Egyptians and 49,700 African immigrants in Australia from countries other than Egypt and South Africa. In 1996, there was an inflow of 4,800 temporary residents from Africa.

International Treaties

- Women's Convention (ratified 1983).
- Children's Rights Convention (ratified 1990).
- Civil and Civil and Political Rights Covenant (ratified 1980).
- Economic, Social and Cultural Rights Covenant (ratified 1975).

National Laws

Constitution

The Australian Constitution outlines the structure of the national government, but does not include a Bill of Rights.[1] Individual rights and liberties have been acknowledged in judicial decisions and in legislation.[2]

Criminal law

Criminal legislation in six out of eight Australian states and territories has made FC/FGM a criminal offense. Australian Capital Territory, Northern Territory, New South Wales, South Australia, Tasmania and Victoria have enacted legislation prohibiting the practice.[3] Two states, Queensland and Western Australia, have not enacted specific legislation.

State and territorial laws prohibiting FC/FGM have several common features.[4] All of the laws explicitly prohibit both the practice of FC/FGM within the jurisdiction and the removal of a child from the jurisdiction for the purposes of subjecting her to FC/FGM. Under all of the laws, a person's consent to undergoing FC/FGM does not relieve a practitioner or accomplice of criminal liability. Finally, all of the laws explicitly state that procedures carried out by health professionals for therapeutic purposes are not considered illegal practices of FC/FGM. The punishments for the crimes relating to FC/FGM range from seven to fifteen years of imprisonment.[5]

Although Queensland has not passed a law specifically prohibiting FC/FGM, the Queensland Law Reform Commission has recommended that Criminal Code provisions addressing "grievous bodily harm" and "unlawful wounding" be applied to FC/FGM. The penalties for such crimes range from seven years for "unlawful wounding"[6] to fourteen years or life imprisonment, depending on intent, for "grievous bodily harm."[7]

Current information on Western Australia was not available.

Provisions

Since New South Wales is the Australian state with the largest population, the full text of its law follows:

New South Wales law

Section 45(1) A person who:

(a) excises, infibulates or otherwise mutilates the whole or any part of the labia majora or labia minora or clitoris of another person; or

(b) aids, abets, counsels or procures a person to perform any of those acts on another person, is liable to penal servitude for 7 years.

(2) An offence is committed against this section even if one or more of the acts constituting the offence occurred outside New South Wales if the person mutilated by or because of the acts is ordinarily resident in the State.

(3) It is not an offence against this section to perform a surgical operation if that operation:

(a) is necessary for the health of the person on whom it is performed and is performed by a medical practitioner; or

(b) is performed on a person in labour or who has just given birth, and for medical purposes connected with that labour or birth, by a medical practitioner or authorised professional; or

(c) is a sexual reassignment procedure and is performed by a medical practitioner.

(4) In determining whether an operation is necessary for the health of a person only matters relevant to the medical welfare of the person are to be taken into account.

(5) It is not a defence to a charge under this section that the person mutilated by or because of the acts alleged to have been committed consented to the acts.

(6) This section applies only to acts occurring after the commencement of the section.

(7) In this section:

"authorised professional" means: (a) a person authorised to practise midwifery under the Nurses Act 1991 or undergoing a course of training with a view to being so authorised; or (b) in relation to an operation performed in a place outside New South Wales – a person authorised to practise midwifery by a body established under the law of that place having functions similar to the functions of the Nurses Registration Board, or undergoing a course of training with a view to being so authorised; or (c) a medical student;

"medical practitioner", in relation to an operation performed in a place outside New South Wales, includes a person authorised to practise medicine by a body established under the law of that place having functions similar to the functions of the New South Wales Medical Board; "medical student" means: (a) a registered medical student within the meaning of the Medical Practice Act 1992; or (b) in relation to an operation performed in a place outside New South Wales – a person undergoing a course of training with a view to being authorised to be a medical practitioner in that place;

"sexual reassignment procedure" means a surgical procedure to alter the genital appearance of a person to the appearance (as nearly as practicable) of the opposite sex to the sex of the person.[8]

Enforcement of the law

Information not available.

Child protection laws

Child protection is the responsibility of the states and territories. Child protection legislation in most states may be applied to protect a child from undergoing FC/FGM.[9] Jurisdictions that have amended their child protection laws to include specific protections against FC/FGM include South Australia.[10] Under South Australia's Children's Protection Act, a court that suspects that a child is at risk of undergoing FC/FGM may make an order for the protection of the child. The order may call for such measures as preventing the removal of the child from the state, requiring that the child's passport be held by the court, or requiring periodic examinations of the child.[11]

Other Measures: Laws, Regulations and Policies

The National Framework for the National Education Program on Female Genital Mutilation has been instituted with the support of the federal government and all of the states and territories.[12] Its objective is "to provide culturally appropriate intervention to prevent the occurrence of female genital mutilation in [Australia] and to assist those women and girls living in Australia who have already been subjected to this practice."[13] In the 1995–6 federal budget, the government allocated approximately Aust.$3 million (approximately US$1,914,486) to the program over five years, used to fund education and health promotion programs implemented by the states and territories.[14] The program also aims to support health care and community workers who provide services to communities in which FC/FGM may be practiced.[15] The federal government also provided a grant to the Royal Australian College of Obstetricians and Gynecologists (RACOG) to develop materials to assist health professionals in caring for girls and women who have undergone FC/FGM.[16]

Standards of Health Professionals

On March 20, 1994, RACOG released a statement affirming its opposition to "any form of female genital circumcision being performed for non-medical reasons," and supporting efforts to eliminate the practice through education of the community and health care providers.[17] RACOG has also produced a publication entitled *Female Genital Mutilation: Information for Australian Health Professionals*, which covers the ethical and legal aspects, as well as practice guidelines for medical practitioners.[18]

Policies for Eliminating FC/FGM in Africa

The policy of the Australian Agency for International Development (AusAID) on FC/FGM is encompassed in its Gender and Development policy, which is aimed at promoting equal opportunities for women and men to participate and benefit from the process of development.[19] AusAID has funded NGOs that are active in campaigns to prevent FC/FGM in Africa.[20] It has also contributed financially to the activities of the WHO, including its Female Genital Mutilation project and its Women's Health and Development Program.[21]

Notes

1. D. Hodgkinson, "Protection of Minority Rights in Australia: The Present Legal Regime," *Loyola of Los Angeles International & Comparative Law Journal*, Vol. XIX, August 1997, p. 859.
2. Ibid., pp. 863–7.
3. Australian Capital Territory, Crimes Amendment Act (No. 3) 1995, No. 50 of

1995, sect. 5, 92V–92Z; Northern Territory, Criminal Code Act (RECP033), 1997, Division 4A, No. 186; New South Wales, Crimes (Female Genital Mutilation) Amendment Act 1994, No. 58, sect. 45; South Australia, Statutes Amendment (Female Genital Mutilation and Child Protection) Act 1995, sects 33–33B; Tasmania, Royal Australian College of Obstetricians and Gynaecologists (RACOG), *Female Genital Mutilation: Information for Australian Health Professionals*, East Melbourne: RACOG, 1997, p. 21; Victoria, Crimes (Female Genital Mutilation) Act 1996, sects 32–43A.

4. Because Tasmania's law prohibiting FC/FGM was not available, it is not reflected in this summary.
5. Australian Capital Territory, Crimes Amendment Act (No. 3) 1995, No. 50 of 1995, sect. 5; Northern Territory, Criminal Code Act (RECP033), 1997; New South Wales, Crimes (Female Genital Mutilation) Amendment Act 1994, No. 58; South Australia, Statutes Amendment (Female Genital Mutilation and Child Protection) Act 1995; Victoria, Crimes (Female Genital Mutilation) Act 1996. Tasmanian legislation not available.
6. See Queensland Law Reform Commission, Report No. 47 – Female Genital Mutilation (1994); Criminal Code Act 1899, sect. 323 (reprinted as in force Apr. 3, 1998).
7. Criminal Code Act 1899, at sects 317 and 320.
8. Crimes (Female Genital Mutilation) Amendment Act 1994, No. 58, sect. 45, amending the Crimes Act of 1900.
9. RACOG, *Female Genital Mutilation*, pp. 24–5.
10. Amendment of Children's Protection Act 1993, sect. 26B(1). The amendments include sects 267A, 26B, 27 and 55.
11. Ibid., sect. 26B(1).
12. Public Health Division, Commonwealth Department of Health and Family Services, *National Education Program on Female Genital Mutilation* (last visited June 8, 1999), <http://www.health.gov.au/pubhlth/strateg/women/fgm/index.htm>.
13. Ibid.
14. Ibid.
15. Ibid.
16. Ibid.
17. Statement from the Royal Australian College of Obstetricians and Gynecologists (March 20, 1994) (on file at the CRLP).
18. RACOG, *Female Genital Mutilation.*
19. Australian Agency for International Development (AusAID), Gender and Development: Australia's Aid Commitment, Policy Statement announced by the Hon. Alexander Downer MP, Minister for Foreign Affairs (March 1997).
20. Letter from Lorraine Breust, Policy Officer, Health Group, Australian Agency for International Development, June 21, 1999.
21. Ibid.

Belgium

Size (1,000 km^2): 33

Income (per capita GNP in US$): 26,730

Population (millions): 10

Immigrant population: In 1997, there were 14,797 immigrants from the Democratic Republic of the Congo, Cameroon and Ghana, and 7,070 of these were women.[1] In 1995, the total immigrant population was 922,300, 429,700 of whom were women.

International Treaties

- Women's Convention (ratified 1985).
- Children's Rights Convention (ratified 1991). Declaration asserting that the state is not obligated to guarantee foreigners the same rights as nationals.
- Civil and Political Rights Covenant (ratified 1983).
- Economic, Social and Cultural Rights Covenant (ratified 1983). Declaration asserting that the state is not obligated to guarantee foreigners the same rights as nationals.
- European Convention (ratified 1955).

National Laws

Constitution

The Belgian Constitution guarantees equality before the law and non-discrimination.[2] Article 10 provides that "Belgians are equal before the law." Article 11 of the Constitution provides that "[e]njoyment of the rights and freedoms recognized for Belgians should be ensured without discrimination."

Article 23 provides that "Everyone has the right to lead a life in conformity with human dignity." Among the specific rights guaranteed in this article are the right "to health care and to social, medical and legal aid" and the right "to enjoy cultural and social fulfillment."

While Article 19 of the Constitution guarantees "freedom of worship," it does not protect "offenses committed when using this freedom."

Criminal law

Since 1986, there have been multiple attempts to modify the Belgian Penal Code to prohibit FC/FGM.[3] Recent legislation would have explicitly included FC/FGM in Penal Code provisions that pertain to acts of violence committed against a minor.[4] The proposed law stated that anyone who "practices, facilitates or promotes acts of sexual mutilation, such as circumcision, excision, or infibulation upon a female minor," would be subject to a punishment provided for violent acts against minors (see below).[5]

Provisions

While FC/FGM is not explicitly prohibited in the Penal Code,[6] Articles 398, 400, 401 and 410 may be applicable.

> Any person who intentionally wounds or strikes shall be punished by imprisonment from eight days to six months and by a fine of 26 francs to 100 francs [approximately US$0.65–2.60], or by either punishment. [Art. 398]
>
> The punishment shall be imprisonment from two to five years and a fine of 200 to 500 francs [approximately US$5.20–13.00], if the strikes or wounds result in an illness that appears to be incurable, a permanent incapacity to work, the complete loss of use of an organ, or a serious mutilation.
>
> In the case of premeditation, the penalty shall be imprisonment (*réclusion*) (5–10 years). [Art. 400]

When intentional wounds or strikes result in unintentional death, the punishment is imprisonment of 5–10 years (Art. 401). The penalties are elevated when these offenses are committed against a child of or below the age of 16 by a parent or by any person having authority over or custody of the child (Art. 410).

Belgian courts have defined the term "strikes" to refer to any violent contact between the human body and any other physical object, potentially causing a contusion or a concussion.[7] Any external or internal lesion, no matter how light, that is inflicted upon the body by mechanical or chemical means may be a "strike" or a "wound."[8] A "wound" is a physical mark, such as a cut, a tear, a contusion, an excoriation, a fracture, a burn, a dislocation or a scratch.[9]

Enforcement of the law

FC/FGM has never been the subject of prosecution under existing penal law.[10]

Child protection laws

Because Belgium is a federal state, child protection is administered at the Community level. These protections may potentially be applied to prevent FC/FGM. For example, in the French Community, an officer on youth assistance oversees efforts to protect children in danger. Upon learning that a child may be in danger, the officer attempts to prevent harm to the child through the voluntary participation of all parties involved. In the case of an immediate and serious threat to the child's physical or psychological integrity, where the child's parents or guardians are unwilling to cooperate with the officer, a youth court (*tribunal de la jeunesse*) may intervene to protect a child. The youth court may take measures to prevent actions on the part of the child, her family or relatives that may be detrimental to the child.[11] Such measures could potentially be taken to prevent a child from undergoing FC/FGM.[12] To date, child protection laws have not been applied in the context of FC/FGM.[13]

Other Measures: Laws, Regulations and Policies

The Ministry of Employment and Labour and Equal Opportunities has issued a policy statement recommending measures to address FC/FGM, including the enactment of a criminal law provision and preventive education and outreach programs.[14]

Standards of Health Professionals

The Code of Medical Deontology, issued in 1975, contains no explicit provisions prohibiting the practice of FC/FGM by a medical professional. Because the practice places the patient at risk without medical justification, however, a physician may still be subject to criminal prosecution for performing the procedure.[15]

Policies for Eliminating FC/FGM in Africa

In December 1997, Belgium's Administration for Development Cooperation (AGCD) released a Plan for the Future, a new policy for development cooperation that strongly emphasizes reproductive health as a priority for Belgian assistance in the health sector.[16] Specific information on AGCD's policy regarding FC/FGM was unavailable.

Notes

1. Proceedings of the Expert Meeting on Female Genital Mutilation, Ghent, Belgium, Nov. 5–7, 1998, p. 11 (figures were obtained from the National Offices of Statistics from each European member state).
2. *Constitution of Belgium*, Belgian Parliament (last visited Aug. 10, 1999), <http://.fed-parl.be/gwuk0002.htm>.
3. Service de Criminologie, Université de Liège, *Les Atteintes à l'intégrité des organes sexuels*, 1996, p. 35.
4. Chambre des Représentants de Belgique, Proposition de Loi (Sept. 13, 1995). Legislation was reintroduced in April 1999 by Minister M. Smet, but failed to pass due to controversy over a provision that was unrelated to FC/FGM (Communication from Els Leye, International Centre for Reproductive Health, Nov. 3, 1999).
5. Ibid.
6. Penal Code, reprinted in Service de Criminologie, Université de Liège, *Les Atteintes à l'intégrité des organes sexuels*, p. 28.
7. Cass. 28 novembre 1932, Pas. 1933, I, 31 cited in Service de Criminologie, Université de Liège, *Les Atteintes à l'intégrité des organes sexuels*, p. 28.
8. Cass. 12 avril 1983, Pas. 1983, I, 852 cited in ibid.
9. Cass. 28 novembre 1949, Pas. 1949, I 197 cited in ibid.
10. Els Leye, International Centre for Reproductive Health, Questionnaire (received April 27, 1998).
11. Service de Criminologie, Université de Liège, *Les Atteintes à l'intégrité des organes sexuels*, p. 34.
12. Ibid., p. 35.
13. Els Leye, International Centre for Reproductive Health, Questionnaire (received April 27, 1998).
14. Avis No. 18 du Conseil de l'Egalité des Chances du 13 juin 1997, relatif aux mutilations génitales.
15. Ibid., p. 15.
16. Population Action International, *Paying Their Fair Share? Donor Countries and International Population Assistance*, Washington, DC: Population Action International, 1998, p. 16.

Benin

Size (1,000 km^2): 113
Income (per capita GNP in US$): 380
Population (millions): 6
Number of women per 100 men: 102
Percentage of young people in the population (under 15 years): 47
Prevalence of FC/FGM: 50%
Type(s) of FC/FGM most commonly practiced: Type II
Ethnic groups that practice FC/FGM: Bariba, Boko, Nago, Peul and Wama.

International Treaties

- Women's Convention (ratified 1992).
- Children's Rights Convention (ratified 1990).
- Civil and Political Rights Covenant (ratified 1992).
- Economic, Social and Cultural Rights Covenant (ratified 1992).
- Banjul Charter (ratified 1986).
- African Charter (ratified 1997).

National Laws

Constitution

The Constitution of Benin[1] guarantees the equality of women and men before the law. Article 26 states that "[t]he State shall assure to everyone equality before the law without distinction of … sex.… Men and women are equal under the law."

The Constitution protects the rights to life and physical integrity. Article 15 states generally that "[e]ach individual has the right to life, liberty, security and the integrity of his person." Article 8 provides that "[t]he human person is sacred and inviolable. The State has the absolute obligation to respect it and protect it. It shall guarantee him a full blossoming out [*épanouissement*]. To that end, it shall assure its citizens equal access to health."

Children receive special protection under the Constitution. Article 26 provides that "the State shall protect the family and particularly the mother and child."

Cultural and religious freedoms may be limited under the law. Article 23 states that "[e]very person has the right to freedom of thought, of conscience, or religion, of creed, of opinion and of expression *with respect for the public order established by law and regulations*" (emphasis added).

Criminal law

The Penal Code contains no provisions specifically prohibiting FC/FGM. Under the current Penal Code, general provisions addressing "intentional wounds or strikes" may be applicable to FC/FGM.

Provisions

Article 309 of the Penal Code imposes sanctions for intentional wounds or strikes, including those that result in mutilation, amputation or loss of the use of a limb, blindness, loss of an eye or other permanent disability.[2] Article 312 increases the punishment for this crime if the violence is committed against a minor of 15 years or younger. Punishments are again elevated where the offender is the mother, father or relative of the victim, or any other person having authority over or guardianship of the child. In addition, punishment varies depending upon the degree of harm that results from the offense.

Enforcement of the law

Information not available.

Other Measures: Laws, Regulations and Policies

The government has taken a position against FC/FGM and has launched some educational activities in rural areas focusing on the health effects of the practice.[3]

Notes

1. *Constitution of the Republic of Benin* (1990), translated in A.P. Blaustein and G.H. Flanz (eds), *Constitutions of the Countries of the World*, Dobbs Ferry, NY: Oceana Publications, 1992.
2. *Code Pénal (France)* (57th edn), Paris: Dalloz, 1960. See also CRLP and Groupe de Recherches Femmes et Lois de Sénégal Réseau de Solidarité des Femmes sous Lois Musulmanes (GREFELS), *Femmes dans le monde: l'Afrique francophone*, New York: CRLP, 1999.
3. Office of the Senior Coordinator for International Women's Issues, Bureau for Global Affairs and the Office of Asylum Affairs, Bureau of Democracy, Human Rights and Labor, U.S. Department of State, *Female Genital Mutilation (FGM) or Female Genital Cutting (FGC) in Benin*, 1999.

Burkina Faso

Size (1,000 km^2): 274

Income (per capita GNP in US$): 250

Population (millions): 10

Number of women per 100 men: 102

Percentage of young people in the population (under 15 years): 45

Prevalence of FC/FGM: 70%

Type(s) of FC/FGM most commonly practiced: Type II

Ethnic groups that practice FC/FGM: Widespread among Christians, Muslims and animists in the provinces of Comeo, Ganzourgou, Houet, Kenedougou, Kossi, Kadiogo, Mouhoun, Nahouri, Yatenga and Zounweogo.

International Treaties

- Women's Convention (ratified 1987).
- Children's Rights Convention (ratified 1990).
- Civil and Political Rights Covenant (ratified 1999).
- Economic, Social and Cultural Rights Covenant (ratified 1999).
- Banjul Charter (ratified 1984).
- African Charter (ratified 1992).

National Laws

Constitution

The Constitution of Burkina Faso[1] guarantees the equality of women and men before the law. Article 1 of the Constitution provides "[a]ll the Burkinabians shall be born free and equal in rights. All shall have an equal right to enjoy all the rights and all the freedoms guaranteed by the present Constitution. Discrimination of all sorts, notably those founded on … sex, … shall be prohibited."

The Constitution further protects the rights to life and physical integrity. Article 2 guarantees "the protection of life, safety, and physical integrity." Article 26 states that "[t]he right to health shall be recognized. The State shall work to promote it."

The Constitution provides special protection to children. Article 24 pledges that the "State shall work to promote the rights of the child."

Cultural and religious practices must conform to constitutional protections of individual rights. Article 7 of the Constitution provides that "[t]he freedom of belief, of non-belief, of conscience, of religious, philosophical opinion, of religious exercise, the freedom of assembly, the free practice of custom ... shall be guaranteed by the present Constitution *subject to respect of the law, of the public order, of good morals and of the human person*" (emphasis added).

Criminal law

The National Assembly enacted a law prohibiting FC/FGM in 1996. It went into effect in February 1997.[2]

Provisions

> Article 380: Any person who violates or attempts to violate the physical integrity of the female genital organ, either by total ablation, excision, infibulation, desensitization, or by any other means, shall be punished by imprisonment for 6 months to 3 years and a fine of 150,000 to 900,000 francs [approximately US$240–1,440], or by either punishment.
>
> If the procedure results in death, the punishment shall be imprisonment for 5 to 10 years.
>
> Article 381: The maximum punishment shall be imposed if the offender is a member of the medical or paramedical field. A court may also suspend his or her license to practice medicine for up to five years.
>
> Article 382: A person having knowledge of the acts outlined in article 380 and who fails to advise the proper authorities will be fined 50,000 to 100,000 francs [approximately US$80–160].[3]

Enforcement of the law

As of July 1998, some 10 excisors and more than 30 accomplices had been prosecuted. Excisors have been punished with prison sentences ranging from one to six months as well as fines ranging from 10,000 to 50,000 francs (approximately US$16–80). The accomplices have been sentenced to prison terms ranging from two to five months, with the majority receiving sentences of three months. Accomplices have also faced fines ranging from 10,000 to 50,000 francs (approximately US$16–80).[4] In a number of instances, prison sentences for both excisors and accomplices have been suspended.[5]

As a means of enforcement, the National Committee against Excision (CNLPE)[6] has established a 24-hour telephone hotline for individuals who wish to report an incident of FC/FGM that has either occurred or is likely to occur. Upon receiving a report of FC/FGM that has already occurred, the CNLPE ensures that the parents of the circumcised girl and the practitioner are served notice to report to the police. When called prior to the excision, the CNLPE provides the family with information about the harmful effects of FC/FGM and about the new law.[7]

Other Measures: Laws, Regulations and Policies

The CNLPE was established in 1990 by presidential decree.[8] The CNLPE, which is administered by the Ministry for Social Action and the Family, oversees activities to prevent excision throughout the country. These include education, research, and evaluating activities aimed at stopping FC/FGM.[9]

Notes

1. *Constitution du Burkina Faso* (1991), translated in A.P. Blaustein and G.H. Flanz (eds), *Constitutions of the Countries of the World*, Dobbs Ferry, NY: Oceana Publications, 1992.
2. M. Lamizana, "The Campaign Against Excision: Burkina Faso's Experience," presentation in New York, Sept. 18, 1997, p. 6.
3. Law No. 43/96/ADP of Nov. 13, 1996 on the Penal Code, arts 380–82, *Journal Officiel du Burkina Faso*, Jan. 27, 1997.
4. Mariam Lamizana, Comité National de Lutte Contre la Pratique de l'Excision (CNLPE), Questionnaire (July 30, 1998).
5. Ibid.
6. In Burkina Faso, the National Committee against Excision is known as the Comité National de Lutte Contre la Pratique de l'Excision (CNLPE).
7. Lamizana, "The Campaign Against Excision," p. 6.
8. Kiti No. AN VII-318/PF/SANS-AS/SEAS, May 18, 1990; Kadiatou Korsaga, Direction de la Promotion de l'Education de la Fille, Ministère de l'Enseignement à la Base et de l'Alphabetisation, Questionnaire (Sept. 1, 1998).
9. Lamizana, "The Campaign Against Excision," p. 6.

Cameroon

Size (1,000 km^2): 475
Income (per capita GNP in US$): 620
Population (millions): 14
Number of women per 100 men: 101
Percentage of young people in the population (under 15 years): 44
Prevalence of FC/FGM: 20%
Type(s) of FC/FGM most commonly practiced: Types I and II
Ethnic groups that practice FC/FGM: In a highly selective study performed by the National Committee on Harmful Traditional Practices in 1994, FGM was found to be practiced by 100% of Muslims and 63.6% of Christians in the southwest and far north provinces.

International Treaties

- Women's Convention (ratified 1994).
- Children's Rights Convention (ratified 1993).
- Civil and Political Rights Covenant (ratified 1984).
- Economic, Social and Cultural Rights Covenant (ratified 1984).
- Banjul Charter (ratified 1989).
- African Charter (ratified 1999).

National Laws

Constitution

The Constitution of the Republic of Cameroon[1] guarantees the equality of women and men before the law. Its Preamble states that the "human person, without distinction as to … sex … possesses inalienable and sacred rights." It further provides that "all persons shall have equal rights and obligations."

The Constitution guarantees the rights to life and physical integrity. Its Preamble provides that "every person has a right to life, to physical and moral integrity and to humane treatment in all circumstances.

Women and children are granted special protection under the Constitution. The Preamble provides that "the Nation shall protect and promote the family.... It shall protect women [and] the young."

Cultural and religious practices must conform to constitutional protections of individual rights. Article 1(2) provides that "[the Constitution] shall recognize and protect traditional value*s that conform to democratic principles, human rights and the law*" (emphasis added).

Criminal law

Provisions

There is no Penal Code[2] provision specifically prohibiting FC/FGM. However, under the heading "Intentional Killing and Harm," Article 277 prohibits "Grievous Harm," providing:

> Whoever permanently deprives another of the use of the whole or of any part of any member, organ or sense shall be punished with imprisonment for from ten to twenty years.

Under the heading "Intentional Force and Interference," Article 279 of the Penal Code prohibits "Assault Occasioning Grievous Harm," providing:

> Whoever by force or interference unintentionally causes to another the injuries described in section 277 of this Code shall be punished with imprisonment for from five to ten years and in a fit case with fine of from five thousand to five hundred thousand francs [approximately US$8–800].

Other criminal provisions that are potentially applicable to FC/FGM are Articles 280 and 281 of the Penal Code. These provide penalties for the intentional and unintentional causing of "simple harm" (sickness or inability to work lasting more than 30 days) (Art. 280) and "slight harm" (sickness or inability to work lasting from eight to 30 days) (Art. 281). Causing "simple harm" is punished with six months to five years in prison and/or a fine of 5,000 to 200,000 francs (approximately US$8–320) (Art. 280). "Slight harm" is punishable with imprisonment for six days to two years and/or a fine of 5,000 to 50,000 (approximately US$8–80) (Art. 281).

Enforcement of the law

Information not available.

Other Measures: Laws, Regulations and Policies

Since 1980, the Ministry of Women's Affairs has conducted a campaign against traditional practices that are harmful to women, including FC/FGM.[3] This ministry participates in and supports educational campaigns organized by women's groups working in this area.[4]

Notes

1. *Constitution of the Republic of Cameroon* (1996), reprinted in G.H. Flanz (ed.), *Constitutions of the Countries of the World*, Dobbs Ferry, NY: Oceana Publications, 1997.
2. *Penal Code of the United Republic of Cameroon*, Law No. 65–LF-24 of Nov. 12, 1965 and Law No. 67–LF-1 of June 12, 1967, art. 277 (1980–1) (official translation).
3. Mpessa Djessi Ndine, Association Camerounaise des Femmes Juristes (ACAFEJ), Questionnaire (June 22, 1998).
4. Ibid.

Canada

Size (1,000 km²): 9,971
Income (per capita GNP in US$): 19,640
Population (millions): 30
Immigrant population: In 1991, there were 166,200 African immigrants in Canada, 77,100 of whom were women. In 1995, there was an inflow of 32,800 permanent settlers from Africa and the Middle East.

International Treaties

- Women's Convention (ratified 1981).
- Children's Rights Convention (ratified 1991).
- Civil and Political Rights Covenant (ratified 1976).
- Economic, Social and Cultural Rights Covenant (ratified 1976).

National Laws

Constitution

The Canadian Charter of Rights and Freedoms[1] guarantees the equality of women and men before the law. Section 15 provides that "[e]very individual is equal before and under the law and has the right to the equal protection and equal benefit of the law without discrimination and, in particular, without discrimination based on ... sex."

The Charter also protects everyone's "right to life, liberty and security of the person" (Sect. 7).

Criminal law

The Criminal Code[2] was amended in April 1997 to prohibit explicitly FC/FGM. Prior to adoption of the amendment, FC/FGM was prosecutable under Section 268 of the Criminal Code, which states that "[e]very one commits an aggravated assault who wounds, maims, disfigures or endangers the life" of another person.

Provisions

Section 268 of the Criminal Code was amended as follows:

> (3) For greater certainty, in this section, "wounds" or "maims" includes to excise, infibulate or mutilate, in whole or in part, the labia majora, labia minora or clitoris of a person, except where
> (a) surgical procedure is performed, by a person duly qualified by provincial law to practice medicine, for the benefit of the physical health of the person or for the purpose of that person having normal reproductive functions or normal sexual appearance or function; or
> (b) the person is at least eighteen years of age and there is no resulting bodily harm.
>
> (4) For the purposes of this section and section 265, no consent to the excision, infibulation or mutilation, in whole or in part, of the labia majora, labia minora or clitoris of a person is valid, except in the cases described in paragraphs (3)(a) and (b).

Under this law, liability extends to numerous persons. The law covers practitioners, those who procure FC/FGM services (such as parents, family members, and guardians), and those who otherwise participate in the procedure.[3] The Criminal Code also makes it a crime for parents or family members to take a girl out of Canada for the purposes of having FC/FGM performed in a country where it is legal. Section 273.3(1) thus provides:

> No person shall do anything for the purpose of removing from Canada a person who is ordinarily resident in Canada and who is …
> (c) under the age of eighteen years, with the intention that an act be committed outside Canada that if it were committed in Canada would be an offence against section … 268 … in respect of that person.[4]
> This offense is punishable with imprisonment of up to five years.[5]

Enforcement of the law

There are no known instances of arrests for FC/FGM.[6]

Child protection laws

The policies of child protection agencies are set at the provincial level. Primary responsibility for child protection lies with the local Children's Aid Society. In 1992, the Ontario Association of Children's Aid Societies (OACAS) announced that FC/FGM "meets the definition of child abuse in the Child and Family Services Act of 1984 [Ontario]."[7]

Other Measures: Laws, Regulations and Policies

The preamble to the federal legislation prohibiting FC/FGM recognizes that education is a tool for eliminating FC/FGM. It states that "the Parliament of Canada believes that a clear statement that the criminal law of Canada applies to the practice of female genital mutilation will facilitate ongoing educational efforts in this area."[8] The government has supported educational programs at the community level, as well as programs designed for health professionals.[9]

Standards of Health Professionals

The Society of Obstetricians and Gynecologists of Canada and the Canadian Medical Association have adopted policies expressing the view that FC/FGM is not a legitimate medical practice and that it should not be performed by health professionals.[10] Each provincial college of physicians and surgeons has adopted the policy that their members have a duty to refuse requests to perform FC/FGM.[11] The Ontario College of Physicians and Surgeons (CPSO), for example, issued a statement banning the practice of FC/FGM by physicians.[12] The practice of FC/FGM is considered professional misconduct.[13] The statement also expressed CPSO's interest in ensuring that women who have undergone FC/FGM receive "sensitivity and compassion."[14]

Policies for Eliminating FC/FGM in Africa

The Canadian International Development Agency (CIDA) addresses FC/FGM in its *Strategy for Health*.[15] It states that one of CIDA's objectives is the improvement of women's health, including reproductive health, and that such matters as violence and FC/FGM are addressed under this rubric.[16]

Notes

1. Constitution Act, 1982, Canadian Charter of Rights and Freedoms, (last visited Aug. 19, 1999), <http://canada.justice.gc.ca/cgi-bin/folioisa.dll/const_e.nfo/query=*/doc/{t390}?>.
2. Criminal Code, *Consolidated Statutes of Canada* (last visited Aug. 26, 1999), <http://canada.justice.gc.ca/cgi-bin/folioisa.dll/estats.nfo/>.
3. Carole Morency, Legal Counsel, Department of Justice, Canada, Questionnaire (received July 3, 1998).

4. Criminal Code, sect. 273.3(1), *Consolidated Statutes of Canada.*
5. Criminal Code, sects 268, 273 3(2), *Consolidated Statutes of Canada.*
6. Carole Morency, Legal Counsel, Department of Justice, Canada, Questionnaire (received July 3, 1998).
7. Khamisa Baya, *FGM: Child Protection, Toronto: Women's Health in Women's Hands (WHIWH)* (factsheet).
8. Bill C-27, Amendment of Section 268 of the Criminal Code, April 25, 1997, p. 6 ; House of Commons of Canada, Second Session, Thirty-Fifth Parliament, 45 Elizabeth II, 1996.
9. Carole Morency, Legal Counsel, Department of Justice, Canada, Questionnaire (received July 3, 1998).
10. Ibid.
11. Ibid.
12. College of Physicians and Surgeons of Ontario, News Release, Jan. 27, 1992.
13. College of Physicians and Surgeons of Ontario, College Notices, Issue No. 25, March 1992.
14. Ibid.
15. Canadian International Development Agency, support by CIDA/Africa and Middle East Branch for Activities Related to the Eradication of Female Genital Mutilation (FGM) 2 (Jan. 15, 1999).
16. Ibid.

Central African Republic

Size (1,000 km^2): 623
Income (per capita GNP in US$): 320
Population (millions): 3
Number of women per 100 men: 106
Percentage of young people in the population (under 15 years): 45
Prevalence of FC/FGM: 43%
Type(s) of FC/FGM most commonly practiced: Types I and II
Ethnic groups that practice FC/FGM: Prevalence greatest among the Banda and Mandjia.

International Treaties

- Women's Convention (ratified 1991).
- Children's Rights Convention (ratified 1992).
- Civil and Political Rights Covenant (ratified 1981).
- Economic, Social and Cultural Rights Covenant (ratified 1981).
- Banjul Charter (ratified 1986).

National Laws

Constitution

The Constitution of the Central African Republic[1] guarantees the equality of women and men before the law. Article 5 declares that "all human beings are equal before the law without distinction of … sex. It further provides that "[t]he law guarantees to man and woman equal rights in all the domains."

The Constitution is also protective of the rights to life and physical integrity. Its first provision states that "[t]he human person is sacred.

Every agent of public power has the absolute obligation to respect it and to protect it." Article 3 provides that "[e]veryone has the right to life and to corporal integrity. Liberty of the person is inviolable. These rights may only be [infringed upon] by application of a law." Article 3 further states that "[e]very person being the object of a measure depriving liberty has the right to be examined and healed by a doctor of his choice if possible."

Special constitutional protections apply to youth and the family. Article 6 recognizes the state's duty "to strike for the physical and moral health of the family and to socially encourage it by appropriate institutions." It further provides that "[t]he protection of the youth against violence … is an obligation for the State and the other public collectivities. This protection is assured by appropriate measures and institutions of the State and the other public collectivities." It is the "natural right and primordial duty" of parents "to raise and educate their children with the end to develop in them good physical, intellectual and moral aptitudes. They are supported in this task by the State and the other public collectivities."

Criminal law

Provisions

In 1966, then President Bokassa issued an ordinance prohibiting the practice of FC/FGM in the Central African Republic.[2] The ordinance states, in part:

> Whereas excision has consequences that are harmful to the physical and mental health of the young girl and it is contrary to basic principles of hygiene;
>
> Whereas the Revolutionary Council has decided to act in conformity with the principles of the Universal Declaration of Human Rights and wishes to ensure the dignity and rank of the women of Central African Republic on both the national and international levels,
>
> [The President of the Republic, in accord with the Council of Ministers] Orders:
>
> Art. 1: The practice of excision is abolished throughout the entire Territory of the Central African Republic.
>
> Art. 2: Any violation of this Ordinance shall be punishable by imprisonment from one month and one day to two years and by a fine of from 5,001 (five thousand and one) to 100,000 (one hundred thousand) francs [approximately US$8–160], or by either punishment.
>
> Art. 3: This Ordinance … shall have the force of national law.

Enforcement of the law

Information not available.

Other Measures: Laws, Regulations and Policies

The Ministry of Social Welfare has been involved in an educational campaign aimed at eliminating the practice.[3]

Notes

1. *Constitution of the Central African Republic* (1995), translated in G.H. Flanz (ed.), *Constitutions of the Countries of the World*, Dobbs Ferry, NY: Oceana Publications, 1995.
2. Ordinance No. 66/16 of Feb. 22, 1966, *Journal Officiel de la République Centrafricaine*, Mar. 15, 1966, p. 158.
3. United States Department of State, *Central African Republic Country Report on Human Rights Practices for 1998* (released Feb. 26, 1999) (last visited June 9, 1999), <http://www.state.gov/www/global/human_rights/1998_hrp_ report/>.

Chad

Size (1,000 km^2): 1,284
Income (per capita GNP in US$): 230
Population (millions): 7
Number of women per 100 men: 103
Percentage of young people in the population (under 15 years): 43
Prevalence of FC/FGM: 60%
Type(s) of FC/FGM most commonly practiced: Type II
Ethnic groups that practice FC/FGM: A UNICEF-supported study undertaken in the south, east and central regions and in N'Djamena, covering nine communities (unpublished data, 1991) found that types I and II were predominant; type III was not reported.

International Treaties

- Women's Convention (ratified 1995).
- Children's Rights Convention (ratified 1990).
- Civil and Political Rights Covenant (ratified 1995).
- Economic, Social and Cultural Rights Covenant (ratified 1995).
- Banjul Charter (ratified 1986).

National Laws

Constitution

The Constitution[1] guarantees the equality of women and men before the law. Article 13 states that "Chadians of either sex have the same rights and the same duties. They are equal before the law." Article 14 further provides that the state "has the duty to see to the elimination of all forms of discrimination with regard to women and to assure the protection of their rights in all areas [*domaines*] of private and public life."

The rights to life and physical integrity are also protected by the Constitution. Article 17 provides that the "human person is sacred and inviolable. Each individual has the right to life, his personal integrity, to security [and] to freedom."

The Constitution provides special protection for the family and youth. Article 37 states that "[t]he State and the Decentralized Territorial Collectivities have the duty to see to the well-being of the family." Article 39 guarantees "the conditions for the blossoming [*epanouissement*] and well-being of youth."

Cultural and religious practices must conform to constitutional protections of individual rights. While Article 27 guarantees "freedoms of opinion and of expression, … conscience, … religion, … [and] of association," it provides that these freedoms may be restricted "by the respect of the liberties and rights of others and the imperative to safeguard the public order and good morals. The law determines the conditions of their exercise."

Criminal law

Provisions

No provisions in the Penal Code[2] specifically prohibit FC/FGM. However, Articles 252 to 254, under the heading of "Attacks on Corporal or Mental Integrity," contain provisions that are potentially applicable to the practice of FC/FGM. The relevant articles provide:

> Any individual who intentionally strikes or wounds or commits any other act of violence or assault upon the person of another, shall be punished by imprisonment from six days to one year and a fine of from 500 to 50,000 francs [approximately US$.80 to $80].… [Art. 252]
>
> The perpetrator shall be punished by imprisonment from five to ten years and with a fine of 10,000 to 500,000 francs [approximately US$16 to $800] when there is a mutilation, amputation or privation of the use of a member, blindness, loss of an eye, or other infirmities or if the strikes or wounds, intentionally inflicted, result in an unintended death.… [Art. 253]

Penalties are elevated in cases of "premeditation" (Arts 252–3). Article 254 provides that "[w]hen the strikes or wounds are carried out against a child under the age of 13, the penalty shall be doubled," that is, the maximum prison sentence will be 20 years and the maximum fine will be 1,000,000 francs (approximately US$1,600). The terms "wounds," "strikes," "violence" and "mutilation" are not defined in the Penal Code.

Enforcement of the law

Information not available.

Other Measures: Laws, Regulations and Policies

The government of Chad has no official policy regarding FC/FGM. Government ministers have, however, declared their intention to work toward eliminating the practice.[3]

Notes

1. *Constitution of the Republic of Chad* (1996), translated in G.H. Flanz (ed.), *Constitutions of the Countries of the World,* Dobbs Ferry, NY: Oceana Publications, 1997.
2. Ordonnance no. 12–67–PR.-MJ. portant promulgation d'un code pénal, *Journal Officiel de la Republique du Tchad,* numéro spécial, Dec. 31, 1967.
3. CRLP and Groupe de Recherches Femmes et Lois de Sénégal Réseau de Solidarité des Femmes sous Lois Musulmanes (GREFELS), *Femmes dans le monde: l'Afrique francophone,* New York: CRLP, 1999.

Côte d'Ivoire

Size (1,000 km^2): 322
Income (per capita GNP in US$): 710
Population (millions): 14
Number of women per 100 men: 97
Percentage of young people in the population (under 15 years): 49
Prevalence of FC/FGM: 43%
Type(s) of FC/FGM most commonly practiced: Type II
Ethnic groups that practice FC/FGM: Female genital mutilation was found to be much more prevalent among the Muslim population (80%) than among Catholics and Protestants (16%).

International Treaties

- Women's Convention (ratified 1995).
- Children's Rights Convention (ratified 1991).
- Civil and Political Rights Covenant (ratified 1992).
- Economic, Social and Cultural Rights Covenant (ratified 1992).
- Banjul Charter (ratified 1992).

National Laws

Constitution

The Constitution[1] guarantees the equality of women and men before the law. Article 6 states that "[t]he Republic shall assure to all equality before the law without distinction as to … sex."

Criminal Law

On December 23, 1998, the Parliament of Côte d'Ivoire passed a law prohibiting FC/FGM,[2] which had been proposed by the Ministry of the Family and Promotion of Women.[3]

Provisions

Art. 1: Genital mutilation is the violation of the integrity of the female genital organ, by total or partial ablation, infibulation, desensitization or by any other procedure;

Art. 2: Any person who commits a genital mutilation shall be punished by imprisonment from one to five years and by a fine of 360,000 to 2,000,000 francs [approximately US$576–3,200].

This punishment shall be doubled when the perpetrator belongs to the medical or paramedical corps.

The punishment shall be imprisonment from five to 20 years when the victim dies as a result of the procedure.

When the perpetrator belongs to the medical or paramedical corps, the court may also suspend his or her license to practice medicine for up to five years.

There is no infraction when the mutilation was done under the conditions indicated in article 350 of the Penal Code [referring to: (1) medical acts that are consistent with scientific data, medical ethics, and professional regulations and that are performed by a licensed practitioner with the patient's consent; and (2) acts committed in the course of a sports activity where the perpetrator was respecting the rules of the sport in question.]

Attempted genital mutilation is punishable.

Art. 3: The infractions provided for in paragraphs 2 and 3 of Article 2 of this law remain misdemeanors [*délits*].

Art. 4: [T]he penalties provided for in the first paragraph of Article 2 shall be imposed upon the victim's mother and father and upon relations by blood and by marriage (to the fourth degree) who have solicited the genital mutilation, or who, knowing it to be imminent, did not report it to the administrative or judicial authorities, or to any person capable of preventing the act.

The penalties provided for in the first paragraph of Article 2 also apply to spouses and relations by blood and by marriage (to the fourth degree) of the perpetrator of the act.

The provisions of the preceding paragraphs do not apply to minors belonging to the families of either the victim or the perpetrator of the act.

[Articles 5 and 6 are omitted.]

Enforcement of the law

Information not available.

Other Measures: Laws, Regulations and Policies

In 1996, the government created a National Anti-Female Circumcision Commission, which has been involved in research and advocacy aimed at stopping the practice throughout the country.[4]

Notes

1. *Constitution of the Republic of Côte d'Ivoire* (1960, amended 1990), translated in A.P. Blaustein and G.H. Flanz (eds), *Constitutions of the Countries of the World* Dobbs Ferry, NY: Oceana Publications, 1998.
2. Loi no. 98–757, Dec. 23, 1998, on the prohibition of various forms of violence against women, *Journal Officiel de la Republique de Côte d'Ivoire*, Jan. 14, 1999, p. 25.
3. Françoise Kaudjhis-Offoumou, Association Internationale pour la Démocratie, Questionnaire (April 15, 1998).
4. Melvis Dzisah, "Human Rights: Invoirian MPs Split on How to Tackle FGM," *Inter Press Service*, Mar. 27, 1998.

Democratic Republic of Congo

Size (1,000 km^2): 2,345
Income (per capita GNP in US$): 110
Population (millions): 47
Number of women per 100 men: 102
Percentage of young people in the population (under 15 years): 48
Prevalence of FC/FGM: 5%
Type(s) of FC/FGM most commonly practiced: Type II
Ethnic groups that practice FC/FGM: Information not available.

International Treaties

- Women's Convention (ratified 1986).
- Children's Rights Convention (ratified 1990).
- Civil and Political Rights Covenant (ratified 1976).
- Economic, Social and Cultural Rights Covenant (ratified 1976).
- Banjul Charter (ratified 1987).

National Laws

Constitution

No constitution is currently in force.[1] A draft constitution was completed in March 1998.[2] No referendum has been scheduled for adoption of the draft constitution.[3]

Criminal law

Provisions

No Penal Code[4] provision specifically prohibits FC/FGM. However, provisions addressing "intentional bodily injuries" may be applicable. Articles 46 through 48 provide:

> Any person who intentionally wounds or strikes shall be punished by imprisonment from eight days to six months and by a fine of 25 to 200 zaïres [approximately US$5 to US$45], or by either of these punishments. [Art. 46]
>
> If the strikes and wounds cause an illness or an incapacity to work, or if they result in the total loss of the use of an organ or in a serious mutilation, the punishment shall be imprisonment from two years to five years and a fine of not more than 1,000 zaïres [approximately US$220]. [Art. 47]

When strikes or wounds, intentionally inflicted, result in an unintended death, the punishment is imprisonment from five to twenty years and a fine of no more than 2,000 zaïres (approximately US$440) (Art. 48). The terms "wounds," "strikes" and "mutilation" are not defined in the Penal Code.

Enforcement of the law

Information not available.

Other Measures: Laws, Regulations and Policies

Information not available.

Notes

1. Bureau of Democracy, Human Rights, and Labor, US Department of State, *Democratic Republic of Congo Country Report on Human Rights Practices for 1998* (last visited April 6, 1999), <http://www.state .gov/www/global/human_rights/1998_hrp_report/congodr.html>.
2. Ibid.
3. Ibid.
4. Code Penal Zaïrois, May 31, 1982 (Dept of Justice, 1983).

Denmark

Size (1,000 km^2): 43

Income (per capita GNP in US$): 34,890

Population (millions): 5

Immigrant population: In 1997, there were 11,105 immigrants from Egypt and Somalia.[1] In 1995, there were 6,900 immigrants from Somalia. There were a total of 222,700 immigrants in 1995, 109,200 of whom were women.

International Treaties

- Women's Convention (ratified 1983).
- Children's Rights Convention (ratified 1991).
- Civil and Political Rights Covenant (ratified 1972).
- Economic, Social and Cultural Rights Covenant (ratified 1972).
- European Convention on Human Rights (ratified 1953).

National Laws

Constitution

Section 71 of the Constitution provides that "[p]ersonal liberty shall be inviolable."[2]

Criminal law

In 1992, the Danish Medical Women's Association proposed to the Ministry of Health legislation prohibiting FC/FGM. The Ministry of Justice responded by stating that FC/FGM could be prosecuted under existing criminal code provisions.[3]

Provisions

The government informed CEDAW that FC/FGM is a crime pursuant to Paragraph 245 of the Danish Criminal Code.[4]

> (1) Any person who commits an assault of a particularly heinous or brutal or dangerous character or who is guilty of cruelty shall be liable to imprisonment for any term not exceeding 4 years.
>
> (2) The same penalty shall apply to any person who, in circumstances other than those covered by subsection (1) above, causes damage to another person or to the health of another person.[5]

Enforcement of the law

Information not available.

Child protection laws

Information not available.

Other Measures: Laws, Regulations and Policies

In 1996, the Ministry of Health appointed a working group to plan and implement an information campaign for young women refugees and immigrants to deter them from going abroad to undergo FC/FGM. The working group was composed of representatives from the Ministry of Health, the National Board of Health, the Danish Refugee Council, the Somali Resource Group, the Association of Somali Women and the Danish Medical Women's Association.[6]

In cooperation with community-based activists, the Danish Refugee Department provides information to incoming refugees and those seeking asylum about the prohibition of FC/FGM in the country.[7]

Standards of Health Professionals

In 1981, the National Board of Health declared that FC/FGM was not medically necessary, and that, therefore, it was illegal for doctors to perform the procedure.[8] In addition, the Danish Medical Women's Association provides educational information to health professionals about how to treat patients, particularly pregnant women, who have undergone FC/FGM.[9]

Policies for Eliminating FC/FGM in Africa

In 1996, the Danish Development Agency (DANIDA) issued *Guidelines on the Prevention of Female Genital Mutilation.*[10] The *Guidelines* discuss DANIDA's goals at the multilateral and bilateral levels. At the bilateral level, DANIDA's activities promote national-level policy-making and program implementation; information, education and communication campaigns; and research.[11]

DANIDA has incorporated FC/FGM prevention activities in its programs in a number of African countries.[12] DANIDA-funded activities include developing alternative economic activities for excisors in Sierra Leone, supporting training for nurses and health assistants in Burkina Faso, and supporting education programs in Kenya.[13]

Notes

1. Proceedings of the Expert Meeting on Female Genital Mutilation, Ghent, Belgium, Nov. 5–7, 1998, p. 11 (figures were obtained from the National Offices of Statistics from each European member state).
2. Constitution of Denmark (1953) (last visited Aug. 17, 1999), <http://www.uni-wuerzburg.de/law/da00000_.html>.
3. J. Smith, *Visions and Discussions on Genital Mutilation of Girls: An International Survey*, Amsterdam: Defence for Children International, 1995, p. 149.
4. Fourth Periodic Report by the Government of Denmark on the Implementation of the Convention on the Elimination of All Forms of Discrimination Against Women (1997) (last visited Oct. 14, 1998), <http://www.um.dk/english/udenrigspolitik/menneskerettigheder/discrimination.5.html>.
5. L.B. Langsted, V. Greve and P. Garde, *Criminal Law in Denmark*, The Hague: Kluwer Law International, 1998, p. 95.
6. Fourth Periodic Report by the Government of Denmark.
7. Smith, *Visions and Discussions on Genital Mutilation of Girls*, p. 149.
8. Ibid.
9. Ibid., p. 150.
10. DANIDA, Ministry of Foreign Affairs, *Guidelines on the Prevention of Female Genital Mutilation*, Copenhagen: DANIDA, 1996.
11. Ibid., pp. 9–12.
12. M. Silberschmidt, *Female Genital Mutilation: A Harmful Act of Trust, Desk Study for DANIDA*, Copenhagen: Centre for Alternative Social Analysis, 1994, pp. 51–4.
13. Ibid.

Djibouti

Size (1,000 km^2): 23.2

Income (per capita GNP in US$): Estimated to be lower middle income (US$766–3,035)

Population (millions): 0.63

Number of women per 100 men: 99

Percentage of young people in the population (under 15 years): 46

Prevalence of FC/FGM: 98%

Type(s) of FC/FGM most commonly practiced: Types II and III
Ethnic groups that practice FC/FGM: FGM is almost universal.

International Treaties

- Women's Convention (ratified 1998).
- Children's Rights Convention (ratified 1990). The government of Djibouti made a declaration asserting the precedence of religion and traditional values over the mandates of the Convention.
- Banjul Charter (ratified 1991).

National Laws

Constitution

The Constitution[1] ensures the equality of women and men before the law. Article 1 provides that the state "shall ensure the equality of all citizens before the law, without distinction as to … sex."

The Constitution also guarantees the rights to life and physical integrity. Article 10 provides that "[t]he person is sacred. The State shall have the obligation to respect and protect it.… Every individual shall have the right to life, liberty, security and the integrity of his person."

Criminal law

In 1995, the Penal Code[2] was amended to include a provision criminalizing FC/FGM.

Provisions

Article 333 of the Penal Code provides that "acts of violence resulting in a genital mutilation are punishable by imprisonment for five years and a fine of 1,000,000 francs [approximately US$5,814]." The Penal Code does not define the term "genital mutilation."

Enforcement of the law

The Union Nationale des Femmes de Djibouti (UNFD), an NGO, has reported one case in which a practitioner of FC/FGM was counseled and advised not to continue her practice after she performed FC/FGM upon a girl who was hospitalized as a result.[3] No formal charges were brought against the woman.[4] While the government is reportedly willing to enforce the law prohibiting FC/FGM,[5] information on instances of enforcement is not available.

Other Measures: Laws, Regulations and Policies

The Ministries of Health, Justice and Education have collaborated with NGOs that are active in addressing FC/FGM in Djibouti.[6] In addition, the Ministry of Health has permitted diffusion of information in public health care facilities about infibulation.[7] The Ministry of Information has encouraged coverage in the media of educational events focused on FC/FGM.[8]

Notes

1. *Draft Constitution of the Republic of Djibouti* (1992), translated in A.P. Blaustein and G.H. Flanz (eds), *Constitutions of the Countries of the World*, Dobbs Ferry, NY: Oceana Publications, 1993.
2. Penal Code, promulgated by Law 59/AN/94 of Jan. 5, 1995.
3. Office of the Senior Coordinator for International Women's Issues, Bureau for Global Affairs and the Office of Asylum Affairs, Bureau of Democracy, Human Rights and Labor, US Department of State, *Female Genital Mutilation (FGM) or Female Genital Cutting (FGC) in Djibouti*, 1999, p. 3.
4. Ibid.
5. Ibid, pp. 2–3.
6. E. Dorkenoo, *Cutting the Rose*, London: Minority Rights Group, 1995, p. 115.
7. Ibid.
8. Ibid.

Egypt

Size (1,000 km^2): 1,001
Income (per capita GNP in US$): 1,200
Population (millions): 60
Number of women per 100 men: 97
Percentage of young people in the population (under 15 years): 38
Prevalence of FC/FGM: 97%
Type(s) of FC/FGM most commonly practiced: Types II (72%), I (17%) and III (9%)
Ethnic groups that practice FC/FGM: FGM is practiced throughout the country by Muslims and Christians.

International Treaties

- Women's Convention (ratified 1981). Reservation asserting precedence of the Islamic Sharia law over Article 2 of the Convention, which prohibits discrimination against women in all forms. Reservation regarding equality in marriage and family relations.
- Children's Rights Convention (ratified 1990).
- Civil and Political Rights Covenant (ratified 1982).
- Economic, Social and Cultural Rights Covenant (ratified 1982).
- Banjul Charter (ratified 1984).

National Laws

Constitution

The Constitution[1] offers only qualified support for women's equality. Article 8 provides that "[t]he State shall guarantee equality of opportunity to all Egyptians" and Article 40 declares that "[a]ll citizens are equal before the law" and "have equal public rights and duties without discrimination due to sex." However, Article 11 provides that "[t]he State shall guarantee coordination between woman's duties towards her family and her work in the society, considering her equal to man in the political, social, cultural and economic spheres *without detriment to the rules of Islamic jurisprudence (Sharia)*" (emphasis added).

The Constitution is protective of the rights of children. Article 10 provides that "[t]he State shall guarantee the protection of motherhood and childhood, look after children and youth and provide the suitable conditions for the development of their talents."

Criminal law

Provisions

The Egyptian Penal Code contains no provisions specifically pertaining to FC/FGM. However, Article 240 on "wounding" can be applied to FC/FGM. It provides that whoever inflicts "harm" (including wounds) leading to the cutting or amputation of a body organ or loss of its function; blindness; loss of an eye; or a permanent disability shall be punished with three to five years of imprisonment and hard labor. If the inflicted harm is intentional, the punishment is raised to ten years' imprisonment.[2]

Article 236 of the Penal Code covers intentional infliction of harm leading to death when death is not the intended result. Punishment ranges from three to seven years of imprisonment, with or without hard labor. Article 241 pertains to intentional and unintentional wounding or striking, resulting in illness or disability. The punishment for this crime is imprisonment or a fine. Article 244 addresses harm resulting from negligence or breaching of laws. The punishment for this crime is imprisonment and/ or a fine.[3]

In addition, articles in the Penal Code prohibit non-medical personnel from performing any form of surgery and prohibit doctors from causing a permanent disability or surgical wound in the absence of medical necessity.[4]

Enforcement of the law

Press reports in 1995 and 1996 covered the prosecution of at least 13 individuals – including physicians, midwives and barbers – accused of performing FC/FGM that resulted in complications such as hemorrhage, shock and death.[5] Similar cases were reported in December 1997 and July 1998.[6]

Other Measures: Laws, Regulations and Policies

In 1994, the then Minister of Health, Dr Ali Abdel Fattah, issued a decree banning the practice of FC/FGM outside of public hospitals. The decree required physicians to discourage parents from having their daughters undergo FC/FGM. If the parents insisted, the procedure was to be carried out by physicians in hospitals. Feminists and human rights activists protested the decree and challenged the policy in administrative court. However, the case was never heard.[7]

In 1995, Dr Abdel Fattah issued a decree reversing the 1994 policy on FC/FGM. On the rationale that Egyptian parents had been successfully convinced to eschew the practice of FC/FGM, the 1995 decree banned physicians from performing FC/FGM in public hospitals.[8] The 1995 decree did not prevent physicians from performing FC/FGM in their private clinics. This was the policy until 1996, when the new Minister of Health, Dr Ismael Sallam, issued a decree prohibiting FC/FGM for non-medical purposes. The decree provides:

> It is forbidden to perform circumcision on females either in hospitals or public or private clinics. The procedure can only be performed in cases of disease and when approved by the head of the obstetrics and gynecology department at the hospital, and upon the suggestion of the treating physician. Performance of this operation will be considered a violation of the laws governing the medical profession. Nor is this operation to be performed by non-physicians.[9]

Shortly after the decree's issuance, it was challenged in administrative court by proponents of FC/FGM and by medical professionals concerned that the ban would lead to increased clandestine practice of FC/FGM with adverse effects on women's health.[10] The court declared the health minister's decree unconstitutional for infringing upon parliamentary functions and for interfering with the right of physicians to perform surgery.[11]

In December 1997, the highest administrative court overturned the lower court's ruling. In response to proponents of FC/FGM who asserted that Islam requires the practice, the court declared that Islam does not sanction FC/FGM and that the practice is punishable under the Penal Code. It concluded:

> With this ruling everybody is banned from performing [female circumcision], even with the proven consent of the girl or her parents, except in cases of medical necessity, which must be determined by the director of the gynecology department in one of the hospitals. Otherwise, all those who do not comply will be subjected to criminal and administrative punishments.[12]

Notes

1. People's Assembly, *Constitution of the Arab Republic of Egypt* (1971), (last visited Feb. 27, 1999), <http://www.parliament.gov.eg/en_aconst4.htm>.
2. Personal communication from Amal Abd-El-Hadi, Women's Program Co-ordinator, Cairo Institute of Human Rights Studies, July 15, 1998 (on file with the CRLP and RAINB♀).
3. Ibid.
4. National NGO Commission for Population and Development, *FGM Task Force Position Paper*, 1997, p. 5.
5. Cairo Institute for Human Rights Studies, "The Health Minister's Decree Crowns NGOs Efforts," *Sawasiah*, No. 12, Sept. 1996, pp. 8–9.
6. "Doctor gets a Year in Jail for Causing Girl's Death," *Associated Press*, Dec. 15, 1997; "Two Doctors Charged with Performing Illegal Female Circumcision in Egypt," *Associated Press*, July 21, 1998.
7. Personal communication from Amal Abd-El-Hadi, Women's Program Co-ordinator, Cairo Institute of Human Rights Studies, July 15, 1998 (on file with the CRLP and RAINB♀).
8. Ibid.
9. Order No. 261 of 8 July, 1996 of the Minister of Health and Population, translated in Office of Asylum Affairs, Bureau of Democracy, Human Rights and Labor, US Department of State, *Female Genital Mutilation (FGM) in Egypt*, 1997, p. 3.
10. Personal Communication from Amal Abd-El-Hadi, Women's Program Co-ordinator, Cairo Institute of Human Rights Studies, July 15, 1998 (on file with the CRLP and RAINB♀).
11. Equality Now, "Egypt," *Awaken*, Dec. 1997, Vol. 1, No. 3, p. 5.
12. "*Egypt: Highest Court Upholds Minister's Ban on Female Genital Mutilation (FGM)*," *Women's Action*, Vol. 8, No. 4 (New York: Equality Now) Feb. 1998.

Eritrea

Size (1,000 km^2): 118
Income (per capita GNP in US$): 230
Population (millions): 4
Number of women per 100 men: Information not available.
Percentage of young people in the population (under 15 years): Information not available.
Prevalence of FC/FGM: 95%
Type(s) of FC/FGM most commonly practiced: Types I (64%), III (34%), and II (4%)
Ethnic groups that practice FC/FGM: FGM is practiced by Eritrean Christians and Muslims.

International Treaties

- Women's Convention (ratified 1995).
- Children's Rights Convention (ratified 1994).

National Laws

Constitution

The Constitution[1] guarantees the equality of women and men before the law. Its Preamble notes that:

> [T]he Eritrean women's heroic participation in the struggle for independence, human rights and solidarity, based on equality and mutual respect, generated by such struggle will serve as an unshakable foundation for our commitment to create a society in which women and men shall interact on the bases of mutual respect, solidarity and equality.

Article 14(2–3) states that "[n]o person may be discriminated against on account of … gender.… The National Assembly shall enact laws that can assist in eliminating inequalities in the Eritrean society."

Article 15 guarantees the right to life and liberty. Article 16 states that "[t]he dignity of all persons shall be inviolable." Article 21(1) expresses the government's commitment to ensuring access to health care. It "shall endeavor, within the limit of its resources, to make available to all citizens health … and other social services."

Religious practices must conform to constitutional protections of individual rights. While Article 19(4) guarantees "the freedom to practice any religion and to manifest such practice," Article 26(1) states that this freedom, like other fundamental freedoms, guaranteed in the Constitution, may be limited "in the interests of … public safety or … health or morals, for the prevention of public disorder or crime or for the protection of the rights and freedoms of others."

Criminal law

Eritrea is in the process of drafting a new Penal Code. The government officially discourages the practice of FC/FGM. Given the prevalence of the practice in Eritrea, however, the government has chosen to address FC/FGM as a public health concern, rather than as a matter for criminal prosecution. FC/FGM will therefore not be specifically prohibited under the new Penal Code. A general provision on grievous harm, however, may potentially be the basis for prosecution in cases of FC/FGM. Under that provision, the consent of the victim or a third party would not be a defense to a charge of grievous harm.[2]

Ethiopia's Penal Code, as modified by proclamations of the transitional Eritrean government, is currently in force in Eritrea.[3]

Provisions

The Penal Code[4] contains no provisions specifically prohibiting FC/FGM. However, several provisions pertaining to "Offenses Against Person and Health" may be applicable. The relevant provisions state:

> Whosoever, intentionally or by negligence, causes bodily injury to another or impairs his health, by any means, is punishable in accordance with the provisions of this chapter.
>
> These provisions embrace all manner of bodily assaults, blows, wounds, maiming, injuries or harm, and all damage to the physical or mental health of an individual, where their causal relation to the offender's prejudicial act is established. [Art 537(1)]

> Whosoever intentionally:
> (a) wounds a person so as to endanger his life or permanently to jeopardize his physical or mental health; or
> (b) maims his body or one of his essential limbs or organs, or disables them, or gravely and conspicuously disfigures him; or
> (c) in any other way inflicts upon another an injury or disease of a serious nature;
> is punishable, according to the circumstances and to the gravity of the injury, with rigorous imprisonment not exceeding ten years, or with simple imprisonment for not less than one year. [Art. 538]

A separate provision on "mistreatment of minors" states that anyone having custody or charge of a child under the age of 15 who "deliberately neglects, ill-treats, over-tasks or beats" that child so as to affect or endanger gravely his or her physical or mental development or health may be punished with a minimum of one month in prison. The offender may also lose his or her "family rights" (Art. 548(1)).

Enforcement of the law

Information not available.

Other Measures: Laws, Regulations and Policies

Prior to independence from Ethiopia, the Eritrean People's Liberation Front (EPLF) forbade the practice of FC/FGM by its members. At the same time, the EPLF carried out educational campaigns aimed at discouraging FC/FGM. Since independence, the government has continued these campaigns with a view to eliminating the practice. The Ministries of Health, Education and Information have collaborated in support of these efforts.[5]

Notes

1. Constitution of Eritrea (1997), preamble (last visited Apr. 7, 1999) <http://wwells.law.usm.maine.edu/~files/eritrea/eritrealie.htm>.
2. Telephone interview by Laura Katzive, CRLP Staff Attorney, with Patrick Healy, Faculty Professor, McGill University Faculty of Law (Aug. 20, 1999). Prof. Healy was one of three drafters of the forthcoming Penal Code of Eritrea.
3. Ibid.
4. *Penal Code of the Empire of Ethiopia*, 158/1957, Proclamation No. 1, Negarit Gazeta, Gazette Extraordinary (July 23, 1957).
5. Telephone interview by Cynthia Eyakuze, former CRLP International Program Associate, with Veronica Rentmeesters, Information Officer, Eritrean Embassy, Washington, DC (Oct. 7, 1998).

Ethiopia

Size (1,000 km^2): 1,104
Income (per capita GNP in US$): 110
Population (millions): 60
Number of women per 100 men: 100
Percentage of young people in the population (under 15 years): 47
Prevalence of FC/FGM: 90%
Type(s) of FC/FGM most commonly practiced: Types I and II
Ethnic groups that practice FC/FGM: FGM is common among Christians and Muslims, and was practiced by Ethiopian Jews, who now live in Israel.

International Treaties

- Women's Convention (ratified 1981).
- Children's Rights Convention (ratified 1991).
- Civil and Political Rights Covenant (ratified 1993).
- Economic, Social and Cultural Rights Covenant (ratified 1993).

National Laws

Constitution

Ethiopia's Constitution,[1] promulgated in 1994, provides clear protection against FC/FGM. Article 35, entitled "Rights of Women," states in part that "[w]omen have the right to protection by the state from harmful customs. Laws, customs and practices that oppress women or cause bodily or mental harm to them are prohibited" (Clause 4). While the text of the Constitution does not refer specifically to FC/FGM, legislative history indicates that the Constitution's drafters identified FC/FGM as a "harmful custom."[2] Article 35(1) also guarantees women "the right to equality with men in the enjoyment and protection of rights provided for by this Constitution."

The Constitution also contains general provisions guaranteeing the right to life and physical integrity. Article 14 protects the "inviolable and inalienable right to life, liberty and the security of the person." Article 16 guarantees all persons "the right to protection from bodily harm."

The Constitution acknowledges a governmental duty to provide health care. Article 41(4) requires the government "to allocate increasing resources to provide public health ... and other social services."

Children are afforded special protections under the Constitution. Article 36(2) provides that "[i]n all actions concerning children undertaken by public and private institutions of social welfare, courts of law, administrative authorities or legislative bodies, the primary consideration shall be the best interests of the child."

Cultural and religious practices must be balanced against constitutional protections of individual rights. Article 9(1) declares that the Constitution is "the supreme law of the land. Any law [or] customary practice ... that contravenes the Constitution is invalid." While Article 27(5) of the Constitution guarantees freedom of religion, "[f]reedom to express or manifest one's religion or belief may be subject only ... to such limitations as are prescribed by law and are necessary to protect public safety, order, health, education, morals or the fundamental rights and freedoms of others."

Criminal law

Provisions

The Penal Code[3] contains no provisions specifically prohibiting FC/FGM. However, several provisions pertaining to "Offenses Against Person and Health" may be applicable. The relevant provisions state:

> Whosoever, intentionally or by negligence, causes bodily injury to another or impairs his health, by any means, is punishable in accordance with the provisions of this chapter.
>
> These provisions embrace all manner of bodily assaults, blows, wounds, maiming, injuries or harm, and all damage to the physical or mental health of an individual, where their causal relation to the offender's prejudicial act is established. [Art 537(1)]
>
> Whosoever intentionally:
> (a) wounds a person so as to endanger his life or permanently to his physical or mental health; or
> (b) maims his body or one of his essential limbs or organs, or disables them, or gravely and conspicuously disfigures him; or

> (c) in any other way inflicts upon another an injury or disease of a serious nature,
>
> is punishable, according to the circumstances and to the gravity of the injury, with rigorous imprisonment not exceeding ten years, or with simple imprisonment for not less than one year. [Art. 538]

A separate provision on "Maltreatment of Minors" states that anyone having custody or charge of a child under the age of 15 who "deliberately neglects, ill-treats, over-tasks or beats" that child so as to affect or endanger his or her physical or mental development or health may be punished with a minimum of one month in prison. The offender may also lose his or her "family rights" (Art. 548(1)).

Enforcement of the law

The government has not officially acknowledged the applicability of the foregoing provisions to the practice of FC/FGM. There have been no arrests for FC/FGM on the basis of the articles discussed above.[4]

Other Measures: Laws, Regulations and Policies

Government support for the elimination of FC/FGM can be found in the national health policy and women's policy. The Health Policy of the Transitional Government of Ethiopia includes among its general strategies for improving national health, "[i]dentifying and discouraging harmful traditional practices while encouraging their beneficial aspects."[5] In reference to customs which include FC/FGM, the National Policy on Ethiopian Women states:

> Such harmful customs and practices must be eliminated, for they stand in the way of progress and endanger lives. They should not be allowed to perpetuate. Both men and women have to be made aware of these harmful practices at all available forums, especially in the classroom.[6]

The government supports efforts to eliminate FC/FGM and has sponsored activities to raise public awareness of the harmful nature of certain customs and practices.[7] The Ministry of Education oversees the Federal Institute for Curriculum Development and Research, which requires regional education bureaus to include in primary school curricula educational materials discouraging harmful traditional practices, including FC/FGM.[8]

Notes

1. *Constitution of the Federal Democratic Republic of Ethiopia* (1994), translated in G.H. Flanz (ed.), *Constitutions of the Countries of the World*, Dobbs Ferry, NY: Oceana Publications, 1996.
2. Hillina Taddesse Tamrat, Ethiopian Women Lawyers' Association, Questionnaire (Mar. 30, 1998).
3. *Penal Code of the Empire of Ethiopia*, Proclamation No. 158/1957, 1 Negarit Gazeta, Gazette Extraordinary (July 23, 1957).
4. Hillina Taddesse Tamrat, Ethiopian Women Lawyers' Association, Questionnaire (Mar. 30, 1998).
5. *Health Policy of the Transitional Government of Ethiopia*, 1993, sect. 4.5.
6. Office of the Prime Minister, Transitional Government of Ethiopia, *National Policy on Ethiopian Women*, 1993, p. 18.
7. Office of the Senior Coordinator for International Women's Issues, Bureau for Global Affairs and the Office of Asylum Affairs, Bureau of Democracy, Human Rights and Labor, US Department of State, *Female Genital Mutilation (FGM) or Female Genital Cutting (FGC) in Ethiopia*, 1999, p. 2.
8. Ibid.

France

Size (1,000 km²): 552

Income (per capita GNP in US$): 26,300

Population (millions): 59

Immigrant population: In 1990, there were 180,997 immigrants from 16 African countries where FGM is practiced: Benin, Burkina Faso, Cameroon, Central African Republic, Chad, Côte d'Ivoire, Democratic Republic of Congo, Djibouti, Egypt, Ghana, Guinea, Mali, Mauritania, Niger, Senegal and Togo.[1]

International Treaties

- Women's Convention (ratified 1983).
- Children's Rights Convention (ratified 1990). Declaration of inapplicability of Article 30, protecting the right of a child belonging to a minority to practice his or her religion, use his or her own language, or enjoy his or her own culture.
- Civil and Political Rights Covenant (ratified 1980). Declaration of inapplicability of Article 27, protecting the right of minorities to enjoy their own culture, profess and practice their own religion, or to use their own language.
- Economic, Social and Cultural Rights Covenant (ratified 1980).
- European Convention (ratified 1974).

National Laws

Constitution

In its Preamble, the 1958 Constitution affirms the continued force of both the Declaration of the Rights of Man and of the Citizen and the Preamble to the 1946 Constitution.[2] The latter guarantees women, "in every domain, rights equal to those of men." It further guarantees "to all, especially to the child, ... protection of health."[3]

Criminal law

Provisions

The French Penal Code[4] contains no provisions specifically prohibiting FC/FGM. However, provisions addressing acts of violence directed toward a minor that result in mutilation are enforced against practitioners of FC/FGM and parents who cause their children to undergo FC/FGM. The relevant provisions of the Penal Code provide:

> Acts of violence resulting in a mutilation or a permanent disability are punishable by imprisonment for 10 years and a fine of 1,000,000 francs [approximately US$160,000]. [Art. 222(9)]
>
> The offense defined in Article 222–9 is punishable with 15 years of criminal imprisonment [*réclusion criminelle*] when it is committed:
> 1: Against a minor under the age of 15 years....The penalty incurred by a violation of Article 222–9 is raised to 20 years of imprisonment [*réclusion criminelle*] when the crime is committed against a minor under the age of 15 by a legitimate, natural or adoptive ascendant or by any other person having authority over the minor. [Art. 222(10)]

Enforcement of the law

Since 1978, there have been at least 25 prosecutions of providers of FC/FGM and of parents of girls who have undergone FC/FGM.[5] Prior to 1983, providers alone were the targets of prosecution and were most often charged with committing "delicts" (*délits*), such as assault of a minor under 15 years of age or involuntary homicide – offenses carrying relatively light sentences.[6] While prison sentences ranged from one to two years, they were generally suspended.[7] In 1983, the French high court (*Cour de Cassation*) recognized that FC/FGM could be charged under a Penal Code provision punishing acts of violence inflicted upon a child under 15 years of age resulting in a mutilation or a permanent disability.[8] Classified as a "crime," a conviction under such a charge gives rise to significantly higher penalties (see above). Since 1983, with some exceptions, FC/FGM has been charged under this provision of the Penal Code.[9]

One provider has served a sentence of five years. Among the parents who have been prosecuted, sentences have ranged from one to five years, but have generally been suspended.[10] Several parents have been required to serve part of their sentences, with prison terms of up to one year.[11] In the most recent case of this type, a practitioner was sentenced to eight years in prison for performing FC/FGM on 48 girls. Most of the 25 parents who were tried as accomplices received suspended sentences from three to five years and are unlikely to go to prison. The mother of the young woman who brought the case received a firm prison sentence of two years. In addition, each of the 48 victims was awarded damages of FF80,000 (approximately US$13,000).[12]

Under Article 2(3) of the French Code of Criminal Procedure, non-governmental organizations dedicated to assisting children who have suffered from child abuse may participate in the prosecution of any offender. They have the status of a "civil party," and represent the victims' interests.[13]

Child protection laws

Juvenile court judges, if they perceive that the health, security or morality of a minor is in danger, may take action to prevent such danger.[14] The law of July 10, 1989 on Child Protection sets out procedures ensuring greater protections for minors under 15 years of age who are subject to violence.[15] Under Article 226(14) of the Penal Code, doctors are exempt from their duty of confidentiality when they discover acts of violence committed against children. They may therefore report cases of FC/FGM to the authorities.

Other Measures: Laws, Regulations and Policies

In 1996, an administrative court in Lyons struck down a prefectoral ruling that would have deported a woman and her two daughters to Guinea. The woman had refused to have her daughters undergo FC/FGM, and the court ruled that she would receive no judicial protection in Guinea.[16]

The French government has explicitly condemned the practice of FC/FGM. Since 1982, an inter-ministerial and inter-organizational working group has undertaken a series of educational initiatives aimed at preventing FC/FGM. A 1994 Circular regarding integration of immigrant groups in France requires FC/FGM prevention activities in jurisdictions with communities that may practice FC/FGM.[17]

Standards of Health Professionals

Article 41 of the Code of Medical Deontology would prohibit physicians from performing FC/FGM. It provides:

> No mutilating procedure may be performed in the absence of very serious medical indications and, except in cases of emergency or impossibility, without information about the patient and without his or her consent.[18]

Policies for Eliminating FC/FGM in Africa

Information not available.

Notes

1. Proceedings of the Expert Meeting on Female Genital Mutilation, Ghent, Belgium, Nov. 5–7, 1998, p. 11 (figures were obtained from the national offices of statistics of each European member state).
2. *Constitution of Oct. 4, 1958*, preamble (last visited Aug. 16, 1999), <http://www.legifrance.gouv.fr/citoyen/constit.htm>.
3. *Constitution of Oct. 27, 1946*, preamble (last visited Aug. 16, 1999), <http://www.conseil-constitutionnel.fr.textes/p1946.htm>.
4. Code Pénal (1992), Paris: Editions Techniques – Juris-Classeurs, 1992.
5. Linda Weil-Curiel, Commission Pour l'Abolition des Mutilations Sexuelles (CAMS), Questionnaire (June 9, 1998).
6. M. Allaix, "Droit et Excision," in E. Rude-Antoine (ed.) *L'Immigration face aux lois de la République*, Paris: Éditions Karthala, 1992, p. 135.
7. Ibid., pp. 135–6.
8. Ibid., p. 136. At the time, Article 312(3) of the Penal Code was the basis of this charge. The comparable provision under the current Penal Code is located in Articles 222(9) and 222(10) (see above).
9. Allaix, "Droit et Excision," p. 137.
10. Linda Weil-Curiel, Commission Pour l'Abolition des Mutilations Sexuelles (CAMS), Questionnaire (June 9, 1998).
11. Ibid.
12. French Ministry of Employment and Solidarity, *Prevention des Mutilations Sexuelles en France* (undated), provided to CRLP on July 26, 1999 (on file with CRLP).
13. Code of Criminal Procedure (last visited June 19, 1990), <http://www.rabenou.org/cpp/P1L1TP.html>.
14. Civil Code, art. 375 (last visited Nov. 3, 1999), <http://www.rabenou.org/civi/L1T9.html>.
15. Loi no. 89–487, July 10, 1989, *Journal officiel de la Republique Française*, July 14, 1989, p. 8869.
16. P. Bernard, "L'Expulsion d'une Guinéene est annulée…," *Le Monde*, June 14, 1996.
17. French Ministry of Employment and Solidarity, *Prevention des Mutilations Sexuelles en France.*
18. Décret no. 95–1000 of Sept. 6, 1995, on the Code de Déontologie Médicale, art. 41.

The Gambia

Size (1,000 km²): 11
Income (per capita GNP in US$): 340
Population (millions): 1
Number of women per 100 men: 102
Percentage of young people in the population (under 15 years): 44
Prevalence of FC/FGM: 80%
Type(s) of FC/FGM most commonly practiced: Type II
Ethnic groups that practice FC/FGM: Practiced by Mandinga and Serehule (100%), Fula (93%), Jola (65.7%) and Wollof (1.9%).

International Treaties

- Women's Convention (ratified 1993).
- Children's Rights Convention (ratified 1990).
- Civil and Political Rights Covenant (ratified 1979).
- Economic, Social and Cultural Rights Covenant (ratified 1978).
- Banjul Charter (ratified 1983).

National Laws

Constitution

The Constitution[1] provides a limited guarantee of equality between women and men before the law. Article 17(2) states that "[e]very person in The Gambia, whatever his or her … gender, … shall be entitled to the fundamental human rights and freedoms of the individual contained in this Chapter, but subject to respect for the rights and freedoms of others and for the public interest." Article 28(1–2) provides that "[w]omen shall be accorded full and equal dignity of the person with men" and that "[w]omen shall have the right to equal treatment with men, including equal opportunities in political, economic and social activities."

A separate provision, however, limits these guarantees of equality. While Article 33(1–4) prohibits laws that discriminate on the basis of gender, this provision is qualified with several exceptions. Exempt from this prohibition of discrimination are laws relating to adoption, marriage, divorce, burial, inheritance or other matters of personal law (Art. 33(5)(c)) and applications of customary law (Art. 33(5)(d)).

Cultural and religious practices must conform to constitutional protections of individual rights. Article 32 declares that "[e]very person shall be entitled to enjoy, practise, profess, maintain and promote any culture, language, tradition or religion *subject to the terms of this Constitution and to the condition that the rights protected by this section do not impinge on the rights and freedoms of others* or the national interest, especially unity [emphasis added]."

On March 9, 1998, International Women's Day, a proposed law was introduced that would amend the Gambian Constitution to protect girl children against FC/FGM.[2]

Criminal Law

Provisions

While no legal provision expressly addresses FC/FGM, the practice may fall under the Penal Code's[3] provisions on "grievous harm." The relevant provisions state:

> Any person who unlawfully does grievous harm to another is guilty of a felony, and is liable to imprisonment for seven years. [Sect. 214]
>
> Any person who, with intent to maim, disfigure, or disable any person, or to do some grievous harm to any person...
> (1) unlawfully wounds or does any grievous harm to any person by any means whatever; or
> (2) unlawfully attempts in any manner to strike any person with any kind of projectile or with a spear, sword, knife, or other dangerous or offensive weapon; ...
> is guilty of a felony, and is liable to imprisonment for life. [Sect. 212]

In addition, the Penal Code contains provisions specifically protecting children, including Section 210, which states:

> If any person over the age of sixteen years, who has the custody, charge, or care of any child under the age of fourteen years, willfully assaults, ill-treats, neglects, abandons or exposes such child, or causes or procures such child to be assaulted, ill-treated, neglected, abandoned, or exposed in a manner likely to cause such child unnecessary suffering or injury to his health (including injury

> to or loss of sight, or hearing, or limb or organ of the body, and any mental derangement), that person shall be guilty of a misdemeanour.

Enforcement of the law

There have been no prosecutions for FC/FGM on the basis of the articles discussed above.[4]

Other Measures: Laws, Regulations and Policies

In July 1997, the Vice President of the Gambia, Isatou Njie-Saidy, who also serves as the Secretary of State for Social Welfare and Women's Affairs, stated that the policy of the government of the Gambia concerning FC/FGM "is to discourage such harmful practices."[5] She also stated that "organisations are not stopped from carrying out activities geared towards the elimination of FGM and all other harmful practices."[6] As recently as January 1999, the Vice President expressed her commitment to eliminating all types of harmful traditional practices, including FC/FGM.[7]

In late 1997, the government of the Gambia announced that matters pertaining to reproductive health, including FC/FGM, could be discussed publicly and that NGOs were permitted to make use of the government media to address FC/FGM.[8] This announcement reversed a directive issued by the Director of Broadcasting Services in May 1997 to the state-owned radio and television stations, which prohibited the broadcasting of programs aimed at the elimination of FC/FGM. The earlier directive stated:

> The broadcast by RG [Radio Gambia] or GTV [Gambia Television] of any programmes which either seemingly oppose female genital mutilation or tend to portray medical hazard about the practice is forbidden, with immediate effect. So also are news items written from the point of view of combating the practice. GTV and RG broadcasts should always be in support of FGM and no other programmes against the practice should be broadcast. All programmes must therefore be previewed to ensure compliance with this directive.[9]

The radio and television stations affected by this policy were those with the largest audiences and the only ones that broadcast to the entire country.[10] The directive was publicly assailed by the Gambian Committee on Traditional Practices (GAMCOTRAP), a non-governmental organization working to eliminate FC/FGM.[11]

In January 1999, President Jammeh reportedly delivered a speech in which he announced that the Gambia would not ban FC/FGM. In his speech, the President declared that FC/FGM was part of Gambian culture and that those campaigning against the practice were working to undermine Islam.[12]

Despite the apparently conflicting government policy statements, the Gambia has taken action to eliminate FC/FGM. In March 1997, concurrently with other World Health Organization member states, the Gambia launched a campaign to eliminate FC/FGM.[13]

Notes

1. *Constitution of the Republic of Gambia* (1996), reprinted in G.H. Flanz, *Constitutions of the Countries of the World*, Dobbs Ferry, NY: Oceana Publications, 1997.
2. Mary Small, Gambia Committee on Traditional Practices Affecting the Health of Women and Children (GAMCOTRAP), Questionnaire (undated, Spring 1998).
3. The Laws of The Gambia, Chapt. 37, Code of Criminal Law (1967).
4. Office of the Senior Coordinator for International Women's Issues, Bureau for Global Affairs and the Office of Asylum, Bureau of Democracy, Human Rights and Labor, US Department of State, *Female Genital Mutilation (FGM) or Female Genital Cutting (FGC) in the Gambia*, 1999, p. 4.
5. Sheriff Bojang, "Gov't Policy is to Discourage FGM – Vice President Declares," *Daily Observer*, July 7, 1997.
6. Ibid.
7. Spice News Services, "Vice President Calls for Elimination of Harmful Traditional Pratices," *Africa News Service*, Jan. 4, 1999.
8. "The Gambia: Government Rescinds Censorship Policy on Female Genital Mutilation (FGM)," *Women's Action* Vol. 13, No. 2 (New York: Equality Now), December 1997.
9. Handing Over Notes from the Director of Broadcasting Services to Manager, Radio Programmes; Manager, TV Operations; Administrative Officer; Principal Producer, Programmes; Typists (May 17, 1997).
10. "The Gambia: Government Censorship of the Campaign to Stop Female Genital Mutilation (FGM)," *Women's Action* Vol. 13, No. 1 (New York: Equality Now), July 1997.
11. "GAMCOTRAP Petitions President Jammeh," *Daily Observer*, May 27, 1997.
12. Spice News Services, "Jammeh Says His Government Will Not Ban FGM," *Africa News Service*, Jan. 22, 1999.
13. "GAMCOTRAP Petitions President Jammeh."

Germany

Size (1,000 km^2): 357

Income (per capita GNP in US$): 28,280

Population (millions): 82

Immigrant population: In 1997, the combined number of female immigrants from Benin, Cameroon, Central African Republic, Chad, Côte d'Ivoire, Democratic Republic of Congo, Djibouti, Egypt, Eritrea, Ethiopia, Gambia, Ghana, Guinea, Guinea-Bissau, Kenya, Liberia, Mali, Niger, Nigeria, Senegal, Sierre Leone, Somalia, Tanzania, Togo and Uganda totaled 38,585. The total number of immigrants (men and women) from these countries was 151,714.[1]

International Treaties

- Women's Convention (ratified 1985).
- Children's Rights Convention (ratified 1992). Declaration asserting the right of the state to pass laws and regulations concerning the entry of aliens and the condition of their stay and the right to make a distinction between aliens and nationals.
- Civil and Political Rights Covenant (ratified 1973).
- Economic, Social and Cultural Rights Covenant (ratified 1973).
- European Convention (ratified 1952).

National Laws

Constitution

The German Constitution[2] guarantees the equality of women and men before the law. Article 3 provides that "[a]ll humans are equal before the law." In particular, it states that "[m]en and women are equal. The state supports the effective realization of equality of women and men and works towards abolishing present disadvantages."

Article 2 recognizes the "right to life and to physical integrity" of all people and provides that the "freedom of the person is inviolable." Article 1 provides that "[h]uman dignity is inviolable. To respect and protect it is the duty of all state authority."

Criminal law

The Bundestag adopted the position that FC/FGM could be prosecuted under Sections 224 and 226 of the Germal Penal Code, which address "serious" and "grave" bodily harm.[3]

Provision

Provisions of the German Penal Code[4] that address "bodily harm" are considered applicable to FC/FGM.

§224. Serious Bodily Harm

(1) Any person who causes bodily harm

1. through administration of poison or other substances harmful to health,
2. by means of a weapon or another dangerous instrument,
3. by means of a deceitful attack,
4. with another person acting in concert or
5. by means of a life-endangering treatment

shall be punished by imprisonment from six months to ten years, in less severe cases, from three months to five years.

(2) Attempt is punishable.

§226. Grave Bodily Harm

(1) If the bodily harm has as a consequence that the injured person

1. loses sight in one or both eyes, hearing, capacity for speech or capacity to procreate,
2. loses an important limb or permanently loses the ability to use such a limb or
3. is permanently disfigured in a significant manner or deteriorates into infirmity, paralysis or mental illness,

then the punishment is imprisonment from one year to ten years.

(2) If the perpetrator causes any of the results listed in paragraph (1) intentionally or deliberately, then the punishment is imprisonment for not less than three years,

(3) In less serious cases under paragraph (1) the sentence shall be imprisonment from six months to five years; in less serious cases under paragraph (2), the sentence shall be imprisonment from one year to ten years.

Enforcement of the law

According to news sources, the German police have generally been reluctant to investigate reports of FC/FGM. Police tend to see FC/FGM as a matter of religious exercise rather than a criminal matter. In March 1999 the then German Minister of Justice, however, stated that "the police and prosecutors need to familiarize themselves with FC/FGM and to investigate incidents of the practice, because religion or tradition do not excuse or justify the practice of FC/FGM."[5]

Child Protection Laws

The Bundestag, as part of a multi-party motion approved on June 17, 1998 (see below), recommended that the federal government and the states develop counseling and information programs aimed at supporting and protecting girls at risk of undergoing FC/FGM.[6]

Other Measures: Laws, Regulations and Policies

On June 17, 1998, the German Bundestag unanimously approved a multipartisan motion condemning FC/FGM as a "serious violation of human rights."[7] The motion made several recommendations to the executive branch of government. The Bundestag recommended that the German government give priority to FC/FGM in the context of multilateral human rights activities and bilateral developmental aid projects.[8] It also asked the government to include FC/FGM prevention in the Foreign Ministries country reports. The Bundestag further recommended that the executive branch consider FC/FGM a violation of human rights for purposes of asylum law and other laws governing the status of foreigners and provide information relating to FC/FGM to the officials conducting asylum hearings.[9] The Bundestag declared that it considers FC/FGM a violation of Article 2 of the German Consitution and as the infliction of serious/grave bodily harm under Sections 224 and 226 of the German Penal Code.[10]

There is only one reported case in which a German court has addressed the question whether FC/FGM can be grounds for asylum. The administrative court in Madgeburg heard the case of a woman from Côte d'Ivoire and found that it was highly probable that she would be subjected to FC/FGM in the event of her return. The court also found that the government of Côte d'Ivoire was highly unlikely to protect her. Holding that performing FC/FGM against a person's will represents a violation of her physical and mental integrity, the court went on to recognize the applicant's right to asylum.[11]

Standards of Health Professionals

The German Medical Association passed resolutions at its annual conventions in 1996 and 1997 condemning the participation of physicians in the practice of FC/FGM.[12] The Medical Association states that the practice is a violation of the professional practice code and renders a doctor subject to disciplinary sanctions.[13] A Berlin doctor was recently recorded on tape agreeing to perform FC/FGM. The Berlin Medical Association has filed a criminal complaint against the doctor and has asked the state licensing board to suspend the doctor's license.[14]

Policies for Eliminating FC/FGM in Africa.

In March 1999, the then German Federal Minister for Economic Cooperation and Development launched a campaign against FC/FGM.[15] As part of this campaign, the German Technical Cooperation (GTZ) will support local organizations and institutions in East and West Africa.[16] GTZ has been granted a total of DM 2 million (approximately US$900,000) for its work in this area over the next four years. Another DM 4 million will follow.[17] The elimination of FC/FGM is also considered a high priority in GTZ-assisted health projects in Kenya, Guinea, Burkina Faso, Senegal, Mali, Mauritania and the Central African Republic.[18]

Notes

1. C. Schmalz-Jacobsen and G. Hansen (eds), *Kleines Lexikon der ethnischen Minderheiten in Deutschland*, Bonn: Bundeszentrale fuer Politische Bildung, 1997.
2. *Constitution of Germany*, (last visited July 31, 1999) <http://www.uni-wuerzburg.de/law/gm00000_.html>.
3. T. Levin, "Female Genital Mutilation: Campaigns in Germany," presentation given at the Conference on Women in Africa and the African Diaspora (WAAD), October 1998, University of Indiana, Indianapolis.
4. German Penal Code (last visited Apr. 28, 1999), <http://www.bib.uni-mannheim.de/bib/jura/gestze/stgb-bt3.shtml.>.
5. Transcript of Report Mainz, March 22, 1999 (last visited Sept. 3, 1999), <http://www.swr-online.de/report>.
6. Beschlußempfehlung, Deutscher Bundestag, 13. Wahlperiod, publication 13/10682, Apr. 3, 1998.
7. Transcript of the session of the Bundestag on June 17, 1998 (last visited Sept. 3, 1999), <http://www.bundestag.de>.
8. Publication 13/10682.
9. Ibid.
10. Ibid.
11. Verwaltungsgericht Madgeburg, June 20, 1996, AZ :1A 185/95.

12. Resolutions passed at the 99th and 100th Deutscher Ärztetag.
13. Ibid.
14. Ärztekammer Berlin, Ärtzekammer erstattet Strafanzeige gegen Berliner Arzt, Pressererklärung, Mar. 23, 1999.
15. German Technical Cooperation, Press Release, Mar. 16, 1999, <http://www.gtz.de/presse/english/990316.htm>.
16. Ibid.
17. Ibid.
18. Ibid.

Ghana

Size (1,000 km^2): 239
Income (per capita GNP in US$): 390
Population (millions): 18
Number of women per 100 men: 101
Percentage of young people in the population (under 15 years): 45
Prevalence of FC/FGM: 30%
Type(s) of FC/FGM most commonly practiced: Type II
Ethnic groups that practice FC/FGM: Practiced by the Bussansi, Frafra, Kantonsi, Kassena, Kussasi, Mamprushie, Moshie and Nankanne in the Upper East region and the Dargarti, Grunshie, Kantonsi, Lobi, Sissala and Walas in the Upper West region.

International Treaties

- Women's Convention (ratified 1986).
- Children's Rights Convention (ratified 1990).
- Banjul Charter (ratified 1989).

National Laws

Constitution

The Constitution[1] provides clear protection against FC/FGM. Article 26(2) states that "[a]ll customary practices which dehumanise or are injurious to the physical and mental well-being of a person are prohibited." Article 39(2) states that a governmental policy objective is to ensure that "traditional practices which are injurious to the health and well-being of the person are abolished."

The Constitution guarantees the equality of women and men before the law. Article 12 states that "[e]very person in Ghana, whatever his … gender, shall be entitled to the fundamental human rights and freedoms of the individual" provided in the Constitution. Article 17(1–2) states that "[a]ll persons shall be equal before the law," noting specifically that discrimination on the basis of gender is prohibited. Article 17(4)(b) states, however, that this guarantee of non-discrimination does not prevent Parliament from "enacting laws that are reasonably necessary" in matters relating to adoption, marriage, divorce, burial, inheritance or other matters of personal law.

Articles 13 and 14 protect the rights to life and liberty. Article 15(1) provides that "[t]he dignity of all persons shall be inviolable." Article 15(2)(b) states further that "[n]o person shall, whether or not he is arrested, restricted or detained, be subjected to … any … condition that detracts or is likely to detract from his dignity and worth as a human being."

Children, defined by Article 28(5) as persons below the age of 18, are accorded special protection under the Constitution. Article 28 states that Parliament "shall enact such laws as are necessary to ensure that … children and young persons receive special protection against exposure to physical and moral hazards."

The freedom to participate in cultural and religious practices is limited under the Constitution. Article 26(1) acknowledges every person's right to "enjoy, practise, profess, maintain and promote any culture, language, tradition or religion *subject to the provisions of th[e] Constitution*"(emphasis added). This provision is qualified by the prohibition of dehumanizing and injurious customary practices cited above (Art. 26(2)).

Criminal law

In 1994, the Parliament of Ghana amended the Criminal Code to make FC/FGM a criminal offense.[2]

Provisions

The 1994 legislation created Article 69A of the Criminal Code, which provides:

> (1) Whoever excises, infibulates or otherwise mutilates the whole or any part of the labia minora, labia majora and the clitoris of another person commits an offence and shall be guilty of a second degree felony and liable on conviction to imprisonment of not less than three years.
>
> (2) For the purposes of this section, "excise" means to remove the prepuce, the clitoris and all or part of the labia minora; "infibulate" includes excision and the additional removal of the labia majora.

Enforcement of the law

The law is reportedly being enforced. In March 1995, an eight-day-old girl was brought into a public hospital, bleeding profusely after having undergone FC/FGM. After the incident was reported in the press, police arrested and charged the practitioner and the infant's parents.[3] In another incident in June 1998, a practitioner of FC/FGM was sentenced to three years in prison for having performed the procedure upon three girls. While the girls – aged between 12 and 15 years – had given their consent to the procedure, it was performed without their parents' knowledge.[4]

Other Measures: Laws, Regulations and Policies

The Ministry of Health has issued the National Reproductive Health Service Policy and Standards (RHSPS), which explicitly discourages FC/FGM.[5] The RHSPS also advocates numerous strategies to stop FC/FGM, including: integration of FC/FGM-related services into all ongoing reproductive health services and activities, and into the school health education programs; encouragement of community involvement; training of service providers; and building a database on harmful traditional practices.[6] In addition, the RHSPS calls for enforcement of the 1994 law prohibiting FC/FGM; the establishment of information, education and communication programs; and the provision of full medical services for those who have undergone FC/FGM.[7] The RHSPS advocates cooperation among law enforcement officers, medical personnel, teachers, government officials, peer counselors, traditional rulers, religious bodies, opinion leaders and *wanzams* (circumcisors).[8]

Notes

1. *Constitution of the Republic of Ghana*, Tema: Ghana Publishing Corp., 1992.
2. Criminal Code (Amendment) Act, 1994, reprinted in *International Digest of Health Legislation*, Vol. 47, No. 1, 1996, pp. 30–31.
3. Inter-African Committee on Traditional Practices Affecting the Health of Women and Children (IAC), "News from Africa," *Newsletter of the IAC*, No. 18, Dec. 1995, p. 12.
4. IAC, "Circumciser Jailed in Ghana," *Newsletter of the IAC*, No. 24, Dec. 1998, p. 10.
5. Ministry of Health, Republic of Ghana, *National Reproductive Health Service Policy and Standards*, 1996, p. 14.
6. Ibid., p. 14.
7. Ibid.
8. Ibid.

Guinea

Size (1,000 km^2): 246
Income (per capita GNP in US$): 550
Population (millions): 7
Number of women per 100 men: 99
Percentage of young people in the population (under 15 years): 47
Prevalence of FC/FGM: 50%
Type(s) of FC/FGM most commonly practiced: Type II
Ethnic groups that practice FC/FGM: Information not available.

International Treaties

- Women's Convention (ratified 1982).
- Children's Rights Convention (ratified 1990).
- Civil and Political Rights Covenant (ratified 1978).
- Economic, Social and Cultural Rights Covenant (ratified 1978).
- Banjul Charter (ratified 1982).

National Laws

Constitution

The Constitution[1] guarantees the equality of women and men before the law. The Preamble recognizes "the equality and solidarity of all nationals without distinction of … sex." Article 1 ensures "equality before the law for all citizens, without distinction of … sex." Article 8 further provides that "[m]en and women have the same rights."

The Constitution also protects the rights to life and physical integrity. Article 5 provides that the "person and the dignity of man are sacred. The State has the duty to respect and protect them." Article 6 guarantees the rights to "life and physical integrity." Article 15 guarantees the "right to health and physical well-being" and charges the state with the "duty to promote the public health."

Children are afforded special protections under the Constitution. Article 16 states that "[p]arents have the right and the duty to assure the education and the physical and moral health of their children." Article 21 requires the state to "create conditions and institutions which permit each child to develop."

The Constitution states that the exercise of fundamental rights and liberties must conform to the law. According to Article 22, "[t]he law shall only set limits on these rights and liberties which are indispensable to the maintenance of public order and democracy."

Criminal law

Provisions

Article 265 of Guinea's Penal Code,[2] which defines the offense of "castration," criminalizes genital mutilation. It provides:

> Castration is the ablation or the mutilation of the genital organs of either a man or a woman.
>
> Any person guilty of this crime shall be sentenced to the punishment of hard labor for life [*perpétuité*].
>
> If death results within 40 days after the crime, the perpetrator will be sentenced to death.

FC/FGM may also be prohibited under Articles 259 through 262 and Article 264, which pertain to assault. Article 264 relates specifically to "wounds or strikes" intentionally inflicted upon a child of 15 years or younger that result in the "mutilation, amputation or privation of the use of a member" or in unintended death. The terms "wounds," "strikes" and "mutilation" are not defined in the Penal Code. These actions are punishable with hard labor for a fixed term, or, if the offender is a parent or other ascendant relative or any other person having authority over the child, the punishment is hard labor for life.

Enforcement of the law

No one has ever been criminally prosecuted for FC/FGM.[3] The term "castration," defined in Article 265, has generally been interpreted to include only castration of men, despite the provision's clear inclusion of females as potential victims of the crime.[4]

Other Measures: Laws, Regulations and Policies

A 1989 governmental declaration, referring to the Constitution's guarantee of the right to physical integrity (see above), condemned harmful traditional practices, including FC/FGM.[5] In collaboration with the World Health Organization, the government has initiated a twenty-year strategy to eliminate FC/FGM. The strategy, planned for the years 1996–2015, will build upon existing efforts to combat FC/FGM through improved coordination with non-governmental organizations, particularly in the process of public education.[6]

Notes

1. *Constitution of the Republic of Guinea* (1990), translated in A.P. Blaustein and G.H. Flanz (eds), *Constitutions of the Countries of the World*, Dobbs Ferry, NY: Oceana Publications, 1993.
2. *Penal Code of the Republic of Guinea*, Conakry: Republic of Guinea, 1965 (unofficial translation).
3. Office of the Senior Coordinator for International Women's Issues, Bureau for Global Affairs and the Office of Asylum Affairs, Bureau of Democracy, Human Rights and Labor, US Department of State, *Female Genital Mutilation (FGM) or Female Genital Cutting (FGC) in Guinea*, 1999, p. 3.
4. La Cellule de Coordination sur les Pratiques Traditionelles Affectant la Santé des Femmes et des Enfants (CPTAFE), Questionnaire (July 1998).
5. Inter-African Committee on Traditional Practices Affecting the Health of Women and Children (IAC), "Guinea: Regional Antennas on FGM and HTPs," *Newsletter of the IAC*, No. 19, June 1996, p. 9.
6. Office of the Senior Coordinator for International Women's Issues, *Female Genital Mutilation (FGM) or Female Genital Cutting (FGC) in Guinea*, p. 2.

Guinea-Bissau

Size (1,000 km^2): 36
Income (per capita GNP in US$): 230
Population (millions): 1
Number of women per 100 men: 103
Percentage of young people in the population (under 15 years): 42
Prevalence of FC/FGM: 50%
Type(s) of FC/FGM most commonly practiced: Types I and II
Ethnic groups that practice FC/FGM: A limited, non-representative survey by the national women's union reported type II FGM in almost 100% of Muslim women (unpublished data, 1990).

International Treaties

- Women's Convention (ratified 1985).
- Children's Rights Convention (ratified 1990).
- Economic, Social and Cultural Rights Covenant (ratified 1992).
- Banjul Charter (ratified 1985).

National Laws

Constitution

The Constitution of Guinea-Bissau[1] guarantees the equality of women and men before the law. Article 23 provides that "[a]ll citizens shall be equal before the law, shall have the same rights, and shall be subject to the same duties, without distinction regarding ... sex." Article 24 states that "[m]en and women shall be equal before the law in all areas of political, economic, social, and cultural life."

The Constitution also protects the rights to life and physical integrity. Article 32(1) guarantees every person "the right to life and to physical and mental well-being." Article 33(1) declares that "[e]very person shall enjoy inviolability of his person."

Article 39 provides that "[e]very citizen shall have the right to protection of his health and the duty to promote and defend it."

The Constitution affords children and mothers special protections. Article 40 provides that "[c]hildren, youth, and mothers shall have the right to the protection of society and of the State."

While freedom of expression and religion is protected under the Constitution, exercise of this right is subject to the law. Article 44 provides that "[f]reedom of expression of thought, of meeting, of association ... as well as freedom of choice of religion, shall be guaranteed *according to conditions provided by law* [emphasis added]."

Criminal law

Upon independence from Portugal in 1974, Guinea-Bissau officially adopted the Portuguese Penal Code.[2] While the Penal Code does not specifically prohibit FC/FGM, provisions on "intentional bodily injury" may be applicable.[3] Punishments vary according to the degree of harm inflicted.[4]

Other Measures: Laws, Regulations and Policies

The Ministries of Women's Affairs and Education participate in the National Committee of the IAC, which was established in 1990.[5]

Notes

1. *Constitution of the Republic of Guinea Bissau* (1991), translated in A.P. Blaustein and G.H. Flanz (eds), *Constitutions of the Countries of the World*, Dobbs Ferry, NY: Oceana Publications, 1994.
2. Telephone interview by Sarah Netburn of CRLP with João Dagama, Legal Advisor, United Nations Permanent Mission of the Republic of Guinea-Bissau (June 1, 1999).
3. M.L.M. Gonçalves, *Código Penal Português*, Coimbra: Livraria Almedina, 1968, pp. 502–24.
4. Ibid.
5. J. Smith, *Visions and Discussions on Genital Mutilation of Girls: An International Survey*, Amsterdam: Defence for Children International, 1995, p. 118.

Italy

Size (1,000 km²): 301

Income (per capita GNP in US$): 20,170

Population (millions): 58

Immigrant population: In 1997, there were 133,847 immigrants from the following countries and regions in Africa: Egypt, Ghana, Nigeria, Senegal, the rest of West Africa, Ethiopia, Somalia, the rest of East Africa and Central Africa. Of these, 46,389 were women.[1] In 1995, there was a total of 24,000 immigrants from Senegal, 17,400 from Somalia, and 12,600 from Ghana. In 1994, there was a total of 10,100 immigrants from Ethiopia. In 1995, the immigrant population in Italy totaled 991,400.

International Treaties

- Women's Convention (ratified 1985).
- Children's Rights Convention (ratified 1991).
- Civil and Political Rights Covenant (ratified 1978).
- Economic, Social and Cultural Rights Covenant (ratified 1978).
- European Convention (ratified 1955).

National Laws

Constitution

The Constitution[2] guarantees the equality of women and men before the law. Article 3(1) states that "[a]ll citizens are … equal before the law, without distinction as to sex." Article 3(2) further provides that "[i]t is the responsibility of the Republic to remove all economic and social obstacles which, by limiting the freedom and equality of citizens, prevent the full development of the individual."

The right to health is explicitly recognized in the Constitution. Article 32(1) states that "[t]he Republic provides health safeguards as a basic right of the individual and in the interests of the community, and grants medical assistance to the indigent free of charge." The right to health encompasses the right to physical integrity. Article 32(2) provides that "[n]o one may be forced to undergo any particular medical treatment, save under the provisions of the law. In no case shall the law violate the limits imposed by proper respect for the human person."

Children and the family are granted special protections under the Constitution. Article 31(2) pledges government support for safeguards for "maternity, infancy, and youth, promoting and encouraging institutions necessary for such purposes."

Religious freedom is protected under the Constitution, with one qualification. Article 19 states that "[a]ll are entitled to freely profess their religious convictions in any form, individually or in associations, to propagate them, and to celebrate them in public or in private, save in the case of rites contrary to morality." The term "morality" is not defined.

Criminal law

Italy has enacted no law specifically criminalizing FC/FGM. However, general provisions of the Penal Code[3] covering "Personal Injury" could potentially apply.

Provisions

Article 582 on "Personal Injury" provides that "[w]hoever causes personal injury to another, which results in physical or mental illness, shall be punished by imprisonment for from three months to three years."

Article 583, which enumerates "aggravating circumstances," provides:

> Personal injury shall be serious, and imprisonment for from three to seven years shall be imposed:
>
> (1) if the act results in an illness which endangers the life of the victim, or an illness or incapacity which prevents his attending to his ordinary occupations for a period in excess of forty days;
> (2) if the act produces the permanent impairment of a sense or organ; ...
>
> Personal injury shall be very serious, and imprisonment for from six to twelve years shall be imposed, if the act results in:
>
> (1) an illness which is certainly or probably incurable;
> (2) the loss of a sense;
> (3) the loss of a limb, or mutilation which renders the limb useless, or the loss of the use of an organ or of the ability to procreate.

Enforcement of the law

Information not available.

Child protection laws

Information not available.

Other Measures: Laws, Regulations and Policies

A committee has been created to establish guidelines to assist health professionals, educators and social workers in addressing FC/FGM.[4]

Standards of Health Professionals

There have been reports that Italian hospitals have permitted physicians to perform FC/FGM in order to reduce the risks associated with the procedure.[5] These reports have never been definitively confirmed and there is no evidence that this practice continues.

Policies for Eliminating FC/FGM in Africa

Information not available.

Notes

1. Proceedings of the Expert Meeting on Female Genital Mutilation, Ghent, Belgium, Nov. 5–7, 1998, p. 12 (figures were obtained from the National Offices of Statistics from each European member state).
2. *Constitution of Italy* (1947), (last visited Aug. 21, 1999), <http://www.uni-wuerzburg.de/law/it00000_.html>.
3. E.M. Wise (trans.), *The Italian Penal Code*, Littleton, NH: Fred B. Rothman, 1978, p. 195.
4. "Political Will for Equality, Gender Sensitivity in National Budgets, etc. addressed at Commission [on the Status of Women]," *M2 Presswire*, Mar. 17, 1999.
5. J. Smith, *Visions and Discussions on Genital Mutilation of Girls*, Amsterdam: Defence for Children International, 1995, p. 158, citing written questions No. 2500/87, Feb. 24, 1988, Official Journal of the European Communities, C 145 of June 12, 1989 and No. 2501/87 Feb. 24, 1988, Official Journal of the European Communities, C 195 of July 25, 1988.

Kenya

Size (1,000 km^2): 580
Income (per capita GNP in US$): 340
Population (millions): 29
Number of women per 100 men: 100
Percentage of young people in the population (under 15 years): 47
Prevalence of FC/FGM: 50%
Type(s) of FC/FGM most commonly practiced: Types I and II
Ethnic groups that practice FC/FGM: Information not available.

International Treaties

- Women's Convention (ratified 1984).
- Children's Rights Convention (ratified 1990).
- Civil and Political Rights Covenant (ratified 1972).
- Economic, Social and Cultural Rights Covenant (ratified 1972).
- Banjul Charter (ratified 1992).

National Laws

Constitution

Section 70 of the Constitution[1] provides that "every person in Kenya is entitled to the fundamental rights and freedoms of the individual ... whatever his ... sex." Section 82(1) and (3) states that "no law shall make any provision that is discriminatory either of itself or in its effect," but prohibits discrimination only on the grounds of "race, tribe, place of origin or residence or other local connexion, political opinions, colour or creed." Gender discrimination is thus not specifically prohibited. In addition, the non-discrimination provision does not apply to laws related to adoption, marriage, divorce, burial, inheritance or other matters of personal law (Sect. 82(4)(b)) and to applications of customary law (Sect. 82(4)(c)).

Section 70(a) of the Constitution protects "the right to life, liberty, security of the person and the protection of the law."

Religious rights must be balanced against individual protections and other state interests under the Constitution. While Section 78 protects "freedom of conscience," which includes "freedom of thought and of religion ... and freedom ... to manifest and propagate his religion or belief in worship, teaching, practice and observance," it reserves the state's right to limit religious freedom "(a) ... in the interests of defence, public safety, public order, public morality or public health; or (b) ... for the purpose of protecting the ... rights and freedoms of other persons."

Criminal law

In 1996, a legislative proposal to criminalize FC/FGM was defeated in the Kenyan Parliament.[2] General criminal provisions on "Offences Endangering Life and Health" may, however, be applicable.

Provisions

Section 250 of the Penal Code,[3] on "Assaults," provides:

> Any person who unlawfully assaults another is guilty of a misdemeanour and, if the assault is not committed in circumstances for which a greater punishment is provided in this Code, is liable to imprisonment for one year.

Section 251 provides:

> Any person who commits an assault occasioning actual bodily harm is guilty of a misdemeanour and is liable to imprisonment for five years, with or without corporal punishment.

Section 234, on "Grievous Harm," provides:

> Any person who unlawfully does grievous harm to another is guilty of a felony and is liable to imprisonment for life, with or without corporal punishment.

"Grievous Harm" is defined in Section 4 as:

> any harm which amounts to a maim or dangerous harm, or seriously or permanently injures health, or which is likely so to injure health, or which extends to permanent disfigurement, or to any permanent or serious injury to any external or internal organ, membrane or sense.

Enforcement of the law

Information on enforcement of the foregoing Penal Code provisions in cases of FC/FGM is unavailable. However, in 1982, following the deaths of 14 girls as a result of circumcision, President Daniel Arap Moi ordered that murder charges be brought against practitioners who carry out circumcisions that result in death.[4]

Other Measures: Laws, Regulations and Policies

In 1982, President Moi issued a statement condemning the practice of FC/FGM.[5] The President's statement was followed by an order from the Director of Medical Services forbidding medical personnel to carry out the operation without specific permission from his office.[6] In 1989, President Moi again called for an end to the practice, and, six months later, the Assistant Minister for Cultural and Social Services announced an official government ban of the practice.[7]

In November 1999, Kenya launched a national plan of action to eliminate FC/FGM, which will emphasize education and outreach over criminal prosecution.[8]

Notes

1. *Constitution of Kenya*, Nairobi: Government Printer, 1992, p. 42.
2. Office of the Senior Coordinator for International Women's Issues, Bureau for Global Affairs and the Office of Asylum Affairs, Bureau of Democracy, Human Rights and Labor, US Department of State, *Female Genital Mutilation (FGM) or Female Genital Cutting (FGC) in Kenya*, 1999, p. 3.
3. *Penal Code*, Nairobi: Government Printer, 1985, p. 90.
4. CRLP and International Federation of Women Lawyers (Kenya Chapter) (FIDA–K), *Women of the World: Laws and Policies Affecting their Reproductive Lives – Anglophone Africa*, New York: CRLP, 1997, p. 69.
5. Ibid.
6. Ibid.
7. Ibid.
8. "Kenya Plans to Eliminate Female Circumcision," Panafrican News Agency, Nov. 18, 1999.

Liberia

Size (1,000 km^2): 97.75

Income (per capita GNP in US$): Estimated to be low income (US$765 or less)

Population (millions): 2.7

Number of women per 100 men: 98

Percentage of young people in the population (under 15 years): 46

Prevalence of FC/FGM: 60%

Type(s) of FC/FGM most commonly practiced: Type II

Ethnic groups that practice FC/FGM: Only three ethnic groups do not perform FGM. The practice, Type II only, is part of the secret Sande or bush school initiation.

International Treaties

- Women's Convention (ratified 1984).
- Children's Rights Convention (ratified 1993).
- Banjul Charter (ratified 1982).

National Laws

Constitution

The Constitution[1] guarantees the equality of women and men before the law. Article 11(b–c) provides that "[a]ll persons, irrespective of … sex,… are entitled to the fundamental rights and freedoms of the individual.… All persons are equal before the law and are therefore entitled to the equal protection of the law."

Article 11(a) also protects the right "of enjoying and defending life and liberty, of pursuing and maintaining the security of the person."

Criminal law

Liberia has no law specifically prohibiting FC/FGM.

Provisions

FC/FGM is potentially covered under the offense of "Mayhem." Section 242 of the Penal Code provides:

> Any person who maliciously and unlawfully injures another by cutting off or otherwise depriving him of any of the members of his body, or in any wise maims him or any part of his body or the members thereof, with intent in so doing unlawfully to disfigure him or to diminish his physical vigor, is guilty of a felony and punishable by imprisonment for not more than five years.[2]

Enforcement of the law

Information not available.

Other Measures: Laws, Regulations and Policies

In 1994, a Grebo girl forced by the Vai Sande Secret Society to undergo FC/FGM took legal action with the assistance of the IAC National Committee of Liberia. Both the Vai Sande Secret Society and the offending *Zoe* (the leader of the Secret Society and the FC/FGM practitioner) were ordered to pay $500 (approximately US$11.75) in compensation for the girl's injuries. As a result of the case and a related information campaign led by the IAC, the government organized a meeting to determine its policy regarding FC/FGM. The participants of this meeting issued a statement condemning FC/FGM and recommending the revocation of licenses of *Zoes* in the Monrovia area and a halt to the issuance of new licenses. It further recommended that practitioners of FC/FGM be criminally prosecuted.[3]

Notes

1. *Constitution of the Republic of Liberia* (1986), reprinted in A.P. Blaustein and G.H. Flanz (eds), *Constitutions of the Countries of the World*, Dobbs Ferry, NY: Oceana Publications, 1985.
2. *Liberian Code of Laws of 1956*, Vol. III, title 27, Sect. 242(1), Ithaca, NY: Cornell University Press, p. 971.
3. Inter-African Committee on Traditional Practices Affecting the Health of Women and Children (IAC), "IAC–Liberia: The Case of the Grebo Girl," *Newsletter of the IAC*, No. 17, Apr. 1995, p. 12.

Mali

Size (1,000 km^2): 1,240

Income (per capita GNP in US$): 260

Population (millions): 10

Number of women per 100 men: 103

Percentage of young people in the population (under 15 years): 47

Prevalence of FC/FGM: 94%

Type(s) of FC/FGM most commonly practiced: Types I (52%) and II (47%)

Ethnic groups that practice FC/FGM: FGM is practiced by all religious groups, ranging from 85% among Christians to 94% among Muslims, and across all ethnic groups. The two groups with the lowest prevalence rates are the Tamachek (16%) and the Sonrai (48%).

International Treaties

- Women's Convention (ratified 1985).
- Children's Rights Convention (ratified 1990).
- Civil and Political Rights Covenant (ratified 1974).
- Economic, Social and Cultural Rights Covenant (ratified 1974).
- Banjul Charter (ratified 1981).
- African Charter (ratified 1998).

National Laws

Constitution

The Constitution[1] guarantees the equality of women and men before the law. It declares in its Preamble that the people of Mali are determined to "defend the rights of Women and Children." Article 2 provides that "[e]very Malian is born and remain[s] free and equal in rights and duties. All discrimination founded on … sex …shall be prohibited."

The right to life and physical integrity is also protected in the

Constitution. Article 1 recognizes that "[t]he human person is sacred and inviolable." It guarantees every individual "the right to life, to liberty, to security and to the integrity of his person." Article 17 states that "health" constitutes a "recognized right."

Freedom of "thought, conscience, religion, [and] worship" are protected, "*with respect to the law*" (Art. 4, emphasis added).

Criminal law

Provisions

There are no Penal Code provisions that specifically prohibit FC/FGM.[2] However, the government of Mali, in its National Plan for the Eradication of Excision by 2007, has stated that FC/FGM may be prohibited under Article 166 (covering voluntary strikes or wounds) and Article 171 (covering harmful experimental treatments).[3] Article 166 provides:

> Any person who intentionally strikes or wounds or commits any other act of violence or assault, resulting in an illness or an inability to work for more than 20 days, shall be punished by imprisonment from one to five years and by a fine of 20,000 to 500,000 francs [approximately US$32–800]....
>
> When the acts of violence, wounds or strikes result in mutilation, amputation, privation of the use of a member or of a sense, blindness, loss of an eye or other infirmities or illness, the punishment shall be five to ten years of hard labor....
>
> In cases provided for [in the previous paragraph], a court may prohibit the perpetrator from appearing in specified places [*intérdiction de séjour*] for one to ten years.

The terms "strikes," "wounds," "violence" and "mutilation" are not defined in the Penal Code. Article 171 provides:

> Any person who, without intending to cause death, intentionally ... subjects a person, even with his or her consent, to practices or maneuvers that result in or could result in an illness or an incapacity to work, shall be punished by imprisonment from six months to three years and, optionally, a fine of 20,000 to 200,000 francs [approximately US$32–320]. In addition, the perpetrator may be prohibited from appearing in specified places for one to ten years.

If these practices result in a permanent illness or incapacity, the punishment is five to ten years of hard labor and the perpetrator may be prohibited from appearing in specified places for five to ten years. If the prohibited practices result in death, the penalty is five to twenty years of hard labor and, optionally, the court may prohibit a person from appearing in specified places for one to twenty years.

Article 169 of the Penal Code also provides that intentionally abandoning a child in a situation in which his or her safety is jeopardized when this abandonment results in a mutilation, an infirmity or a permanent illness is punishable with five to ten years of hard labor.

Enforcement of the law

As of July 1998, no one had ever been criminally prosecuted for FC/FGM.[4]

Other Measures: Laws, Regulations and Policies

In 1996, the government formed the National Action Committee for the Eradication of Practices Harmful to the Health of Women and Children, whose mandate is to develop strategies for the elimination of harmful practices, including FC/FGM.[5] The National Action Committee, which is directed by the Commissioner for the Promotion of Women, is composed of representatives from every government ministry and from NGOs, national health and science research institutions, and religious groups.[6] In June 1997, the National Action Committee devised the first phase of the Plan of Action for the Eradication of Excision by 2007.[7] The Plan, which will cover the entire national territory, is to be implemented by the government and by NGOs, with the help of the donor community.[8] The first phase of this Plan will take place between 1998 and 2002.[9] Its specific objectives include the creation of a database containing information and statistics on the practice of FC/FGM in Mali, the development and implementation of programs to prevent FC/FGM, and improved coordination between national-level organizations and international organizations working to eliminate the practice.[10]

Notes

1. *Constitution of the Republic of Mali* (1992), translated in G.H. Flanz (ed.), *Constitutions of the Countries of the World*, Dobbs Ferry, NY: Oceana Publications, 1997.
2. *Penal Code*, Law No. 99 AN-RM of Aug. 3, 1961.
3. Republic of Mali, *National Plan for the Eradication of Excision by 2007, Phase I: 1998–2002*, 1998, p. 5.
4. Ibid.
5. Office of the Senior Coordinator for International Women's Issues, Bureau of Global Affairs and the Office of Asylum Affairs, Bureau of Democracy, Human Rights and Labor, US Department of State, *Female Genital Mutilation (FGM) or Female Genital Cutting (FGC) in Mali*, 1999, p. 3
6. Ibid., p. 4.
7. Republic of Mali, *National Plan for the Eradication of Excision by 2007*, p. 3.
8. Ibid.
9. Ibid., p. 6.
10. Ibid., pp. 6–10.

Mauritania

Size (1,000 km^2): 1,026
Income (per capita GNP in US$): 440
Population (millions): 2
Number of women per 100 men: 102
Percentage of young people in the population (under 15 years): 45
Prevalence of FC/FGM: 25%
Type(s) of FC/FGM most commonly practiced: Types I and II
Ethnic groups that practice FC/FGM: Information not available.

International Treaties

- Children's Rights Convention (ratified 1991). Reservation asserting precedence of the beliefs and values of Islam over the mandates of the Convention.
- Banjul Charter (ratified 1986).

National Laws

Constitution

The Constitution of Mauritania[1] guarantees the equality of women and men before the law. The Preamble recognizes the "right to equality" and the "fundamental freedoms and rights of human beings." Article 1 provides for "equality before the law … without distinction as to … sex."

The Constitution guarantees the right to physical integrity. Article 13 protects the "inviolability of [the] person" of each citizen and provides that "[a]ll forms of moral or physical violence shall be proscribed."

Criminal law

No law specifically prohibits FC/FGM. General provisions related to assault may be applicable.

Provisions

Article 285 of the Penal Code provides penalties for any adult who intentionally wounds or strikes or amputates a member, or commits any other acts of violence or assault against an innocent party. This law would be enforceable against practitioners of FC/FGM, those who procure the services of practitioners of FC/FGM, and those who assist during the procedure. Penalties include imprisonment from ten days to two years, fines of 5,000 to 20,000 Ouguiya (approximately US$23–92), and retaliation.[2]

Enforcement of the law

There has been at least one arrest for FC/FGM, in May 1998, pursuant to Article 285 of the Penal Code. The case was never prosecuted.[3]

Other Measures: Laws, Regulations and Policies

A law amending the Family Code has been proposed, but the bill has been blocked at the parliamentary level.[4]

The Secretariat of Women's Affairs initiated discussions and seminars on the subject of FC/FGM in 1996 and 1997. However, no legislative proposals grew out of those activities.[5]

In 1996, the government produced a Guide to the Rights of Women in Mauritania, which was endorsed by religious leaders. It asserts that Islam does not require FC/FGM and that individuals should follow the advice of medical personnel and refrain from practicing FC/FGM.[6]

A civil court permitted a family member of a girl who had undergone FC/FGM to bring a suit. The case was dismissed after the plaintiff withdrew the complaint.[7]

Notes

1. *Constitution of the Islamic Republic of Mauritania* (1991), translated in A.P. Blaustein and G.H. Flanz (eds), *Constitutions of the Countries of the World*, Dobbs Ferry, NY: Oceana Publications, 1993.
2. Fatimata M'Baye, Association Mauritanienne des Droits de l'Homme, Questionnaire (July 26, 1998).
3. Ibid.

4. Ibid.
5. Ibid.
6. Bureau of Democracy, Human Rights and Labor, US Department of State, *Mauritania Country Report on Human Rights Practices for 1998* (last visited Aug. 16, 1999), <http://www.state.gov/www/global/human_rights/1998_hrp_report/>.
7. Fatimata M'Baye, Association Mauritanienne des Droits de l'Homme, Questionnaire (July 26, 1998).

The Netherlands

Size (1,000 km^2): 41

Income (per capita GNP in US$): 25,830

Population (millions): 16

Immigrant population: In 1997, there was a total of 56,534 immigrants from the following African countries where FGM is practiced: The Democratic Republic of Congo, Egypt, Ethiopia, Ghana, Kenya, Liberia, Nigeria, Sudan, Somalia and Tanzania. Of this total, 21,508 were women.[1]

International Treaties

- Women's Convention (ratified 1991).
- Children's Rights Convention (ratified 1995).
- Civil and Political Rights Covenant (ratified 1978).
- Economic, Social and Cultural Rights Covenant (ratified 1978).
- European Convention on Human Rights (ratified 1954).

National Laws

Constitution

The Constitution[2] guarantees the equality of women and men before the law. Article 1 of the Constitution declares that "[a]ll persons in the Netherlands shall be treated equally in equal circumstances. Discrimination on the grounds of ... race ... or sex or on any other grounds whatsoever shall not be permitted."

Article 11 guarantees the right to physical integrity, stating that "[e]veryone shall have the right to inviolability of his person, without prejudice to restrictions laid down by or pursuant to Act of Parliament."

The government's commitment to protecting health is recognized in the Constitution. Article 22(1) declares that "[t]he authorities shall take steps to promote the health of the population."

Religious freedom is balanced against governmental interests, as defined under law. Article 6(1) states that "[e]veryone shall have the right to manifest freely his religion or belief, either individually or in community with others, without prejudice to his responsibility under the law."

Criminal law

The Netherlands has enacted no law specifically criminalizing FC/FGM. The government has stated, however, that Articles 300–309 and Article 436 of the Penal Code[3] are applicable to FC/FGM.[4]

Provisions

Article 300 provides:

1. Physical abuse is punishable by a term of imprisonment of not more than two years or a fine of the fourth category.
2. Where serious bodily harm ensues as a result of the act, the offender is liable to a term of imprisonment of not more than four years or a fine of the fourth category.
3. Where death ensues as a result of the act, the offender is liable to a term of imprisonment of not more than six years or a fine of the fourth category.
4. Intentionally injuring a person's health is equivalent to physical abuse.
5. An attempt to commit the serious offense of physical abuse is not punishable.

Article 302 provides:

1. A person who intentionally inflicts serious bodily harm on another person is guilty of aggravated physical abuse and is liable to a term of imprisonment of not more than eight years or a fine of the fifth category.
2. Where death ensues as a result of the act, the offender is liable to a term of imprisonment of not more than ten years or a fine of the fifth category.

Punishments for these offenses are elevated in the case of "premeditation" (Arts 301, 303). In addition, they may be increased by one-third where "the offender commits the serious offense against ... his child" (Art. 304(1)).

Negligence or carelessness that results in death or serious bodily harm is punishable under Articles 307 and 308 of the Penal Code. Article 309 provides that where these offenses are committed "in any official or professional capacity," the term of imprisonment may be raised by one-third and the offender may be disqualified from practicing his or her profession.

Finally, Article 436 provides, in part:

1. A person who, without being licensed to practice a profession for which a license is required by law, practices that profession without necessity, is liable to a fine of the second category.
2. A person who is licensed to practice a profession for which a license is required by law and who, without necessity, exceeds the limits of his license, is liable to a fine of the second category.

Enforcement of the law

Information not available.

Child protection laws

Information not available.

Other Measures: Laws, Regulations and Policies

In 1993, the government issued an official statement condemning FC/FGM in all of its forms. It stated that FC/FGM "is viewed here as a form of repression, and as Dutch policy aims to combat the repression of women, it opposes all forms of female circumcision."[5] The government did not endorse a proposal to permit health professionals to perform "non-mutilating" forms of FC/FGM, such as the light incision or puncturing of the skin covering the clitoris.[6] In the government's view, such a policy would lead to confusion and would imply toleration of the practice of FC/FGM.[7]

The government stated that its policy "must be geared towards prevention, with judicial intervention as a last resort."[8] The primary strategy for preventing FC/FGM has been the use of information campaigns directed at immigrant groups, health professionals and other organizations and bodies that serve or work in collaboration with these groups.[9] These campaigns are carried out primarily by the Pharos Association, a semi-independent agency formed in 1993.[10]

Standards of Health Professionals

It is the position of the Dutch Association of Obstetricians and Gynaecologists (NVOG) that physicians should not participate in the practice of any form of FC/FGM.[11] The Dutch Association of Female Doctors (VNVA) and the Dutch Royal Association for the Furtherance of Medicine (KNMG) also oppose the involvement of health professionals in the practice of FC/FGM.[12]

Policies for Eliminating FC/FGM in Africa

In 1992, the Ministry for Development Cooperation issued a statement declaring its position that "the circumcision of women and young girls is unacceptable in any country and should be eradicated."[13] In 1994, the Ministry issued a policy memorandum stating that the Netherlands would advocate for the enactment of legal measures prohibiting FC/FGM in countries in which no applicable laws were in force.[14] Finally, the Dutch government provides support to women's organizations in Africa that are working to eliminate FC/FGM.[15]

Notes

1. Proceedings of the Expert Meeting on Female Genital Mutilation, Ghent, Belgium, November 5–7, 1998, p. 12 (figures were obtained from the National Offices of Statistics from each European member state).
2. *Constitution of the Netherlands* (1983) (last visited Aug. 18, 1999), <http://www.uni-wuerzburg.de/law/n100000_.html>.
3. L. Rayar and S. Wadsworth (trans.), *The Dutch Penal Code*, Universiteit Maastricht, American Series of Foreign Penal Codes, 1997, p. 202.
4. J. Smith, *Visions and Discussions on Genital Mutilation of Girls: An International Survey*, Amsterdam: Defence for Children International, 1995, p. 165.
5. Netherlands policy on the elimination of female genital mutilation (1993) (on file with the CRLP). See also Smith, *Visions and Discussions on Genital Mutilation of Girls*, p. 165.
6. Netherlands Policy on the elimination of female genital mutilation.
7. Ibid.
8. Ibid.
9. Ibid.
10. Ibid.
11. Smith, *Visions and Discussions on Genital Mutilation of Girls*, p. 166.
12. Ibid., p. 167.
13. Ibid., pp. 163–4.
14. Ibid.
15. Ibid., p. 166.

New Zealand

Size (1,000 km²): 271
Income (per capita GNP in US$): 15,830
Population (millions): 4
Immigrant population: According to a 1997 survey, there are approximately 3,040 women and girls in New Zealand from parts of Africa where FC/FGM is practiced, the majority of whom are from Somalia. New Zealand also has Egyptian, Ethiopian, Eritrean and Sudanese communities.[1]

International Treaties

- Women's Convention (ratified 1985).
- Children's Rights Convention (ratified 1993). New Zealand retains the right to distinguish in its law and practice between persons according to the nature of their authority to be in New Zealand.
- Civil and Political Rights Covenant (ratified 1978).
- Economic, Social and Cultural Rights Covenant (ratified 1978).

National Laws

Constitution

The 1990 Bill of Rights protects individual rights and freedoms.[2] While Parliament has the duty to uphold the Bill of Rights and refer to it as a guide,[3] it is empowered to override the Bill of Rights in legislation.[4]

The Bill of Rights guarantees the equality of women and men before the law. Section 19 ensures everyone's right to freedom from discrimination on the grounds of sex.[5]

The right to life and security of the person are protected under Title 1 of the Bill of Rights. In particular, Section 11 protects the right "to refuse to undergo any medical treatment."

In addition, the Bill of Rights protects the rights of minorities, with Section 20 providing that any "person who belongs to an ethnic, religious, or linguistic minority in New Zealand shall not be denied the right, in community with other members of that minority, to enjoy the culture, to profess and practice the religion, or to use the language, of that minority."

Criminal law

Provisions

An amendment to the Crimes Amendment Act on FC/FGM was passed in 1995 and went into effect on January 1, 1996.[6] The law states:

> 204 bis. Female Genital Mutilation[7]
>
> (2) Subject to subsection (3) of this section, every one is liable to imprisonment for a term not exceeding 7 years who performs, or causes to be performed, on any other person, any act involving female genital mutilation.
>
> (3) Nothing in subsection (2) of this section applies in respect of–
> (a) Any medical or surgical procedure (including a sexual reassignment procedure) that is performed on any person–
> (i) For the benefit of that person's physical or mental health; and
> (ii) By a medical practitioner:
> (b) Any medical or surgical procedure that is performed on any person–
> (i) While that person is in labour or immediately after that person gives birth; and
> (ii) For the benefit of that person's health or the health of the child; and
> (iii) By a medical practitioner or a registered midwife or a trainee health professional, or by any other person in any case where the case is urgent and no medical practitioner or registered midwife or trainee health professional is available.
>
> (4) In determining, for the purposes of subsection (3) of this section, whether or not any medical or surgical procedure is performed on any person for the benefit of that person's physical or mental health, no account shall be taken of the effect on that person of any belief on the part of that person or any other person that the procedure is necessary or desirable as, or as part of, a cultural, religious, or other custom or practice.
>
> (5) Nothing in subsection (3) of this section limits or affects any enactment or rule of law relating to consent to any medical or surgical procedure or treatment.
>
> (6) It is no defence to a charge under this section that the person on whom the act involving female genital mutilation was performed consented to that act, or that the person charged believed that such consent had been given.
>
> (7) No person shall be charged as a party to an offence committed upon her against this section.
>
> 204B. Further offences relating to female genital mutilation–
>
> (1) Every one is liable to imprisonment for a term not exceeding 7 years who, with intent that there be done, outside New Zealand, to or in relation to any child under the age of 17 years (being a child who is a New Zealand citizen or

is ordinarily resident in New Zealand), any act which, if done in New Zealand, would be an offence against section 204A of this Act,–

(a) Causes that child to be sent or taken out of New Zealand; or

(b) Makes any arrangements for the purposes of causing that child to be sent or taken out of New Zealand.

(2) Every one is liable to imprisonment for a term not exceeding 7 years who, in New Zealand, aids, incites, counsels, or procures the doing, outside New Zealand, in relation to any person who is a New Zealand citizen or is ordinarily resident in New Zealand, of any act which, if done in New Zealand, would be an offence against section 204A of this Act, whether or not the act is in fact done.

(3) Every one is liable to imprisonment for a term not exceeding 7 years who, in New Zealand, incites, counsels, procures, or induces any person who is a New Zealand citizen or is ordinarily resident in New Zealand –

(a) To submit, outside New Zealand, to any act which, if done in New Zealand, would be an offence against section 204A of this Act; or

(b) To acquiesce in the doing, outside New Zealand, on that person, of any such act; or

(c) To permit any such act to be done, outside New Zealand, on that person, – whether or not, in any case, the act is in fact done.

(4) It is no defence to a charge under subsection (2) or subsection (3) of this section that the person on whom the act was done consented to that act, or that the person charged believed that such consent had been given.

(5) No person shall be charged as a party to an offence committed in relation to her against subsection (2) or subsection (3) of this section.

Enforcement of the law

There have been no criminal investigations based on the FC/FGM law.[8]

Child protection laws

Under the Children, Young Persons, and Their Families Act 1989, a guiding principle for child protection authorities is that "children and young persons must be protected from harm, their rights upheld, and their welfare promoted" (Sect. 13(a)). In all cases, "the welfare and interests of the child or young person shall be the first and paramount consideration" (Sect. 6). While FC/FGM is not specifically addressed under this law, a child who is likely to undergo FC/FGM would meet the Act's definition of a child or young person "in need of care or protection" (Sect. 13(d)).[9] To date, there have been no interventions in cases of FC/FGM under the Act.[10]

The Children, Young Persons and Their Families Agency (CYPFA) is charged with overseeing interventions on behalf of children who are believed to be at risk of undergoing FC/FGM. An experienced social worker will be appointed to work with the family and monitor the child at risk. It is recommended that the social worker collaborate with someone known to the family, such as a health professional. The social worker should also coordinate with a community worker of the same ethnic/cultural group as the child at risk and with an interpreter. Agency guidelines emphasize the importance of handling the situation respectfully and with sensitivity.[11] Removal of the child from her immediate family may occur when she is in imminent danger of undergoing FC/FGM.[12] While it is not recommended that children who have already undergone FC/FGM be removed from their families, the CYPFA is obliged to contact the police because FC/FGM is a criminal offense.[13]

Other Measures: Laws, Regulations and Policies

A National FGM Education Programme has been established to prevent FC/FGM through "community education, support, and health promotion." The program is also intended to assist women and girls who are either at risk of undergoing FC/FGM or who have already undergone the procedure. The program's activities include: the development of national guidelines and protocols for obstetric care, including an FC/FGM clinic; the creation of guidelines for child protection strategies; the creation of educational resources for health care professionals, child protection professionals, and the media; the development of regional educational programs; and community education and support programs for relevant African immigrant communities.[14]

Standards of Health Professionals

While there are no medical ethics provisions pertaining to FC/FGM, a set of guidelines has been developed by the National FGM Education Programme in collaboration with the New Zealand College of Obstetricians and Gynaecologists for antenatal, delivery and postnatal care of women who have undergone FC/FGM. According to the guidelines, midwives and doctors should have a sound knowledge of the physiological aspects of FC/FGM, the obstetric, gynecological and rehabilitative clinical care of women who have undergone FC/FGM, and the psychological and cultural issues surrounding the practice.[15]

Policies for Eliminating FC/FGM in Africa

Because most of New Zealand's bilateral development assistance is directed toward the South Pacific and Asia regions, it has not directly addressed the practice of FC/FGM in Africa.[16] It has, however, supported FC/FGM programs indirectly, through such multilateral channels as the UNFPA.[17]

Notes

1. Nikki Denholm, FGM Healthcare Survey, FGM Programme, Auckland Healthcare, 1997.
2. *Bill of Rights Act 1990*, sect. 3 (last visited May 27, 1999), <http://www.uni-wuerzburg.de/law/nz01000_.html>.
3. Charles Alan Wright, *A Bill of Rights: Does It Matter?*, 32 Tex. Int'l LJ 381, 390 (1997).
4. Ibid., note 25, at 382 (quoting *Ministry of Transport* v. *Noort* [1992] 3 NZLR 260, 286. (Hardie Boys, J.).
5. See also *Human Rights Act 1993*, sect. 21 (last visited Aug. 24, 1999), <http://www.knowledge-basket.co.nz/gpprint/acts.html>.
6. Crimes Act Amendment 1995 049.
7. Section 1 provides the following definitions for terms used in the law:

   "Female genital mutilation" means the excision, infibulation, or mutilation of the whole or part of the labia majora, labia minora, or clitoris of any person;

   "Registered midwife" means a person who is registered as a midwife under the Nurses Act 1977;

   "Sexual reassignment procedure" means any surgical procedure that is performed for the purposes of altering (whether wholly or partly) the genital appearance of a person to the genital appearance of a person of the opposite sex;

   "Trainee health professional" means any person who is receiving training or gaining experience under the supervision of–

   (a) A medical practitioner for the purpose of gaining registration as a medical practitioner; or

   (b) A registered midwife for the purpose of gaining registration as a registered midwife.
8. Nikki Denholm, New Zealand FGM Education Programme, Questionnaire (updated Spring 1998).
9. See also N. Denholm and S. Sligo, *Female Genital Mutilation and Child Protection in New Zealand: Resource Kit*, FGM Education Programme and Children, Young Persons and Their Families Agency (CYPFA), 1998, p. 18.
10. Electronic mail message sent by Nikki Denholm, Director, National FGM Education Programme, to Laura Katzive, Staff Attorney, CRLP, Aug. 26, 1999.
11. Denholm and Sligo, *Female Genital Mutilation and Child Protection in New Zealand: Resource Kit*, p. 5.
12. Ibid., p. 11.
13. Ibid., pp. 11–12.
14. New Zealand National FGM Programme (policy document), p. 1, supplied by Nikki Denholm, Director, National FGM Education Programme.

15. Guidelines for Antenatal, Delivery and Postnatal Care of Genitally Mutilated Women, FGM Education Programme, supplied by Nikki Denholm, Director, National FGM Education Programme.
16. Ministry of Foreign Affairs and Trade, New Zealand Official Development Assistance (last visited Aug. 25, 1999), <http://www.mft.govt.nz/nzoda/nzoda.html>.
17. Population Action International (PAI), *Paying Their Fair Share? Donor Countries and International Population Assistance*, Washington, DC: PAI, 1998, p. 58.

Niger

Size (1,000 km^2): 1,267
Income (per capita GNP in US$): 200
Population (millions): 10
Number of women per 100 men: 102
Percentage of young people in the population (under 15 years): 48
Prevalence of FC/FGM: 20%
Type(s) of FC/FGM most commonly practiced: Type II
Ethnic groups that practice FC/FGM: Practiced by the Arabes (Shuwa), Gourmanche, Kourtey, Peulh, Songhai and Wogo.

International Treaties

- Women's Convention (ratified 1999).
- Children's Rights Convention (ratified 1990).
- Civil and Political Rights Covenant (ratified 1986).
- Economic, Social and Cultural Rights Covenant (ratified 1986).
- Banjul Charter (ratified 1986).
- African Charter (ratified 1996).

National Laws

Constitution

The Constitution[1] guarantees the equality of women and men before the law. Article 8 states that "[e]quality is assured everyone under the law without distinction [of] sex."

The right to life and physical integrity is protected under the Constitution. Article 10 states that "[e]ach human being is sacred. The State has an absolute obligation to respect and protect the individual. The full nurturing of each individual is guaranteed." Article 11 provides "[e]ach person has the right to life, health, liberty, security, physical and mental well being, education, and instruction according to conditions established by law."

Freedom of conscience is protected, subject to the rights of others. Article 14 provides that "[e]ach person has the right to full ... spiritual development, *as long as such development does not violate the right[s] of others or infringe on the constitutional or legal order* [emphasis added]."

Criminal law

The Penal Code[2] contains no provisions specifically prohibiting FC/FGM. However, provisions under the heading "Intentional Strikes and Wounds" may be applicable.

Provisions

Article 222 provides:

> Any person who intentionally wounds or strikes, or commits any other act of violence or assault, shall be punished by imprisonment from three months to two years and by a fine of 10,000 to 100,000 francs [approximately US$16–160], or by either punishment....
>
> If the acts described in the preceding paragraph were committed with premeditation or resulted in a mutilation, amputation, or privation of the use of a member, blindness, loss of an eye or any other permanent infirmities, imprisonment from one to eight years shall be imposed....
>
> If the strikes or wounds carried out intentionally result in unintended death, the perpetrator shall be punished by imprisonment from 10 to 20 years.

Penalties for all of the acts described above are increased when committed with "premeditation, lying in wait, or with use of a weapon." Article 226 provides that when the acts described in Article 222 resulting in mutilation are committed "upon the person of a child of thirteen years or younger," the term of imprisonment shall be raised by two to ten years.

Enforcement of law

Information not available.

Other Measures: Laws, Regulations and Policies

In March 1997, the Ministry of Health announced the launch of its Program of Action for the Elimination of All Forms of Female Genital Mutilation, which will be carried out in cooperation with the World Health Organization – Africa Region. The announcement noted the Ministry's firm support for "all initiatives aimed at protecting and promoting the rights of girls and women, including the right to preserve their physical integrity." The Ministry also expressed its commitment to supporting "all efforts aimed at permitting [girls and women] to attain the highest level of physical, mental, and social well-being."[3]

In July 1990, the Ministry of Social Affairs and the Promotion of Women issued an Order creating a Niger Committee to Fight Harmful Traditional Practices (CONILPRAT). The Committee's functions included: taking a census of the harmful traditional practices affecting maternal and child health; raising public awareness of the medical, social and economic consequences for maternal and child health of some of these practices; researching strategies for promoting maternal and child health; and disseminating all information, documents and research pertaining to harmful traditional practices.[4] In 1993, in recognition of the fact that certain practices are positive and should be promoted, the Committee changed its name to the Niger Committee on Traditional Practices (CONIPRAT).[5] In 1993, by governmental decree, CONIPRAT was given the status of an NGO. It is the national chapter of the IAC, and continues to work closely with the Ministry of Public Health and the Ministry of Social Development, Population and Promotion of Women.[6]

Notes

1. *Constitution of the Republic of Niger* (1996), translated in G.H. Flanz (ed.), *Constitutions of the Countries of the World*, Dobbs Ferry, NY: Oceana Publications, 1997.
2. Penal Code of the Republic of Niger (1961).
3. Allocution du Ministre de la Santé Publique, Lancement du Plan d'Action pour Accelerer l'Elimination des Mutilations Genitales Feminines, Mar. 17, 1997 (on file with the CRLP and RAINB♀).
4. Order No. 09/MAS/PF of July 8, 1990 of the Ministry of Social Affairs and the Promotion of Women creating a Niger Committee to Fight Harmful Traditional Practices, summarized in R. Boland and J. Stepans (eds), *Annual Review of Population Law*, Vol. XVII, 1990, p. 176.
5. Comité Nigerien sur les Pratiques Traditionnelles (CONIPRAT), *Plan d'Action 1997–1999*, 1996, p. 4.
6. Ibid., p. 5.

Nigeria

Size (1,000 km^2): 924
Income (per capita GNP in US$): 280
Population (millions): 118
Number of women per 100 men: 102
Percentage of young people in the population (under 15 years): 47
Prevalence of FC/FGM: 60%
Type(s) of FC/FGM most commonly practiced: Types I and II
Ethnic groups that practice FC/FGM: FGM is widely practiced among the three major tribes: the Hausa, Ibo and Yoruba.

International Treaties

- Women's Convention (ratified 1985).
- Children's Rights Convention (ratified 1991).
- Civil and Political Rights Covenant (ratified 1993).
- Economic, Social and Cultural Rights Covenant (ratified 1993).
- Banjul Charter (ratified 1983).

National Laws

Constitution

The Constitution of Nigeria[1] guarantees the equality of women and men before the law. Section 17(2)(a) provides that "every citizen shall have equality of rights, obligations and opportunities before the law." Section 42(1) prohibits the enactment of discriminatory laws and other acts of discrimination by the government.

The Constitution is protective of the rights to life and physical integrity. Section 17(2)(b) provides that "the sanctity of the human person shall be recognized and human dignity shall be maintained and enhanced." The rights to life, dignity of one's person and personal liberty are protected in Sections 33, 34 and 35, respectively.

The protection of health is a government priority. Section 17(3)(d) provides that "the State shall direct its policy toward ensuring that ... there are adequate medical and health facilities for all persons."

Religious rights must be balanced against individual protections and other state interests under the Constitution. Section 38 guarantees "freedom of thought, conscience and religion" and freedom "to manifest and propagate ... religion or belief in worship, teaching, practice and observance." Section 45, however, declares that this protection is among those that may not invalidate "any law that is reasonably justifiable in a democratic society (a) in the interest of ... public safety, public order, ... or public health; or (b) for the purpose of protecting the rights and freedom of other persons."

Criminal law

Provisions

There is currently no national law specifically prohibiting FC/FGM in Nigeria. FC/FGM could be prohibited under provisions of both the Penal Code, the body of criminal law in force in the northern states of Nigeria, and the Criminal Code, which is applicable in the southern states.

Penal Code

Provisions of the Penal Code[2] falling under the heading "Hurt" could theoretically apply to FC/FGM. Sections 240 and 241 state:

> 240. Whoever causes bodily pain, disease or infirmity to a person is said to cause hurt.
>
> 241. The following kinds of hurt only are designated as grievous– ...
> (c) deprivation of any member or joint;
> (d) destruction or permanent impairing of the powers of any member or joint;...
> (g) any hurt which endangers life or which causes the sufferer to be during the space of twenty days in severe bodily pain or unable to follow his ordinary pursuits.

If death results from an act intended to cause hurt or grievous hurt, the offender may be sentenced to imprisonment for up to 14 years and/or may be fined (Sect. 225).

Criminal Code

The Criminal Code[3] also has provisions that are potentially applicable to FC/FGM. Sections 335, 338 and 343 state:

335. Any person who unlawfully does grievous harm to another is guilty of a felony, and is liable to imprisonment for seven years.

338. Any person who–
(1) unlawfully wounds another; ...
is guilty of a felony, and is liable to imprisonment for three years.

343. Any person who in a manner so rash or negligent as to endanger human life or to be likely to cause harm to any other person– ...
(e) gives medical or surgical treatment to any person whom he has undertaken to treat; ...
is guilty of a misdemeanour, and is liable to imprisonment for one year.

Enforcement of the law

There have been no arrests for FC/FGM on the basis of the provisions discussed above.[4]

Other Measures: Laws, Regulations and Policies

The government drafted a "Children's Decree" in 1993 and revised it in 1996.[5] The Children's Decree, which would incorporate into Nigerian law the Convention on the Rights of the Child, the Organization of African Unity Charter on the Rights and Welfare of the Child, and the principles adopted at the Fourth World Conference on Women in Beijing, would make FC/FGM an offense.[6] This instrument has not yet been adopted.

The Federal Ministry of Health has drafted a national policy on the elimination of FC/FGM. The policy's stated goal is "to eliminate the practice of Female Genital Mutilation in Nigeria in order to improve the health and quality of life of girls and women."[7] Its specific objectives are: to increase awareness of the dangers of FC/FGM, particularly among family decision-makers and FC/FGM providers; to increase the number of health personnel who undergo training on prevention and treatment of FC/FGM; and to provide educational programs directed at health workers, women and men's groups, adolescents and youth, traditional rulers, religious and other community leaders, and traditional birth attendants. The policy also calls for the monitoring of intervention programs, the integration of units on FC/FGM into the school curriculums at every level, the promotion of the enactment of laws prohibiting FC/FGM and the promotion of inter-sectoral collaboration and networking.[8]

In November 1999, Edo State, one of Nigeria's thirty-six states, adopted a state-level law prohibiting FC/FGM.[9]

Notes

1. Nigeria Web, *Constitution of the Federal Republic of Nigeria 1999*, (last visited June 8, 1999) <http://www.odili.net/republic/constitution/constitution.html>.
2. Penal Code Act (Laws of Northern Nigeria 1963) (Nig.), Vol. III, ch. 89.
3. Criminal Code Act (Laws of the Federation 1990) (Nig.), Vol. V, ch. 77.
4. Theresa U. Akumadu, Women's Centre for Peace and Development, Questionnaire (updated Spring 1998).
5. Ibid.
6. Ibid.
7. Dept of Primary Health Care and Disease Control, Fed. Ministry of Health, Abuja, Draft National Policy on the Elimination of Female Genital Mutilation (May 1998), p. 5.
8. Ibid., *passim*.
9. Inter-African Committee on Traditional Practices Affecting the Health of Women and Children (IAC), "FGM Banned in Edo State, Nigeria," *Newsletter of the IAC*, No. 26, January 2000, p. 14.

Norway

Size (1,000 km²): 324

Income (per capita GNP in US$): 36,100

Population (millions): 4

Immigrant population: In 1995, there were 3,700 immigrants from Somalia, 1,700 of whom were women. In 1995, the total immigrant population was 160,800, of whom 80,300 were women.

International Treaties

- Women's Convention (ratified 1981).
- Children's Rights Convention (ratified 1991).
- Civil and Political Rights Covenant (ratified 1972).
- Economic, Social and Cultural Rights Covenant (ratified 1972).
- European Convention on Human Rights (ratified 1952).

National Laws

Constitution

The Constitution provides that "[i]t is the responsibility of the authorities of the State to respect and ensure human rights."[1]

Criminal law

In 1995, Norway enacted a law specifically criminalizing FC/FGM.

Provisions

Section 1.

Any person who intentionally performs an intervention on a woman's sexual organs, thereby damaging those organs or causing them to undergo permanent changes, shall be convicted of sexual mutilation. The penalty imposed shall be imprisonment for a maximum period of three years, or six years if the intervention results in disease or an incapacity to work of more than two weeks' duration or if the intervention is the cause of an incurable deformation, defect, or injury, and imprisonment for a maximum period of eight years if the intervention results in death or considerable damage to the body or health of the person concerned. Assisting in such activities shall be punishable in the same manner.

The reconstruction of a sexual mutilation shall be punished in the manner described in the first paragraph.

Consent shall not be a ground for exemption from sanctions.[2]

Enforcement of the law

To date, there have been no prosecutions under this new law.[3]

Child protection laws

The 1992 Child Welfare Services Act is intended to ensure the provision of necessary care and assistance to "children and young people who live in conditions which may be detrimental to their health and development." More generally, the Act is intended to "help ensure that children and young people are brought up in a secure environment."[4] The Child Welfare Service Act makes no specific reference to FC/FGM. However, given the serious and irreparable damage caused by FC/FGM and the fact that the practice is prohibited in Norway, the Child Welfare Services could potentially take measures to prevent a child from undergoing FC/FGM.[5] All actions taken by the Child Welfare Services follow a full assessment of the situation of the child in question.[6]

Other Measures: Laws, Regulations and Policies

The Health Department has provided funding for NGO-sponsored education and outreach programs.[7]

Standards of Health Professionals

There are no medical ethics provisions or guidelines for health professionals that pertain directly to FC/FGM.[8]

Policies for Eliminating FC/FGM in Africa

Information not available.

Notes

1. *Constitution of the Kingdom of Norway* (1995), art. 110c (last visited Nov. 5, 1999), <http://odin.dep.no/html/nofovalt/depter/ud/nornytt/uda-121.html>.
2. Law No. 74 of December 15, 1995 prohibiting female genital mutilation (Norsk Lovtidend, Part 1, 9 January 1996, No. 25, pp. 1619–20), translated in *International Digest of Health Legislation*, Vol. 47, No. 2, 1996, p. 173.
3. Agnete Strøm, Women's Front of Norway, Questionnaire (July 9, 1998).
4. Act no. 100 of July 17, 1992 on Child Welfare Services (as amended June 1993), sect. 1–1, Ministry of Children and Family Affairs, 1993, Norway.
5. Letter to Laura Katzive, CRLP Staff Attorney, from Tone G. Smith, Deputy Director General, and Tone Furuhovde, Senior Executive Officer, Royal Ministry of Children and Family Affairs, Aug. 3, 1999 (ref. no. 99/02903 K TFU) (on file with CRLP).
6. Ibid.
7. Agnete Strøm, Women's Front of Norway, Questionnaire (July 9, 1998).
8. Ibid.

Senegal

Size (1,000 km²): 197
Income (per capita GNP in US$): 540
Population (millions): 9
Number of women per 100 men: 100
Percentage of young people in the population (under 15 years): 45
Prevalence of FC/FGM: 20%
Type(s) of FC/FGM most commonly practiced: Type II
Ethnic groups that practice FC/FGM: Information not available.

International Treaties

- Women's Convention (ratified 1985).
- Children's Rights Convention (ratified 1990).
- Civil and Political Rights Covenant (ratified 1978).
- Economic, Social and Cultural Rights Covenant (ratified 1978).
- Banjul Charter (ratified 1982).
- African Charter (ratified 1998).

National Laws

Constitution

The Constitution of the Republic of Senegal[1] guarantees the equality of women and men before the law. Article 1 provides that "[the Republic of Senegal] shall ensure equality before the law for all citizens, without distinction as to … sex." Article 7 provides that "[a]ll human beings shall be equal before the law. Men and women shall be equal in law."

The Constitution also protects the rights to life and physical integrity. Article 6 states that "[t]he person is sacred. The state shall have the obligation to respect it and to protect it.... Everyone has the right to life and to physical integrity under the conditions defined by law."

The rights of the child receive special protection under the Constitution. Article 14 states that "[t]he state and the public collectivities shall have the social duty to watch over the physical and moral well-being of the family."

Article 19 guarantees freedom of conscience and the freedom to practice religion, "subject to the respect for public order."

Criminal law

In January 1999, Senegal amended its Penal Code to prohibit FC/FGM.[2]

Provisions

Article 299 bis of the amended Penal Code provides:

> Any person who violates or attempts to violate the integrity of the genital organs of a female person by total or partial ablation of one or several of the organ's parts, by infibulation, by desensitization or by any other means shall be punished by imprisonment from six months to five years.
>
> The maximum penalty shall be imposed when these sexual mutilations are performed or abetted by a member of the medical or paramedical corps.
>
> When they result in death, the punishment shall be hard labor for life.
>
> Any person who, through gifts, promises, influences, threats, intimidation, or abuse of authority or of power, provokes these sexual mutilations or gives instructions for their commission shall be subject to the same punishments.[3]

Enforcement of the law

The first arrests under the new law were made in early August 1999. The father of a five-year-old girl reported to the police that the girl's mother and grandmother had caused the girl to undergo FC/FGM, and the two women were arrested. At the time of the arrest, the police had not located the woman who performed the FC/FGM.[4]

Other Measures: Laws, Regulations and Policies

President Abdou Diouf has been a vocal supporter of efforts to stop FC/FGM. In November 1997 he made the following statement:

> We must fight relentlessly against excision. The promulgation of a specific law might be necessary in order to show government commitment. But, and above all, governments and NGOs should join efforts to convince the populations of the danger this practice represents to the health of women and induce attitudinal changes.... Every village should initiate debates on excision in order to make

everybody realize that the time has come to ban such traditional practices forever.[5]

In March 1997, the Ministry of Health of Senegal launched a National Reproductive Health Program, which contains a Sub-Program on Female Genital Mutilations and Violence against Women, Adolescents and Girls. The general objectives of the program are to "support the struggle to abolish FC/FGM and other forms of violence against women, girls and adolescents in order to protect their reproductive health, promote respect for their fundamental rights and improve their social and economic status." The specific objectives of the program, as they relate to FC/FGM, are to reduce the practice by 50 per cent by the year 2001 and eventually to eliminate it altogether. The program also calls for the prevention of violence and the provision of care for women, adolescents and girls who are subjected to it.[6]

Strategies of the Sub-Program include: adopting political and legislative measures that would advance efforts to stop FC/FGM and other forms of violence; reinforcing the institutional capacity of the bodies working to eliminate FC/FGM; developing multimedia sensitization, education and information programs; and developing research and documentation.[7]

Women have organized at the local level to stop the practice of FC/FGM. At least fourteen villages, home to about 13,000 women, have banned FC/FGM.[8]

Notes

1. *Constitution of the Republic of Senegal* (1991), translated in A.P. Blaustein and G.H. Flanz (eds), *Constitutions of the Countries of the World*, Dobbs Ferry, NY: Oceana Publications, 1998.
2. A.D. Soumare, "Senegal has Law against Female Genital Mutilation," *Panafrican News Agency*, February 1999.
3. Republic of Senegal, Proposed Law Modifying Certain Provisions of the Penal Code (adopted January 1999).
4. "Premieres Arrestations pour Excision au Senegal," *Agence France Presse*, August 5, 1999.
5. Statement before the 33rd Congress of the International Federation of Human Rights, Nov. 20, 1997, Dakar, translated in Canadian International Development Agency (CIDA), *Support by CIDA/Africa and Middle East Branch for Activities Related to the Eradication of Female Genital Mutilation (FGM)*, 1999, pp. 5–6.
6. Ministry of Health, Programme National en Santé de la Reproduction, Sous-programme sur les Mutilations Génitales Féminines et les Violences à l'Encontre des Femmes, des Adolescentes et de Petites Filles, 1997, p. 6.
7. Ibid., pp. 7–9.
8. El Hadj Youga Ndiaye, "Human Rights–Senegal: Rural Women Ban Genital Mutilation," *Inter Press Service*, March 1998.

Sierra Leone

Size (1,000 km^2): 72
Income (per capita GNP in US$): 160
Population (millions): 5
Number of women per 100 men: 103
Percentage of young people in the population (under 15 years): 45
Prevalence of FC/FGM: 90%
Type(s) of FC/FGM most commonly practiced: Type II
Ethnic groups that practice FC/FGM: All Christian and Muslim ethnic groups practice FGM except for the Krios. Only types I and II are performed as part of the initiation rituals into the Bundo and Sande secret societies.

International Treaties

- Women's Convention (ratified 1998).
- Children's Rights Convention (ratified 1990).
- Civil and Political Rights Covenant (ratified 1996).
- Economic, Social and Cultural Rights Covenant (ratified 1996).
- Banjul Charter (ratified 1983).

National Laws

Constitution

Article 6(2) of the Constitution[1] calls upon the state to "discourage discrimination on the grounds of ... sex" and Article 15 guarantees "fundamental human rights and freedoms" without regard to sex. Article 27(1) prohibits the passage of laws or other governmental actions that discriminate on the basis of sex. However, discrimination is not prohibited in matters related to adoption, marriage, divorce, burial, inheritance, or other matters of personal law (Art. 27(4)(d)) and in the application of customary law (Art. 27(4)(e)).

Article 15(a and c) guarantees the rights to "life, liberty, security of the person" and respect for privacy. Article 8(2)(b) provides for state recognition, protection and enhancement of "the sanctity of the human person and human dignity." Article 8(3)(d) also calls upon the state to provide "adequate medical and health facilities for all persons" to the extent permitted by state resources.

Children are afforded special protections under the Constitution. Article Article 8(3)(f) provides that "the care and welfare of the ... young ...shall be actively promoted and safeguarded."

Criminal law

Sierra Leone has no law specifically prohibiting FC/FGM. However, general criminal law provisions may theoretically be applicable.

Provisions

The Ordinance on Prevention of Cruelty to Children provides that any person over the age of 16 years, who has the "custody, charge, or care of any child" and who "exposes the child or causes or procures the child to be exposed, in a manner likely to cause such child unnecessary suffering or injury to his health (including...loss of...organ of the body...)," is guilty of a misdemeanor, and shall be liable:

> (a) on conviction before the Supreme Court to a fine not exceeding one hundred pounds, or alternatively, or in default of payment of such fine, or in addition thereto, to imprisonment, with or without hard labour, for any period not exceeding two years; and
> (b) on summary conviction to a fine not exceeding twenty five pounds [approximately one US cent], or alternatively, or in default of payment of such fine, or in addition thereto, to imprisonment, with or without hard labour, for any period not exceeding six months.[2]

Enforcement of the law

According to news reports, FC/FGM is not considered a crime in Sierra Leone if the woman who undergoes the procedure has given her consent.[3]

Other Measures: Laws, Regulations and Policies

Information not available.

Notes

1. *Constitution of Sierra Leone* (1991), reprinted in A.P. Blaustein and G.H. Flanz (eds), *Constitutions of the Countries of the World.*: Dobbs Ferry, NY: Oceana Publications, 1992.
2. The Laws of Sierre Leone, Prevention of Cruelty to Children, Cap. 31, Part I, art. 4(1)(a) and (b) (1960).
3. R. MacJohnson, "Supporters of Female Excision Fight Back in Sierra Leone," *Agence France Presse*, Aug. 30, 1996.

Somalia

Size (1,000 km²): 637.66

Income (per capita GNP in US$): Estimated to be low income (US$765 or less).

Population (millions): 10.7

Number of women per 100 men: 102

Percentage of young people in the population (under 15 years): 47

Prevalence of FC/FGM: 98%

Type(s) of FC/FGM most commonly practiced: Type III

Ethnic groups that practice FC/FGM: Almost universally practiced.

International Treaties

- Civil and Political Rights Covenant (ratified 1990).
- Economic, Social and Cultural Rights Covenant (ratified 1990).
- Banjul Charter (ratified 1985).

National Laws

Since 1991, when former President Mohamed Siad Barre fled the country, Somalia has had no central government.[1] The information contained in this report refers to the Somali Democratic Republic prior to 1991.

Constitution

The Constitution[2] guarantees the equality of women and men before the law. Article 6 provides that "[a]ll citizens regardless of sex … shall be entitled to equal rights and duties before the law." In addition, Article 20 guarantees that "[e]very citizen shall be entitled to participate fully in the political, economic, social and cultural activities in accordance with the constitution and laws."

The Constitution is protective of the rights to life and physical integrity. Article 25(1) guarantees "the right to life and personal security." Article 26(1) further provides that "[e]very person shall have the right to personal integrity."

Article 55 commits the state to fulfilling a "policy of general health care." To that end, the government shall encourage "general hygiene" and "free medical treatment."

Special protections are provided for family and child welfare. Article 56 provides that the state "shall protect the family and shall assist the mother and child."

The Constitution provides for state intervention in the practice of culture. Article 51(1) provides that "[t]he state shall promote the progressive culture of the Somali people, while benefiting from the international culture of human society." Article 52 provides that "[t]he state shall preserve the good customs, and shall liberate society from outdated customs."

Criminal law

The Somali Democratic Republic has no law specifically prohibiting FC/FGM. However, some provisions of the Penal Code[3] of the former government may theoretically be applicable to FC/FGM.

Provisions

According to Article 440(1), any person who causes "hurt" to another resulting in physical or mental illness shall be punished with imprisonment from three months to three years. "Grievous" hurt is punishable with imprisonment from three to seven years. The hurt is considered "grievous" under the following conditions:

(a) where the act results in an illness which endangers the life of the person injured, or an illness or incapacity which prevents him from attending to his ordinary occupation for a period exceeding forty days;
(b) where the act produces a permanent weakening of a sense or organ;
(c) where the party injured is a pregnant woman and the act results in the acceleration of the birth. [Art. 440(2)]

"Very grievous" hurt is punishable with imprisonment of from six to twelve years. The hurt is considered "very grievous" when the act results in:

(a) an illness certainly or probably incurable;
(b) the loss of a sense;

(c) the loss of a limb, or a mutilation which renders the limb useless, or the loss of the use of an organ or the capacity to procreate … ;
(e) the miscarriage of the person injured. [Art. 440(3)]

Enforcement of the law

The Penal Code is not enforced in cases of FC/FGM. There is currently no functioning national judicial branch of government. Regional courts apply a combination of traditional and customary law, Islamic law and the Penal Code of the former government.[4]

Other Measures: Laws, Regulations and Policies

In June 1988, the government endorsed a campaign to stop the practice of FC/FGM in all of its forms. Concrete efforts to pursue that agenda were interrupted in 1991, when the national government fell into disarray.[5]

Notes

1. Bureau of Democracy, Human Rights and Labor, US Dept of State, *Somalia Country Report on Human Rights Practices for 1998* (last visited Aug. 29, 1999), <http://www.state.gov/www/global/human_rights/1998_hrp_report/>.
2. Constitution of the Somali Democratic Republic (1979), reprinted in A.P. Blaustein and G.H. Flanz (eds), *Constitutions of the Countries of the World*, Dobbs Ferry, NY: Oceana Publications, 1981.
3. M.R. Ganzglass, *Penal Code of the Somali Democratic Republic*, New Brunswick, NJ: Rutgers University Press, 1971, p. 491.
4. Bureau of Democracy, Human Rights and Labor, *Somalia Country Report on Human Rights Practices for 1998*.
5. J. Smith, *Visions and Discussions on Genital Mutilation of Girls: An International Survey*, Amsterdam: Defence of Children International, 1995, p. 128.

Sudan

Size (1,000 km^2): 2,506
Income (per capita GNP in US$): 290
Population (millions): 28
Number of women per 100 men: 99
Percentage of young people in the population (under 15 years): 44
Prevalence of FC/FGM: 89%
Type(s) of FC/FGM most commonly practiced: Types III (82%), I (15%) and II (3%) [in the North]
Ethnic groups that practice FC/FGM: Information not available.

International Treaties

- Children's Rights Convention (ratified 1990).
- Civil and Political Rights Covenant (ratified 1986).
- Economic, Social and Cultural Rights Covenant (ratified 1986).
- Banjul Charter (ratified 1986).

National Laws

Constitution

The Constitution[1] guarantees the equality of women and men before the law. Article 21 provides that "[a]ll people are equal before the courts of law. Sudanese are equal in rights and duties as regards to functions of public life; and there shall be no discrimination only by reason of … sex." In addition, among the Constitution's "Directive Principles" is the provision in Article 15 that "[t]he State shall emancipate women from injustice in all aspects and pursuits of life and encourage the role thereof in family and public life."

The Constitution protects the right to life and physical integrity. Article 20 guarantees "the right to life, freedom, safety of person and dignity of honour save by right in accordance with the law."

The rights of the family and children are given additional protections. In a "Directive Principle," Article 14, the Constitution declares that "[t]he State shall care for children and youth and protect them against … physical and spiritual neglect." In another Directive Principle, Article 15, the Constitution proclaims that the "State shall care for the institution of the family, facilitate marriage and adopt policies to purvey progeny, child upbringing, pregnant women and mothers."

Cultural and religious practices must conform to constitutional protections of individual rights. Article 24 provides that "[e]very human being shall have the right of freedom of conscience and religious creed, and he shall have the right to … manifest the same by way of worship, education, practice or performance of rites or ceremonies." This protection is qualified by Article 24's guarantee that "no one shall be coerced to adopt such faith, as he does not believe in, nor to practice rites or services he does not voluntarily consent to." Article 27 guarantees "every community or group of citizens the right to preserve their particular culture … and rear children freely within the framework of their particularity, and the same shall not by coercion be effaced."

Criminal law

From 1946 until 1983, the Penal Code explicitly prohibited infibulation, the most severe form of FC/FGM. The offense was punishable with imprisonment for a maximum of five years and/or a fine.[2] Permitted, however, was the removal of the "free and projecting part of the clitoris."[3] The law, initially enacted under British colonial rule, was ratified again in 1957, following Sudan's independence from Great Britain.[4] However, this provision was apparently repealed with the promulgation of the 1983 Penal Code, which included no provision on infibulation.[5] The 1991 Penal Code contains no provisions explicitly prohibiting FC/FGM.

Provisions

There are currently no Penal Code provisions that explicitly prohibit FC/FGM. The definition of "injury" in Article 138 of the Penal Code, however, is potentially applicable to FC/FGM. Article 138(1) provides:

> One who causes the loss of a body part, or the loss of a mental function or sense or organ or limb of a person, or causes a cut or excessive blood flow to a person's body has caused injury.

Penalties include fines and/or prison sentences ranging from a maximum of six months to a maximum of five years, depending upon the degree of premeditation on the part of the offender (Arts 139–41).

Enforcement of the law

Some FC/FGM practitioners have reportedly been placed under arrest.[6] Further information on the legal bases of these arrests and the penalties imposed, if any, is unavailable.

Other Measures: Laws, Regulations and Policies

Government health authorities have sanctioned traditional birth attendants and village midwives who participate in FC/FGM. Offenders have had their midwifery kits confiscated and been placed under close supervision.[7]

In 1984, the Minister of the Interior and Social Welfare established, by resolution, the Organization for Eradication of Traditional Harmful Practices Affecting the Health of Women and Children (ETHP). The ETHP succeeded the Sudanese National Committee for the Eradication of Female Circumcision, founded in 1981 by a decree of the same ministry. Concurrently with non-governmental organizations, the ETHP conducts workshops, seminars, courses and discussions on FC/FGM, targeting key groups, such as midwives.[8]

Notes

1. *Constitution of the Republic of the Sudan* (1998), translated in G.H. Flanz (ed.), *Constitutions of the Countries of the World* , Dobbs Ferry, NY: Oceana Publications, 1999.
2. Penal Code 1974 (1974 Act No. 64), art. 284A(1), in 9 Laws of the Sudan 1974–5 (revised up to Dec. 31, 1981).
3. Ibid.
4. J. Smith, *Visions and Discussions on Genital Mutilation of Girls: An International Survey*, Amsterdam: Defence of Children International, 1995, p. 131.
5. Office of the Senior Coordinator for International Women's Issues, Bureau of Global Affairs and the Office of Asylum Affairs, Bureau of Democracy, Human Rights and Labor, US Department of State, *Female Genital Mutilation (FGM) or Female Genital Cutting (FGC) in Sudan*, 1999, p. 4.
6. Inter-African Committee on Traditional Practices Affecting the Health of Women and Children (IAC), "Sudan: Turning Point in the Sensitization Campaign," *Newsletter of the IAC*, No. 19, June 1996, p. 8.
7. Ibid.
8. Office of the Senior Coordinator for International Women's Issues, *Female Genital Mutilation (FGM) or Female Genital Cutting (FGC) in Sudan*, p. 2.

Sweden

Size (1,000 km^2): 450

Income (per capita GNP in US$): 26,210

Population (millions): 9

Immigrant population: In 1997, there were 31,798 immigrants from the following African countries where FGM is practiced: Eritrea, Ethiopia, the Gambia, Kenya, Somalia and Uganda. Of these, 14,557 were women.[1]

International Treaties

- Women's Convention (ratified 1980).
- Children's Rights Convention (ratified 1990).
- Civil and Political Rights Covenant (ratified 1971).
- Economic, Social and Cultural Rights Covenant (ratified 1971).
- European Convention on Human Rights (ratified 1952).

National Laws

Constitution

The Constitution of Sweden[2] explicitly provides non-Swedish citizens some of the protections enjoyed by citizens of Sweden. Article 20(1)(7) ensures protection from discrimination on the grounds of "race, skin color, ethnic origin, or sex." Unless otherwise provided by special rules of law, non-Swedish citizens also enjoy protection against "physical violations" and "deprivation of liberty" (Art. 20(2)(3, 4)). The rights to freedom of expression and worship are also among these conditional protections (Art. 20(2)(1)).

Criminal law

Provisions

Sweden enacted a law criminalizing FC/FGM in 1982 and revised it in 1998 to make the penalties more severe. The 1982 law prohibiting FC/FGM had a maximum penalty of two years if the crime was not "serious."[3] The current law states:

> Section 1: Operations on the external female genital organs which are designed to mutilate them or produce other permanent changes in them (genital mutilation) must not take place, regardless of whether consent to this operation has or has not been given.
>
> Section 2: Anyone contravening Section 1 will be sent to prison for a maximum of four years.
>
> If the crime has resulted in danger to life or serious illness or has in some other way involved particularly reckless behavior, it is to be regarded as serious. The punishment for a serious crime is prison for a minimum of two and a maximum of ten years. Attempts, preparations, conspiracy and failure to report crimes are treated as criminal liability in accordance with Section 23 of the Penal Code.[4]

Swedish law also provides for the prosecution of any resident of Sweden who arranges for FC/FGM to take place in another country where the practice is prohibited.[5]

Enforcement of the law

While there have been reports of one arrest for the practice of FC/FGM, no information is available regarding the outcome of the case. There have been no prosecutions under the FC/FGM law.[6]

Child protection laws

FC/FGM may be viewed as a form of "abuse," and may thus be the basis for government intervention under Section 2 of the Act relating to the Welfare of Minors (LVU),[7] which provides:

> A decision to take the child into care is to be made if, as a result of physical abuse, improper exploitation, a lack of care or some other situation in the home, there is a definite risk that the health or development of the child could be impaired.[8]

Section 71 of the Social Service Act (SoL) provides that government "[a]uthorities whose activities relate to children and young people and other authorities in the health and medical service and the social services" have an obligation to report to the social welfare board cases of minors in need of protection.[9] Teachers, doctors, nurses and midwives are among those obligated to comply with these reporting requirements.[10]

Other Measures: Laws, Regulations and Policies

The National Board of Health and Welfare has undertaken various activities to address FC/FGM, supporting programs aimed at both preventing the practice and assisting those who have undergone it. A three-year project entitled "Mother and Child Health Care – Female Genital Mutilation" was instituted in Gothenburg beginning in April 1993.[11] The aim of the project was to organize FC/FGM prevention efforts and to provide medical and psychosexual care to women who have undergone FC/FGM, particularly during pregnancy, delivery and post-natal care.[12] The project was implemented by the Immigrant Services Administration of Gothenburg.[13]

Standards of Health Professionals

As part of the Mother and Child Health Care – Female Genital Mutilation project, guidelines were drawn up for health care professionals in Gothenburg.[14] These guidelines are intended to assist health care professionals in meeting the health care needs of women who have undergone FC/FGM.[15] They also outline the responsibilities of health care professionals in preventing girls from undergoing the practice. Health care professionals are directed to approach the issue of FC/FGM "in a respectful manner."[16] Where necessary, an interpreter should be used, preferably one who is female.[17] Discussion of FC/FGM should begin at the time of enrollment of a new baby and be raised again at the check-up at five and a half.[18] Health care professionals are instructed to inform parents of the health risks of FC/FGM and of the fact that the practice is prohibited under Swedish law.[19]

Policies for Eliminating FC/FGM in Africa

The Swedish International Development Agency (SIDA) has made the prevention of FC/FGM a priority of its reproductive health and rights program.[20] SIDA's projects focus on: dissemination of knowledge about the harmful effects of FC/FGM among health personnel and practitioners of FC/FGM; advocacy aimed at changing attitudes among all sectors of society; and legislative reform and monitoring of enforcement of existing laws and treaties prohibiting the practice.[21] SIDA has funded activities of NGOs and inter-governmental organizations aimed at eliminating FC/FGM.[22]

Notes

1. Proceedings of the Expert Meeting on Female Genital Mutilation, Ghent, Belgium, Nov. 5–7, 1998 p. 12 (figures were obtained from the National Offices of Statistics from each European member state).
2. Instrument of Government (Constitution) (1989), (last visited Nov. 6, 1999), <http:www.uni-wuerzburg.de/law/sw00000_.html>.
3. Act Prohibiting the Female Genital Mutilation of Women (1982: 316).
4. Act Prohibiting the Female Genital Mutilation of Women (1982: 316, as amended in July 1998).
5. Ibid.
6. Suzanne Julin, Swedish National Board of Health and Welfare, Questionnaire (Sept. 29, 1998).
7. Immigration Services Administration, Gothenburg (1996), Female Genital Mutilation – Administration Routines Within Social Services, pp. 5–6.
8. Ibid., p. 6.
9. Ibid.
10. Ibid.
11. Immigration Services Administration, Gothenburg (undated), Mother and Child Health Care Project – Female Genital Mutilation, p. 1.
12. Ibid.
13. Ibid.
14. Immigration Services Administration, Gothenburg (undated), Female Genital Mutilation: Guidelines for Medical and Health Care Staff.
15. Ibid., pp. 1–4.
16. Ibid., p. 5.
17. Ibid.
18. Ibid.
19. Ibid.
20. Population Action International (PAI), *Paying Their Fair Share? Donor Countries and International Population Assistance*, Washington, DC: PAI, 1998, p. 71.
21. Department for Democracy and Social Development Health Division, Swedish International Development Agency (SIDA), *Strategy for Development Cooperation, Sexual and Reproductive Health and Rights*, 1997, p. 28.
22. SIDA, *Health Division Facts and Figures*, 1997, p. 21.

Tanzania

Size (1,000 km²): 945
Income (per capita GNP in US$): 210
Population (millions): 31
Number of women per 100 men: 102
Percentage of young people in the population (under 15 years): 48
Prevalence of FC/FGM: 18%
Type(s) of FC/FGM most commonly practiced: Types II and III
Ethnic groups that practice FC/FGM: There is a high prevalence rate among some groups such as the Shaga of Mount Kilimanjaro. Type III is performed by Somali settlers and refugees.

International Treaties

- Women's Convention (ratified 1985).
- Children's Rights Convention (ratified 1991).
- Civil and Political Rights Covenant (ratified 1976).
- Economic, Social and Cultural Rights Covenant (ratified 1976).
- Banjul Charter (ratified 1984).

National Laws

Constitution

The Constitution[1] guarantees the equality of women and men before the law. Article 9(1)(g) provides that "the Government and all its instruments of the people offer equal opportunities for all citizens, men and women, regardless of color, tribe, religion, or creed." Article 13(1) further provides that "[a]ll people are equal before the law, and have the right, without discrimination of any kind, to be protected and to be accorded equal justice before the law." However, in defining "discrimination," the Constitution refers only to differential treatment on the basis of nationality, tribe, origin, political affiliation, color, religion, or lifestyles; it excludes sex as a prohibited basis of discrimination (Art. 13(5)).

The rights to life and personal freedom are protected under the Constitution. Article 14 states that "[e]veryone has the right to exist and to receive from society protection for his life, in accordance with the law." Article 15(1) protects the "right to be free and to live as a free person."

Religious rights must be balanced against individual protections and other state interests under the Constitution. Article 19(2) of the Constitution protects freedom of religion and the freedom to worship "[w]ithout jeopardising the laws applicable in the Union Republic." Religious rights, like all individual rights, may be limited by laws intended to ensure the protection of "justice and freedom of others" and "security, safety of the society, peace of the community, good conduct in the community, community health, development programs in cities and villages" (Art. 30(2)(a–b)).

Criminal law

The Parliament of Tanzania enacted a law on April 21, 1998 amending the Penal Code to prohibit FC/FGM.[2]

Provisions

Section 169A of the Penal Code, in effect as of July 1998, provides:

> (1) Any person who, having the custody, charge or care of any person under eighteen years of age, ill treats, neglects or abandons that person or causes female circumcision or procures that person to be assaulted, ill-treated, neglected or abandoned in a manner likely to cause him suffering or injury to health, including injury to, or loss of, sight or hearing, or limb or organ of the body or mental derangement, commits the offence of cruelty to children.
>
> (2) Any person who commits the offence of cruelty to children is liable on conviction to imprisonment for a term of not less than five years and not exceeding fifteen years or to a fine not exceeding three hundred thousand shillings [approximately US$380] or to both the fine and imprisonment, and shall be ordered to pay compensation of an amount determined by the court to the person in respect of whom the offence was committed for the injuries caused to that person.[3]

Enforcement of law

Information not available.

Other Measures: Laws, Regulations and Policies

The Committee on Harmful Traditional Practices, which engages in educational programs and campaigns, operates within the Ministry of Health.[4]

Notes

1. *Constitution of the United Republic of Tanzania* (1984), translated in A.P. Blaustein and G.H. Flanz (eds), *Constitutions of the Countries of the World*, Dobbs Ferry, NY: Oceana Publications, 1986.
2. Ananilea Nkya and Lella Sheikh Hashim, Tanzania Media Women's Association, Questionnaire (1998).
3. The Sexual Offences Special Provision Act, 1998, sect. 169A.
4. Committee on the Elimination of Discrimination Against Women (CEDAW), *Consideration of Reports Submitted by States Parties Under Article 18 of the Convention on the Elimination of All Forms of Discrimination Against Women, Second and third periodic reports of States parties: United Republic of Tanzania*, CEDAW/C/TZA/2–3, 30 Sept. 1996, para. 32.

Togo

Size (1,000 km²): 57
Income (per capita GNP in US$): 340
Population (millions): 4
Number of women per 100 men: 102
Percentage of young people in population (under 15 years): 46
Prevalence of FC/FGM: 50%
Type(s) of FC/FGM most commonly practiced: Type II
Ethnic groups that practice FC/FGM: Information not available.

International Treaties

- Women's Convention (ratified 1983).
- Children's Rights Convention (ratified 1990).
- Civil and Political Rights Covenant (ratified 1984).
- Economic, Social and Cultural Rights Covenant (ratified 1984).
- Banjul Charter (ratified 1982).
- African Charter (ratified 1998).

National Laws

Constitution

The Constitution[1] guarantees the equality of women and men before the law. Article 2 provides that "[t]he Togolese Republic shall assure equality before the law for all citizens without distinction as to … sex." Article 11 states that "[e]very human being shall enjoy equal dignity and equal rights. Both sexes shall be considered equal before the law."

Several provisions protect the rights to life and physical integrity. Article 13 provides that "[t]he State shall be required to guarantee the physical and mental integrity, life and safety of each person living on any national territory." Article 21 states that "[e]ach human being shall be considered sacred and inviolable."

Article 34 provides that "[t]he State shall recognize and shall work to promote the citizen's right to health." Further, Article 12 provides that "[e]ach human being shall have the right to develop toward his physical, intellectual, moral and cultural potential."

Finally, protections of cultural and religious rights are subject to the limitations of the law. Article 25 provides that "[e]very person shall have the right to freedom of thought, conscience, religion, worship, opinion and expression. These rights and liberties shall be exercised *with respect to the liberties of others and to the maintenance of public order and standards established by laws and regulations* [emphasis added]."

Criminal law

In November 1998, Togo adopted a law explicitly prohibiting FC/FGM.[2]

Provisions

General provisions

> Art. 1: All forms of female genital mutilations (FGM) practiced by any person, whatever his or her position, are prohibited in Togo.
>
> Art. 2: For purposes of this law, female genital mutilations are understood to mean any partial or total removal [*ablation*] of the external genital organs of little girls, young girls, or women and/or any other operations affecting these organs. Excluded from this category are surgical operations of the genital organs performed pursuant to medical prescription.

Sanctions

> Art. 3: Any person who by traditional or modern methods practices or promotes female genital mutilations or participates in these activities shall be guilty of an act of intentional violence against the person of the excised girl or woman.
>
> Art. 4: Any person who commits the intentional acts of violence defined in Article 3 shall be punished by imprisonment from two months to five years and by a fine of 100,000 to 1,000,000 francs [approximately US$160–1,600], or by either of these punishments.
>
> The punishment shall be doubled in the case of recidivism.
>
> Art. 5: If the mutilations result in the death of the victim, the penalty will be 5 to 10 years of imprisonment [*réclusion*].
>
> Art. 6: When by denunciation it might have been possible to prevent one or more perpetrators from committing additional female genital mutilations, anyone having knowledge of an excision already planned, attempted or practiced, who fails to inform immediately the public authorities, shall be punished with

one month to one year of imprisonment or with a fine of 20,000 to 500,000 francs [approximately US$32–800].

Exempt from these provisions are relatives to the fourth degree, by blood or by marriage, of the perpetrator of or accomplice to the prohibited activities.

Final provisions

Art. 7: The directors of both public and private health facilities are required to ensure the most appropriate medical care to the victims of female genital mutilations arriving in their centers or establishments.

The competent public authorities should be informed without delay in order to permit them to follow the evolving state of the victim and to meet the requirements of this provision.

Art. 8: This law shall have the force of national law.

Enforcement of the law

Information not available.

Other Measures: Laws, Regulations and Policies

In 1984, the Ministry of Social Affairs supported the formation of the National Committee of the IAC.[3]

Notes

1. *Constitution of the Republic of Togo* (1992), translated in A.P. Blaustein and G.H. Flanz (eds), *Constitutions of the Countries of the World*, Dobbs Ferry, NY: Oceana Publications, 1994.
2. Loi No. 98–016 of Nov. 17, 1998 concerning the prohibition of female genital mutilations in Togo, *Journal Officiel de la Republique Togolaise*, Nov. 21, 1998, pp. 2–3.
3. E. Dorkenoo, *Cutting the Rose*, London: Minority Rights Publications, 1995, p. 110.

Uganda

Size (1,000 km²): 241
Income (per capita GNP in US$): 330
Population (millions): 20
Number of women per 100 men: 101
Percentage of young people in the population (under 15 years): 49
Prevalence of FC/FGM: 5%
Type(s) of FC/FGM most commonly practiced: Types I and II
Ethnic groups that practice FC/FGM: Information not available.

International Treaties

- Women's Convention (ratified 1985).
- Children's Rights Convention (ratified 1990).
- Civil and Political Rights Covenant (ratified 1995).
- Economic, Social and Cultural Rights Covenant (ratified 1987).
- Banjul Charter (ratified 1986).
- African Charter (ratified 1994).

National Laws

Constitution

Article 33(b) of the Constitution[1] explicitly notes that "[l]aws, cultures, customs or traditions which are against the dignity, welfare or interest of women or which undermine their status are prohibited by this Constitution."

The Constitution also contains more general protections to ensure the equality of women and men before the law. Article 21(1) provides that "[a]ll persons are equal before and under the law in all spheres of political, economic, social and cultural life and in every other respect and shall enjoy equal protection of the law." The Constitution also specifically prohibits discrimination on the basis of sex (Art. 21(2)). In a separate section, the Constitution affirms that "[w]omen shall be accorded full and equal dignity of the person with men" (Art. 33(1)).

The Constitution permits state intervention to protect children's health and other social and economic needs. Article 34(3) provides that "[n]o child shall be deprived by any person of medical treatment, education or any other social or economic benefit by reason of religious or other beliefs."

The application of customary law and the exercise of religious freedom must conform to the Constitution. Article 2(1–2) states that the Constitution "is the supreme law of Uganda" and that "[i]f any other law or any custom is inconsistent with any of the provisions of this Constitution, the Constitution shall prevail, and that other law or custom shall, to the extent of the inconsistency, be void." Finally, Article 29(c) of the Constitution provides that every person has the right to "freedom to practise any religion and manifest such practise which shall include the right to belong to and participate in the practices of any religious body or organisation *in a manner consistent with the Constitution* [emphasis added]."

Criminal law

There are no Penal Code provisions explicitly prohibiting FC/FGM. In 1998, the State Minister for Gender and Community Development announced that the government was formulating a law prohibiting FC/FGM.[2] There are currently several provisions of the Penal Code[3] that may be applicable to FC/FGM.

Provisions

Section 212 of the Penal Code provides that "[a]ny person who unlawfully does grievous harm to another is guilty of a felony and is liable to imprisonment for seven years." Section 4 of the Penal Code defines "grievous harm" as "any harm which amounts to a maim or dangerous harm, or seriously or permanently injures health or which is likely so to injure health, or which extends to permanent disfigurement, or to any permanent or serious injury to any external or internal organ, membrane or sense."

In addition, Section 215 provides that any person who "unlawfully wounds another ... is guilty of a misdemeanour and is liable to imprisonment for three years." The term "wound" is defined in Section 4 of the Penal Code as "any incision or puncture which divides or pierces any exterior membrane of the body, and any membrane is exterior for the purpose of this definition which can be touched without dividing or piercing any other membrane."

Section 219 of the Penal Code also states that "consent by a person to the causing of ... his own maim does not affect the criminal responsibility of any person by whom such ... maim is caused."

Enforcement of the law

There have been no criminal prosecutions for cases of FC/FGM.[4]

Other Measures: Laws, Regulations and Policies

The Children Statute,[5] enacted in 1996, is a comprehensive child welfare law. Section 8 of the Children's Statute provides that "[i]t shall be unlawful to subject a child to social or customary practices that are harmful to the child's health."

In February 1996, a girl upon whom FC/FGM was to be performed successfully secured the intervention of a court and the circumcision was prevented.[6]

Notes

1. *Constitution of Uganda* (1995), reprinted in G.H. Flanz (ed.), *Constitutions of the Countries of the World*, Dobbs Ferry, NY: Oceana Publications, 1996.
2. Inter-African Committee on Traditional Practices Affecting the Health of Women and Children (IAC), "Uganda, Togo, Tanzania and Ivory Coast Propose Legislation Banning FGM," *Newsletter of the IAC*, No. 23, June 1988, p. 3.
3. Penal Code Act, Cap. 106 (1964).
4. Dr Josephine Kasolo, Safe Motherhood Initiative in Uganda, Questionnaire (undated, Spring 1998).
5. Children Statute, 1996, Statute No. 6, Apr. 4, 1996, Statutes Supplement to the Uganda Gazette, Volume LXXXIX, No. 21.
6. Dr Josephine Kasolo, Safe Motherhood Initiative in Uganda, Questionnaire (undated, Spring 1998).

United Kingdom

Size (1,000 km^2): 245

Income (per capita GNP in US$): 20,870

Population (millions): 59

Immigrant population: In 1997, there were 303,454 immigrants from the following African countries: Egypt, the Gambia, Ghana, Kenya, Nigeria, Sierre Leone, Tanzania and Uganda. Of this total, 148,291 were women.[1]

International Treaties

- Women's Convention (ratified 1986).
- Children's Rights Convention (ratified 1991).
- Civil and Political Rights Covenant (ratified 1976).
- Economic, Social and Cultural Rights Covenant (ratified 1976).
- European Convention on Human Rights (ratified 1951).

National Laws

Constitution

The United Kingdom currently has no written constitution or bill of rights. Parliament is empowered to revise or amend statutes as it chooses and there is no mechanism for judicial review of legislation. This situation changes in October 2000 when the Human Rights Act[2] comes into effect.[3] Under the Human Rights Act, the UK will incorporate the European Convention on Human Rights[4] into domestic law. The European Convention guarantees to all individuals within its jurisdiction the rights and freedoms traditionally protected in constitutional bills of rights.

As noted in Chapter 3 of this book, the Convention ensures the equality of women and men, stating that "[t]he enjoyment rights and freedoms set forth in this Convention shall be secured without discrimination on any ground such as sex" (Art. 14).

The Convention also guarantees "the right to liberty and security of the person" (Art. 5(1)) and "the right to respect for … private and family life" (Art. 8).

Freedom of religion is protected by Article 9(1), which provides that "[e]eryone has the right to freedom of thought, conscience and religion," including the right "in public or private, to manifest [one's] religion or belief, in worship, teaching, practice and observance." This right is subject to "such limitations as are prescribed in a democratic society in the interests of public safety, for the protection of public order, health or morals, or for the protection of the rights and freedoms of others" (Art. 9(2)).

Criminal law

Provisions

Female genital mutilation is a criminal offense in the United Kingdom under the Prohibition of Female Circumcision Act of 1985.[5] The law provides:

> 1.– (1) Subject to section 2 below, it shall be an offence for any person–
> (a) to excise, infibulate or otherwise mutilate the whole or any part of the labia majora or labia minora or clitoris of another person; or
> (b) to aid, abet, counsel or procure the performance by another person of any of those acts on that other person's own body.
>
> (2) A person guilty of an offence under this section shall be liable–
> (a) on conviction on indictment, to a fine or to imprisonment for a term not exceeding five years or to both; or
> (b) on summary conviction, to a fine not exceeding the statutory maximum (as defined in section 74 of the Criminal Justice Act 1982) or to imprisonment for a term not exceeding six months, or to both.
>
> 2.– (1) Subsection (1)(a) of section 1 shall not render unlawful the performance of a surgical operation if that operation–
> (a) is necessary for the physical or mental health of the person on whom it is performed and is performed by a registered medical practitioner; or
> (b) is performed on a person who is in any stage of labour or has just given birth and is so performed for purposes connected with that labour or birth by–
> (i) a registered medical practitioner or a registered midwife; or
> (ii) a person undergoing a course of training with a view to becoming a registered medical practitioner or a registered midwife.
>
> (2) In determining for the purposes of this section whether an operation is necessary for the mental health of a person, no account shall be taken of the effect on that person of any belief on the part of that or any other person that the operation is required as a matter of custom or ritual.

Enforcement of the law

As of 1998, there had been no prosecutions under the law.[6] In 1993, a doctor charged with contracting to perform female genital mutilation was brought before the General Medical Council (GMC), the licensing and disciplinary body of the medical profession in the United Kingdom. The police arrested and interviewed this physician in February 1993. While investigators sent a preliminary file to the Crown Prosecution Service, it did not proceed with the prosecution, citing lack of evidence.[7]

Child protection laws

In addition to being a criminal offence, FC/FGM is considered a form of child abuse and is thus a basis for state intervention to safeguard or promote the child's welfare. The Children Act of 1989, a comprehensive child welfare law, provides that when a local authority has "reasonable cause to suspect that a child who lives, or is found, in [its] area is suffering, or is likely to suffer, significant harm, the authority shall make, or cause to be made, such enquiries as they consider necessary to enable them to decide whether they should take any action to safeguard or promote the child's welfare."[8] According to an inter-agency guide for government agents, local authorities should be alert to the possible practice of FC/FGM, particularly in areas where "there are significant numbers of children of particular ethnic minority or cultural backgrounds."[9]

Child welfare officials, when they suspect that a child is at risk of FC/FGM, can intervene by filing for a "prohibited steps order." Such an order prevents a child's parents or legal guardians from taking specified actions – such as removal of the child from the country – without the court's consent.[10] In addition, a court could make a "care" order, which would take the child out of the custody of the parent or guardian, or a "supervision" order, which would put the child under the supervision of a designated local authority or probation officer.[11] Since 1989, there have been at least seven interventions by local authorities that have prevented parents from having their daughters or wards undergo FC/FGM.[12]

Other Measures: Laws, Regulations and Policies

The Department of Health has provided financial support to non-governmental organizations carrying out awareness-raising campaigns through workshops, dissemination of literature, and use of the mass media.[13]

Standards of Health Professionals

The GMC has condemned the practice of FC/FGM by medical personnel. In 1993, as noted above, a doctor charged with contracting to perform FC/FGM was brought before the GMC. He was found guilty of seven charges of serious misconduct and his license was suspended.[14] Professor Sir Herbert Duthie, who chaired the GMC hearing, was reported to have told the doctor, "[t]he committee is appalled by your willingness to perform an abhorrent, illegal and mutilating operation with no possible medical benefit to a patient."[15] The British Medical Association has stated that doctors have a duty to make a report to social services when they suspect that a child is at risk of FC/FGM.[16]

Policies for Eliminating FC/FGM in Africa

As part of its Health and Population Innovation Scheme, the Department for International Development (DFID) encourages project proposals that address sexual and reproductive health, and, in particular, initiatives that focus on FC/FGM.[17] FC/FGM is considered an important priority within the British population assistance program.[18]

Notes

1. Proceedings of the Expert Meeting on Female Genital Mutilation, Ghent, Belgium, Nov. 5–7, 1998, p. 12 (figures were obtained from the National Offices of Statistics from each European member state).
2. Human Rights Act 1998, chap. 42 (Eng.).
3. S. Lyall, "Britain Says it's Time to Adopt a Bill of Rights," *New York Times*, October 3, 1999, Week in Review, p. 6.
4. European Convention for the Protection of Human Rights and Fundamental Freedoms, adopted Nov. 4, 1950, 312 UNTS 222 (entered into force Sept. 3, 1953).
5. Prohibition of Female Circumcision Act, 1985, ch. 38.
6. Jenny Davidson, FORWARD, Questionnaire (March 10, 1998).
7. O. Dyer, "Gynaecologist Struck Off Over Female Genital Circumcision," *British Medical Journal*, 307 (6917), Dec. 4, 1993, pp. 1441–2 (abstracted on POPLINE, Population Information Program, Center for Communication Programs, Johns Hopkins School of Public Health).
8. Children Act, 1989, part V, sect. 47.
9. Home Office et al., *Working Together Under the Children Act 1989*, 1989, p. 11.
10. Children Act, 1989, part II, sect. 8.
11. Ibid., part IV, sect. 31.
12. Jenny Davidson, FORWARD, Questionnaire (March 10, 1998).
13. Ibid.

14. Dyer, "Gynaecologist Struck Off Over Female Genital Circumcision."
15. Helen Davidson and Andrew Alderson, "'Mutilation' Doctor Banned," *Sunday Times*, Nov. 28, 1993.
16. British Medical Association, *Guidance for Doctors Approached by Victims of Female Genital Mutilation*, 1996, p. 5.
17. Department for International Development, Health and Population Research, Sexual and Reproductive Health and Communicable Diseases: Guidelines for Applicants (last visited May 27, 1999), <http://www.dfid.gov.uk/public/working/hpdis.html>.
18. Population Action International (PAI), *Paying Their Fair Share? Donor Countries and International Population Assistance*, Washington, DC: PAI, 1998, p. 79.

United States

Size (1,000 km^2): 9,364
Income (per capita GNP in US$): 29,080
Population (millions): 268
Immigrant population: In 1990, there were 1,285,200 immigrants of origins other than Mexico, the Caribbean, Canada, Central America, South America, Asia and Europe. In 1995, there was an inflow of 42,500 permanent settlers from Africa.

International Treaties

- Civil and Political Rights Covenant (ratified 1992).

National Laws

Constitution

The United States Constitution protects against the deprivation of "life, liberty and property" without "due process" by either the federal[1] or state[2] governments. The 14th amendment to the Constitution also guarantees that no individual shall be denied "equal protection of the laws."[3] While these rights only protect individuals against government action, Congress is empowered to regulate against civil rights violations by private actors.[4]

Criminal law

In 1996, Congress passed several legislative measures related to FC/FGM, one of which criminalized the practice. In addition to the federal law, fifteen states have also criminalized FC/FGM. This report focuses primarily on efforts at the federal level.

Legislation on FC/FGM was first introduced in Congress in 1993 by Representative Patricia Schroeder, as part of the Women's Health Equity Act. It did not pass.[5] However, legislation on FC/FGM was enacted as part of the Illegal Immigration Reform and Immigrant Responsibility Act of 1996.[6]

Provisions

Section 116 of the Illegal Immigration Reform and Immigrant Responsibility Act of 1996 follows:

(a) Exept as provided in subsection (b), whoever knowingly circumcises, excises, or infibulates the whole or any part of the labia majora or labia minora or clitoris of another person who has not attained the age of 18 years shall be fined under this title or imprisoned not more than 5 years, or both.

(b) A surgical operation is not a violation of this section if the operation is–
  (1) necessary to the health of the person on whom it is performed, and is performed by a person licensed in the place of its performance as a medical practitioner; or
  (2) performed on a person in labor or who has just given birth and is performed for medical purposes connected with that labor or birth by a person licensed in the place it is performed as a medical practitioner, midwife, or person in training to become such a practitioner or midwife.

(c) In applying subsection (b)(1), no account shall be taken of the effect on the person on whom the operation is to be performed of any belief on the part of that person, or any other person, that the operation is required as a matter of custom or ritual.[7]

At the state level, the following fifteen states have criminalized FC/FGM: California, Colorado, Delaware, Illinois, Maryland, Minnesota, Nevada, New York, North Dakota, Oregon, Rhode Island, Tennessee, Texas, West Virginia and Wisconsin.[8] With few exceptions, these laws have criminal provisions similar to the federal law. Illinois, Minnesota, Rhode Island and Tennessee prohibit the practice upon all women, including those over 18 years of age. Colorado, Delaware, Maryland, New York, Oregon and West Virginia also explicitly hold parents or legal guardians of children under 18 liable for FC/FGM if they knowingly consent to the procedure. In California, the law states that a person convicted of practicing FC/FGM will receive a sentence increase of one year in addition to the regular penalty for child endangerment. California, Colorado, Minnesota, New York and Oregon have additional provisions for education and outreach to the relevant communities.

Enforcement of the law

To date, there have been no criminal prosecutions at federal or state level.

Child protection laws

A legislative measure requiring the Immigration and Naturalization Service to provide information about the health and legal consequences of practicing FC/FGM notes that specific mention should be made of the consequences under criminal or child protection statutes of allowing a child under one's care to undergo the procedure.[9] See the following section for more information.

Other Measures: Laws, Regulations and Policies

In addition to the criminalization of FC/FGM, Congress passed three other legislative measures relating to the practice.

The first law, adopted prior to the criminal law, required the Secretary of Health and Human Services to undertake a study on FC/FGM in the US to determine the population that was at risk.[10] The Department of Health and Human Services (DHHS) commissioned the Centers for Disease Control (CDC) to carry out a study to determine the prevalence of the practice. Using data from the 1990 US Census, the CDC estimated that, in 1990, there were approximately 168,000 girls and women in the country "with or at risk for FC/FGM."[11] The Secretary of DHHS was also required to carry out educational outreach to affected communities and to develop and disseminate recommendations for students in medical and osteopathic schools.[12] Between February and September 1997, DHHS held community consultation meetings in Washington DC, New York, Boston, San Diego, Houston, Atlanta and Chicago. DHHS also completed a survey of medical schools, medical osteopathy schools, nursing schools, midwifery schools and schools of social work and has formed a working group with representatives from these schools to work on incorporating FC/FGM into their curricula.[13] DHHS commissioned RAINBQ to produce a manual for use by health professionals.

The second legal measure, which was passed as part of the Illegal Immigration Reform and Immigrant Responsibility Act of 1996, requires the Immigration and Naturalization Service (INS), in cooperation with the Department of State, to provide information to immigrants and non-immigrants entering the USA from countries where FC/FGM is practiced about the harmful effects of FC/FGM and the potential legal consequences of its performance in the USA. The legislation required that the information be compiled and presented in a culturally appropriate manner.[14]

Finally, as part of the fiscal year 1997, Congress enacted legislation requiring the US executive directors of international financial institutions to oppose non-humanitarian loans to countries where FGM is practiced and whose governments have not implemented any educational programs to prevent the practice.[15]

The issue of FC/FGM has also arisen in the context of US asylum law. In 1995 the Office of International Affairs issued the INS Gender Guidelines.[16] Elaborating on the relevant substantive and procedural law, Federal Judges have referred to the Guidelines as statements of INS policy.[17] The INS Gender Guidelines explicitly recognize FC/FGM as a form of persecution directed primarily at women and girls.[18]

Following the promulgation of the INS Gender Guidelines, the Board of Immigration Appeals heard the case of Fauziya Kassindja,[19] a Togalese woman who sought asylum on the grounds that if she returned to her country she would be subjected to FC/FGM. In 1996, the Board granted asylum to Kassindja, finding that she had a well-founded fear of persecution. However, the Board declined to establish standards for granting asylum in future FC/FGM cases.[20]

Standards of Health Professionals

In 1991, the American Medical Association (AMA) adopted a resolution encouraging obstetric/gynecologic and urologic societies to develop educational material addressing medically unnecessary surgical modification of female genitalia, complications arising therefrom, and possible corrective surgical procedures. The AMA also opposed all forms of "medically unnecessary surgical modification of female genitalia."[21] The AMA followed up with a policy in which it condemned the practice, characterizing FC/FGM as a form of child abuse. The policy states the Association's support for legislation to eliminate FC/FGM and protect those at risk. Furthermore, the policy recommends that physicians who are asked to perform FGC/FGM discourage families from pursuing the procedure. Doctors are encouraged to provide culturally sensitive counseling to inform the patient and her family about the negative health consequences of the procedure and to refer patients to social support groups.[22]

In 1995, the American College of Obstetricians and Gynecologists (ACOG) released a statement noting its opposition to all forms of surgical modification of female genitalia that are medically unnecessary. [23]

The American Academy of Pediatrics (AAP) has also issued recommendations opposing all forms of FC/FGM.[24] It recommends that its members not carry out any medically unnecessary procedure that alters the genitalia of female infants, girls and adolescents. The statement calls upon the AAP actively to dissuade family members from carrying out the practice while also providing them with compassionate education about the physical and psychological effects of the practice.[25]

Policies for Eliminating FC/FGM in Africa

In 1993, in response to interest from Congress, the US Agency for International Development (USAID) began to work on the prevention of FC/FGM in the countries where it was practiced.[26] To date, the agency has provided assistance to Kenya, Egypt and the IAC.

USAID strategies have been categorized as "Knowledge-building," "Prevention" and "Treatment of Consequences of FGM." Activities include data collection, support for local organizations working to eliminate the practice, and training of medical providers and community-based health workers on methods for dealing with the consequences of FC/FGM. In addition, a Working Group on FC/FGM was formed in 1994 in response to public outcry against the practice.[27] Using a "multi-sectoral and gender-based approach" to FC/FGM, the Working Group seeks to "incorporate attention to FGM into ongoing activities in reproductive health, and to build on areas of expertise in gender and reproductive rights to address FGM."[28] Among other things, the Working Group will convene a technical working group to review existing programs and activities and conduct a systematic review of USAID activities to formulate a strategy for integrating FC/FGM into reproductive health programs.[29]

Notes

1. US Constitution, amend. V.
2. Ibid., amend. XIV, sect. 1.
3. Ibid.
4. Ibid. art. I, sect. 8 (Commerce Clause and Necessary and Proper Clause); amend. XIV, sect. 5 (Enforcement Clause).
5. Federal Prohibition of Female Genital Mutilation Act of 1993, 103rd Congress, 1st Session, HR 3247 (1993).
6. Illegal Immigration Reform and Immigrant Responsibility Act of 1996, Pub. L.104–208, sect. 645, 110 Stat.3009–546 (1996)
7. 18 USCA sect. 116.
8. See Cal. Penal Code sect. 273.4 (West 1996); Cal. Health & Safety Code sect. 124170 (1996); Col. Rev. Stat. tit. 18, art. 6, sect. 401(1)(b)(1); Del. Code Ann. tit. 11, sect. 780 (1996); Ill. Comp. Stat. Ann. sect. 5/12–34 (1997); tit. 25, art. 30, 101–03; Md. Code Ann., Health sects 20–601–20–603; Minn. Stat. sects 609.2245(1) & 144.3872 (West 1996); Nev. Rev. Stat. Ann. sect. 200.5083 (Michie 1999); NY Penal Law sect. 130.85 (1997); ND Cent. Code sect. 12.1–36–01 (1996); OR. Rev. Stat. sects 163.207, 431.827 (1999); R.I. Gen. Laws

sect. 11–5–2 (1996); Tenn. Code Ann. sect. 39–13–110 (1996); Texas Health and Safety Code, ch. 166, sect. 166.001; W.VA Code, sect. 61–8D–3a; and Wis. Stat. sect. 146.35 (West 1995).

9. 8 USCA sect. 1374 (to be recodified as 8 USCA sect. 904, pursuant to HR 2716, 105th Cong.).
10. Pub. L. 104–134, Title I, sect. 101(d)[Title V sect. 520] Apr. 26, 1996, 110 Stat. 1321–250; renumbered Title I Pub.L. 104–140, sect. 1(a), May 2, 1996, 110 Stat. 1327 (see 42 USCA sect. 241, Historical and Statutory notes (1998 Supp.)).
11. Wanda K. Jones et al., "Female Genital Mutilation/Female Circumcision: Who Is at Risk in the US?", *Public Health Report*, No. 112, 1997, pp. 368, 372.
12. See note 10.
13. Telephone interview by Kathy Hall Martinez, Dep. Dir. Int. Prog., CRLP, with Dr David Smith, HHS Office of International and Refugee Health, regarding the status of implementation on Oct. 24, 1997.
14. Pub. L. 104–208, sect. 644, 110 Stat. 3009–546 (1996).
15. 22 USCS sect. 262k–2 (1996).
16. Memorandum from Phyllis Coven, INS Office of International Affairs, to All INS Asylum Officers and HQASM Coordinators, Considerations For Asylum Officers Adjudicating Asylum Claims From Women (May 26, 1995), reproduced in Deborah E. Anker, *Women Refugees: Forgotten No Longer?*, 32 San Diego L. Rev. 771, 794–817 (1995).
17. Deborah E. Anker, *Law of Asylum in the United States*, Boston: Refugee Law Center, 1999, p. 9.
18. Ibid., p. 263.
19. Her name was misspelled as Kasinga when she entered the country. Consequently, all legal documents referring to her case use the incorrect spelling of her name. See F. Kassindja and L.M. Bashir, *Do They Hear You When You Cry*, New York: Delacorte Press, 1998.
20. See *in re* Fauziya Kasinga, Interim Dec. 3278, Bd of Immig. Appeals, File A73 476 695, 1996 BIA LEXIS 15 (June 13, 1996).
21. American Medical Association, Proceedings of the 140th Annual Meeting, June 1991, Res. No. 13.
22. American Medical Association Policy Compendium, 1997 edn, AMA Policy #525.980 – Expansion of AMA Policy on Female Genital Mutilation.
23. American College of Obstetricians and Gynecologists, Committee Opinion 151 on Female Genital Mutilation, Jan. 1995.
24. American Academy of Pediatrics, Policy Statement on Female Gential Mutilation (RE 9749), 102 Pediatrics, 153–6 (1998).
25. Ibid.
26. Agency for International Development, USAID's Approach to Female Genital Mutilation (undated) (on file with CRLP).
27. Ibid.
28. Ibid., p. 8.

Select Bibliography

African Charter on Human and People's Rights, adopted June 26, 1981, OAU Doc. CAB/LEG/67/3/Rev.5, 21 ILM 58 (1982).

African Charter on the Rights and Welfare of the Child, adopted 1991, art. 21, OAU Doc. CAB/LEG/24.9/49 (1990).

Alston, P., "The Best Interests Principle: Towards a Reconciliation of Culture and Human Rights," in P. Alston (ed.), *The Best Interests of the Child*, Oxford: Clarendon Press, 1994.

Amnesty International, "Female Genital Mutilation and International Human Rights Standards," *Female Genital Mutilation: A Human Rights Information Pack*, London: Amnesty International, 1997.

Beijing Declaration and Platform for Action, Fourth World Conference on Women, Beijing, China, Sept. 4–15, 1995, 1 UN Doc. DPI/1766/Wom (1996).

Committee on the Elimination of Discrimination Against Women (CEDAW), General Recommendation No. 14 (Ninth session, 1990): Female Circumcision, A/45/38 (General Comments).

Convention Against Torture and Other Cruel, Inhuman or Degrading Treatment or Punishment, opened for signature Dec. 10, 1984, GA res. 39/46, annex, 39 UN GAOR Supp. (No. 51) at 197, UN Doc. A/39/51 (1984) (entered into force June 26, 1987).

Convention on the Elimination of All Forms of Discrimination Against Women, opened for signature Dec. 18, 1979, art. 2(e), 1249 UNTS 14 (entered into force Sept. 3, 1981).

Cook, R.J., "Human Rights and Reproductive Self-Determination," *American University Law Review*, Vol. XLIV, 1995.

CRLP and Groupe de Recherches Femmes et Lois de Sénégal Réseau de Solidarité des Femmes sous Lois Musulmanes (GREFELS), *Femmes dans le monde: l'Afrique francophone*, New York: CRLP, 1999.

Declaration of the Principles of International Cultural Co-operation, proclaimed by the General Conference of the United Nations Educational, Scientific and Cultural Organization (UNESCO) (14th Session, Nov. 4, 1966), art. XI(2), in United Nations, *Human Rights: A Compilation of International Instruments*, Vol. 1 (2nd Part), New York: United Nations, 1993.

Declaration on the Elimination of All Forms of Intolerance and of Discrimination Based on Religion or Belief, adopted Nov. 25, 1981, 21 ILM 205 (1982).

Declaration on the Rights of Persons Belonging to National or Ethnic, Religious and Linguistic Minorities, adopted by General Assembly resolution 47/135 of Dec. 18, 1992, in United Nations, *Human Rights: A Compilation of International Instruments*, Vol. 1 (2nd Part), New York: United Nations, 1993.

Eide, A., "The Right to an Adequate Standard of Living Including the Right to Food," in A. Eide, C. Krause and A. Rosas (eds) *Economic, Social and Cultural Rights: A Textbook*, Boston: Martinus Nijhoff, 1995.
El Dareer, A., *Women, Why Do You Weep?*, London: Zed Books, 1982.
Equality Now, *Awaken* (periodical), New York: Equality Now.
Final Report on the International Conference on Population and Reproductive Health in the Muslim World, Cairo, Egypt, Feb. 21–24, 1998.
Fitzpatrick, J., "The Use of International Human Rights Norms to Combat Violence Against Women," in R. Cook (ed.) *Human Rights and Women: National and International Perspectives*, Philadelphia: University of Pennsylvania Press, 1994.
Henkin, L., R.C. Pugh, O. Schachter and H. Smit, *International Law, Cases and Materials* (3rd edn), St Paul: West Publishing, 1993.
Inter-African Committee on Traditional Practices Affecting the Health of Women and Children (IAC), *Newsletters*, Addis Ababa: IAC.
International Covenant on Civil and Political Rights, opened for signature Dec. 16, 1966, 999 UNTS 171, 6 ILM 368 (entered into force March 23, 1976).
International Covenant on Economic, Social and Cultural Rights, opened for signature Dec. 16, 1966, 993 UNTS 3 (entered into force Jan. 3, 1976).
Kiss, A.C., "Permissible Limitation on Rights," in L. Henkin (ed.), *The International Bill of Rights*, New York: Columbia University Press, 1981.
Koso Thomas, O., *The Circumcision of Women: A Strategy for Eradication*, London: Zed Books, 1987.
Lai, S.Y., and R.E. Ralph, "Recent Development: Female Sexuality and Human Rights," *Harvard Human Rights Journal*, Vol. VIII, 1995.
Marks, S.P., "Emerging Human Rights: A New Generation for the 1980s," *Rutgers Law Review*, Vol. XXXIII, 1981.
National NGO Commission for Population and Development, *FGM Task Force Position Paper*, 1997.
Newman, F., and D. Weissbrodt, *International Human Rights: Law, Policy, and Process* (2nd edn), Cincinnati: Anderson Publishing, 1996.
OECD, *Trends in International Migration: Annual Report 1996*, Paris: OECD, 1997.
Office of the Senior Coordinator for International Women's Issues, Bureau for Global Affairs and the Office of Asylum Affairs, Bureau of Democracy, Human Rights and Labor, US Department of State, *Female Genital Mutilation(FGM) or Female Genital Cutting (FC)* (information pack), 1999.
Population Action International, *Paying Their Fair Share? Donor Countries and International Population Assistance*, Washington, DC: PAI, 1998.
Programme of Action of the International Conference on Population and Development, Cairo, Egypt, Sept. 5–13, 1994, in Report of the International Conference on Population and Development, UN Doc. A/CONF.171/13/Rev. I, UN Sales No. 95.XIII.18 (1995).
Rahman, A., and R. Pine, "An International Human Right to Reproductive Health Care," *Health and Human Rights*, Vol. I, No. 4, 1995.
Rich, S., *Historical Perspective of FC/FGM Movement*, Presentation given at the National Conference of the Ethiopian Community Development Council, Washington, DC, Sept. 12, 1997.
Smith, J., *Visions and Discussions on Genital Mutilation of Girls: An International Survey*, Amsterdam: Defence for Children International, 1995.
Toebes, B.C.A., *The Right to Health as a Human Right in International Law*, Antwerp: Intersentia, 1999.

Toubia, N., *Caring for Women with Circumcision: A Technical Manual for Health Care Providers*, New York: RAINB♀, 1999.
Toubia, N., *Female Genital Mutilation: A Call for Global Action* (2nd edn), New York: RAINB♀, 1995.
Toubia, N., and S. Izett, *Female Genital Mutilation: An Overview*, Geneva: World Health Organization, 1998.
United Nations, *The World's Women 1995: Trends and Statistics*, New York: United Nations, 1995.
United Nations General Assembly, Declaration on the Elimination of Violence Against Women (85th Plenary Meeting, 1993), A/RES/48/104.
United Nations General Assembly, Principles for the Protection of Persons with Mental Illness and the Improvement of Mental Health Care, Resolution 46/119, Dec. 17, 1991, Principle 11, 2.
United Nations General Assembly, Traditional or Customary Practices Affecting the Health of women, Report of the Secretary-General (53rd Session, Sept. 10, 1998), A/53/354.
United Nations Population Fund (UNFPA), *The State of the World Population 1999: 6 Billion, A Time for Choices*, New York: UNFPA, 1999.
Universal Declaration of Human Rights, adopted Dec. 10, 1948, GA Res. 217A (III), UN Doc. A/810 (1948).
Welch, C.E., Jr, *Protecting Human Rights in Africa: Strategies and Roles of Non-Governmental Organizations,* Philadelphia: University of Pennsylvania Press, 1995.
World Bank, *World Development Indicators 1999*, Washington, DC: World Bank, 1999.
World Health Organization, Constitution of the World Health Organization, in Basic Documents, adopted on July 22, 1946 (14th edn, 1994).
X and Y v. *The Netherlands*, European Court of Human Rights (1986), 8 EHRR 235, Mar. 26, 1985.

Index

Lightning Source UK Ltd.
Milton Keynes UK

176730UK00002B/4/P

9 781856 497732